The Guru,
the Bagman
& the Sceptic

The Guru, the Bagman & the Sceptic

A story of
science, sex &
psychoanalysis

Seamus O'Mahony

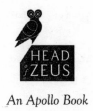

HEAD
of ZEUS

An Apollo Book

First published in the UK in 2023 by Head of Zeus Ltd,
part of Bloomsbury Publishing Plc

9 7 5 3 1 2 4 6 8

A catalogue record for this book is available from the British Library.

ISBN (HB): 9781803285658
ISBN (XTPB): 9781804548523
ISBN (E): 9781803285634

Typeset by Adrian McLaughlin

Printed and bound in Great Britain by
CPI Group (UK) Ltd, Croydon CR0 4YY

Head of Zeus Ltd
First Floor East
5–8 Hardwick Street
London ECIR 4RG

WWW.HEADOFZEUS.COM

To Karen

Whoever undertakes to write a biography binds himself to lying, to concealment, to hypocrisy, to flummery, and even to hiding his own lack of understanding, since biographical truth is not to be had, and even if it were it could not be used.

—SIGMUND FREUD, letter to Arnold Zweig, 1936

As to Freud. I think you write greatly about this business ... but I do not get the sense of illumination, the sense of splendour that you do.

—WILFRED TROTTER, letter to Ernest Jones, 1908

Foreword

This book is about three doctors whose lives intersected over the period from 1908 to 1939. The first, Sigmund Freud, achieved a level of fame that might be called iconic; the second, Ernest Jones, is well known within a single community – that of psychoanalysis; the third, the surgeon and author Wilfred Trotter, is all but forgotten, even in the hospital where he was once so revered. If Jones's fame is slight, Trotter's is even less: it died with the last of his pupils.

Freud remains a cultural figure of the same stature as Karl Marx or Charles Darwin. The twenty-four volumes of his collected writings are afforded a biblical reverence; his every utterance and scribbled letter has been analysed, annotated and interpreted by an academic industry devoted to his thought. Even if his creation – psychoanalysis – is no longer fashionable (or even slightly disreputable), Freud's status seems unassailable. A century after he achieved global fame, many are puzzled by how Freud's ideas became so widely accepted. It may be – as Gibbon wrote of Christianity – 'that it was owing to the convincing evidence of the doctrine itself', but I doubt it.

Although I admire Freud, psychoanalysis has always *bothered* me; I have written this book partly to find out why.

In an aside in his 1916 book *Instincts of the Herd in Peace and War*, Wilfred Trotter observed: 'we tend to get at the summit of our professions only those rare geniuses who combine real specialist capacity with the arts of the bagman.' Ernest Jones was Freud's bagman. A born disciple, the object of his adoration before Freud was Trotter. Even after Jones transferred his loyalties to Freud and psychoanalysis, he remained connected to Trotter – they were, after all, brothers-in-law – and their lives crossed at key moments, almost novelistically. If Jones was a disciple and bagman, Trotter was a sceptic and his own man. This is a story of three men, two opposing views of the world, and the fathomless foolishness of humans.

1

In 1902, Ernest Jones, a twenty-four-year-old house officer at University College Hospital (UCH) London, assisted Wilfred Trotter, a surgical registrar six years his senior, with a double amputation in a man whose legs had been crushed beyond repair. They took a leg each. In his punningly titled memoir *Free Associations* (1959), Jones takes up the story:

> He was what is called a 'peeper' – that is, he achieved sexual excitement by witnessing some erotic scene – and presumably unable to do so in any other way, the poor fellow used to haunt the Underground Railway (of course in pre-electric times), wait until he observed a likely couple in the separate compartments that made up the trains, and then in the tunnels creep along the footboard to catch the desired glimpse. It was a sprightly occupation, because he had to return to his own compartment before reaching the next station, but doubtless he knew the stretches well from experience and had become skilful at timing it. On the fatal day in question, however, the excitement overcame him; he

lost his hold and fell on the line, and a train came along from the opposite direction and cut his legs off. What effect this retaliatory mutilation had on his later mentality I do not know, but one can well imagine it to have been immense; it was a supreme example of a physical and a psychological trauma combined.

With its combination of paraphilia and gristle, Jones's story is what we might now lazily label as 'Freudian', and hints at his future career as psychoanalytic *capo*.

When he was still in his late twenties, and completely unknown, Sigmund Freud told his fiancée, Martha, with a Messianic certainty, that he would be the subject of *many* biographies. In 1944, in a characteristically deferential gesture, Jones abandoned *Free Associations* to concentrate instead on his biography of Sigmund Freud, published in three volumes, and to great acclaim, between 1953 and 1957. Jones's monumental biography may have been a critical and commercial success and may have done much to spread Freud's ideas in the English-speaking world, but nearly all subsequent biographers – for, as Freud predicted, there have been several – have been at pains to highlight its many errors, both factual and doctrinal. This great hagiographical tribute completed, he took up the memoir again, but died in 1958 at the age of seventy-nine before completing it.

Those who are puzzled by the success of psychoanalysis and the global acceptance of Freud's ideas in the early to mid-twentieth century often blame (or credit) Ernest Jones. The psychiatrist and author Anthony Daniels (who usually writes as Theodore Dalrymple) is a confirmed psychoanalytic sceptic, but even he expressed a grudging admiration for Jones's success as a proselytiser, while meditating on his undeserved obscurity:

> It is, of course, quite true that Dr. Jones's current fame is not equal to his importance. Indeed, I have often thought of conducting the following experiment: to count the number of people it is necessary to accost in the various streets of New York, London, or Sydney before encountering someone who has heard of Ernest Jones. My experiment is a rare opportunity to establish an important law in the field of cultural studies: that in the era of celebrity, fame is inversely related to importance.

Jones saw his relationship to Freud as that of T. H. Huxley to Darwin: 'we were both "bonny fighters"'. He did all the political, administrative and publishing work that Freud couldn't or didn't want to do. Jones loved this labour: he founded and ran psychoanalytic associations and societies (he was de facto president for life of two); he recruited English translators for Freud's vast written output; he was a one-man intelligence operation, sniffing out heresy and banishing dissenters, feeding information back to Freud in a correspondence lasting thirty years; he almost single-handedly saved Freud after the *Anschluss* in 1938, when he deployed his extensive diplomatic and political contacts to rescue the sick old man.

Jones combined the Huxleyan role with those of Boswell and St Paul.

Although he was legendarily – and mysteriously – 'irresistible' to women, nearly all the men he came across disliked Jones. A small, humourless, bossy man, he was, in his own words, 'opinionated, tactless, conceited'. A fellow psychoanalyst recalled that Jones's face was 'pale but pungent – like a salad dressing'. A clever outsider, Jones studied medicine at UCH in London, winning numerous medals and prizes; he was ashamed of his lower middle class Swansea origins, and swiftly lost his Welsh accent. He had many talents, including a facility for languages, a winning and readable prose style, stamina, and a capacity for organisation. When he was a boy, Jones startled his mother by telling her that he knew the quality he most longed to possess: 'energy'. He was a confident and articulate public speaker; he was astoundingly resilient, recovering from setbacks that would have finished the careers of most other men – Jones never lacked for courage. Conceited and arrogant though he may have been, Jones realised, even as a young man, that he lacked originality. This insight was not a deflation, but a revelation: he was a disciple in search of a master. Although he idolised Sir Victor Horsley and Sir John Rose Bradford, the great clinician-aristocrats at UCH, his first intense attachment was to the elder-brother figure of Wilfred Trotter: 'my best friend and – apart from Freud – the man who mattered most in my life.'

Trotter too was an outsider, from Coleford in Gloucestershire's Forest of Dean; he had survived spinal tuberculosis, or 'caries', which consigned him to bed rest for much of his childhood and early adolescence. This enforced solitude made him pathologically shy; Jones was his only close male friend. A prolonged childhood illness is sometimes the making of a writer: Trotter devoured the canonical works of English literature; he read, and reread, the Bible, and thereafter had a remarkable facility for scriptural quotation. He was an intellectual, with interests in psychology, philosophy and sociology. Surgery colonises its practitioners so comprehensively that surgeon-intellectuals are as rare as unicorns; Trotter was once memorably described as 'a philosopher in a profession where there are none'. In his old age, Jones was still star-struck: 'I have never known anyone who excelled Wilfred Trotter in the sobriety of his judgment; in the philosophic calm with which he apprehended experience, however arresting; in his penetrating understanding of human nature, both individual and general; or in his profound grasp of the essentials of the scientific attitude and its significance for mankind.' Jones's own less than profound grasp of 'the scientific attitude', however, would lead him to Freud and sunder his friendship with Trotter. Although he vehemently denied it, Jones was by nature credulous, while Trotter's instinctive intellectual position was one of scientific scepticism. Trotter was willing to take personal risks in the exercise of this scepticism: he famously had seven of his cutaneous nerves severed as part of an experiment that he undertook purely to challenge a paper whose 'findings' he simply didn't believe.

The young Trotter had a permanent stoop and looked older than his years. If he managed to overcome his crippling shyness, his rare pronouncements were witty and wise. When Trotter was still a lowly house officer, the great neurosurgeon Sir Victor Horsley told anyone who would listen that he was the only doctor in UCH whose opinion he respected.* (This was simultaneously a sincere tribute to Trotter and an expression of profound contempt for his senior colleagues.) Trotter's judgement was so sound and his hands so skilled that Horsley routinely delegated major operations to him. His choice of career was inspired by Horsley and by the fact that surgery was then far more innovative than other branches of medicine.

Ernest Jones somehow penetrated Wilfred Trotter's thick carapace, but wondering what Trotter saw in him, asked him directly: 'He said it was my capacity for imagination, but I suspect it was that I provided the sympathetic audience of which, in spite of, or rather because of, his general aloofness, he stood in need.' They got on so well that in 1905 they jointly took out a lease on consulting rooms in Harley Street, where they lived and worked.† It was an intense relationship, but such intimate friendships between young men were then quite common; the sexes still occupied entirely different spheres educationally and

---

* Horsley (1857–1916) was professor of surgery at UCH, the first ever doctor to be appointed by any hospital as a 'neurosurgeon'. He was a pioneer in the treatment of brain tumours and pituitary disease. As a young man, he had worked on rabies with Pasteur. Horsley was unconventional: he was a supporter of women's suffrage and one of the first anti-smoking campaigners. According to the neurosurgeon Michael Powell, he 'was loved by his trainees and patients, but profoundly disliked by a legion of enemies and former friends whom he had argued with and insulted. His lack of interpersonal skills was his greatest failing. Despite being so gifted, he was unable to accept another's point of view.' He died in 1916 at the age of fifty-nine of heat stroke and malaria while on military service in Basra (in what was then Mesopotamia).

† Harley Street was not then as prestigious an address as it is now, and it was not uncommon for younger non-consultant hospital doctors to see private fee-paying patients in consulting rooms.

professionally. And then, as now, the long hours and brutality of hospital work fostered a camaraderie among junior doctors.

'In spite of being a professional surgeon,' Jones recalled, 'Trotter was really always more interested, and I should say remained so, in mind than in matter, and so he encouraged me in my predilection.' They subscribed to dozens of journals and learned publications, 'but mostly,' recalled Jones, 'we talked and talked and talked'. This being the prelapsarian heyday of belief in social and scientific progress, the pair had vague notions about the reorganisation of society along scientific principles, and the application of biology to psychology. Their utopianism and seriousness are strangely touching; the world was yet to be corrupted by irony and enervated by cynicism. I can't imagine two house-sharing young men having such earnest conversations now.

Jones credited Trotter with making him aware of the Viennese neurologist Sigmund Freud, drawing his attention to a review of his book *Studies in Hysteria* (1895), co-written with Josef Breuer. This prompted Jones to read Freud's account of the 'Dora' case, in *Fragment of an Analysis of a Case of Hysteria* (1905). So much of what they read was written in German that Jones and Trotter engaged a tutor in the language, who visited their rooms three times a week. This man was a Berliner, and Jones eventually became a fluent German speaker, with – so he claimed – a pronounced Prussian accent. Trotter didn't much care for abroad and foreigners but learned enough German to read the journals and books that interested him.

As a young man, Trotter (like Freud) was influenced by Nietzsche and Schopenhauer, and (also like Freud) was attracted to grand unifying theories of human behaviour. In

Free Associations, Jones recalled that he and Trotter drew up a plan for a book, 'a detailed, and no doubt scathing indictment of the maladies of civilisation'. Years later, when Trotter was the most eminent surgeon in England, he denied any recollection of this unwritten book. He must have squirmed with embarrassment to be reminded of his younger self, flirting with megalomaniacal ideas, such as 'the idea of breeding a better race' and renaming cities after the founders (including himself and Jones) of a utopia founded on the abolition of 'the cruel, aggressive, exploiting tendencies in man'. On the other hand, Jones was such an unreliable memoirist that it is entirely possible that no such conversation ever took place, and no such book was ever mooted, for biographical truth is not to be had.

Wilfred Trotter: 'my best friend and – apart from Freud – the man who mattered most in my life.'

2

On 20 March 1906, Ernest Jones was arrested in his Harley Street rooms, charged with 'gross indecency'. Many years later, he described his trial for this charge as 'the most disagreeable experience of my life'.

After his house jobs at UCH, Jones had hoped to train as a neurologist, but failed in his bid to be appointed to the much-coveted post of resident physician at the National Hospital for the Relief and Cure of the Paralysed and Epileptic* (now the National Hospital for Neurology and Neurosurgery) at Queen Square in London; his reputation for being 'difficult' had spread beyond UCH. This was a major blow for Jones, whose career up to that point had been a triumphant procession of gold medals and first-class honours. With his customary resilience, he developed a portfolio of activities: coaching candidates for medical exams, lecturing, writing for a medical newspaper and carrying out medical inspections of schools

* Hospital names were then wonderfully descriptive. My favourite is the Home for Protestant Incurables, later Marymount Hospice, Cork.

for 'mentally deficient and epileptic children' run by London County Council (LCC).

One of the schools allocated to Jones was the Edward Street School for Mentally Defective Children in Deptford. He visited this school on Friday 2 March 1906, where, during the morning, he examined (unchaperoned) twenty-five children. That afternoon, three girls – Dorothy Freeman (aged thirteen), Fanny Harrigan (also thirteen) and Elizabeth Overton (fourteen) – complained to the headmistress, Mrs Hall, about Jones's behaviour. Mrs Hall contacted Jones's immediate superior, Dr James Kerr. Kerr, in the presence of Jones and Mrs Hall, questioned the children. Elizabeth Overton told him that Jones had asked what the court later referred to as 'an objectionable question'; Fanny Harrigan accused Jones of speaking and acting 'in a grossly indecent manner'; Dorothy Freeman, who attended with her mother, made the same accusation. Kerr told Mrs Freeman that the girls must have made up this story, that such a thing could never have happened. 'If you try to quieten me,' retorted Mrs Freeman, 'you cannot quieten my husband.'

Kerr suspended Jones from the school but took no further action. On Monday 12 March, Dorothy Freeman's father – who, as his wife predicted, was not to be quietened – made a formal complaint against Jones at Blackheath Police Station. Detective Sergeant Beavis took a statement from Fanny Harrigan, following which he visited the teachers' room (where Jones had examined the children) to examine a green baize tablecloth for 'stains'. The divisional police surgeon Dr Dudley Burney found 'certain marks upon it which were

12

regarded of great importance'. Jones was arrested and spent that night at Blackheath Police Station. He appeared the next day before Mr Ernest Baggallay at Blackheath Police Court and was released on bail, to appear again at this court on 28 March and 10 April. The press reported that Jones, 'dapper and alert-looking, occupied a seat behind his solicitor. Although a trifle pale, he frequently laughed and seemed quite unembarrassed.'

Jones's barrister, Archibald Bodkin, cross-examined Dorothy Freeman for two hours, and Fanny Harrigan for one hour. Giving evidence on the tablecloth, Dr Dudley Burney told the court that 'in his opinion the stains were of a character that should not have been there'. In the final hearing on 1 May, held at Greenwich Police Court, Bodkin cross-examined Dr Kerr; *The Kentish Mail and Greenwich & Deptford Observer* reported the court proceedings:

he [Dr Kerr] was under the impression that the girls had made up the charge amongst themselves. They were mentally defective, and children of that description were given to romancing. The girls Freeman and Harrigan were of a nervous type. His experience led him to the opinion that mentally defective children were not ignorant in such matters, some of them, in fact, were precocious. It was his deliberate opinion at the time that there was no truth in the girls' statement. He came to that conclusion before hearing anything about the tablecloth. At this point Ladies were requested to withdraw, and Dr. Kerr gave evidence to account for the stains on the tablecloth and carpet.

The Kentish Mail and Greenwich & Deptford Observer, mindful of the delicacy of its readers, did not record any further discussion on the stains, but did, however, report this exchange:

BODKIN: Romancing with illustrative detail is not unknown, even in courts of justice. (*Laughter*)
BAGGALLAY: Particularly by women. (*More laughter*)

Baggallay acquitted Ernest Jones of all charges; no jury, he said, would convict him, because the court could not rely on the evidence of the children involved.

The acquittal was celebrated by the London medical community: the *Lancet* congratulated Jones 'on his complete exoneration from the infamous and perfectly incredible charges brought against him', while the *British Medical Journal* printed an appeal for contributions to a fund to pay his legal costs. Sir Victor Horsley threw a party at his house in Cavendish Square, where the President of the Royal College of Surgeons presented Jones with a cheque for his legal expenses. He was guest of honour at the annual dinner of the Wandsworth Division of the British Medical Association. Many years later, Jones rationalised the experience: 'My view was that the children had really been concerned in some sexual scene, and that I was being made the scapegoat for their sense of guilt.' He must have been very relieved indeed that in 1906, the testimony of intellectually disabled children was not taken seriously by the courts.

Less than two years later, on 23 March 1908, Jones was in trouble again. He was formally asked to resign from his post as registrar and pathologist at the West End Hospital for Diseases of the Nervous System, Paralysis and Epilepsy (later the West End Hospital for Nervous Diseases) by Ian Malcolm, chairman of the hospital committee:

It has come to my knowledge that twice recently you have examined female patients in this hospital without the presence of any third person in the room and I am also informed that you had previously been told by the matron that such procedure was contrary to the rules of this Hospital as well as others. It is the fact that, after your examination of Rebecca Levi the child asserted that certain questions had been asked her by you, which may have been misunderstood by your patient, but which may form the basis of subsequent investigation of a painful character. I must therefore ask you tender your resignation, both for your own sake and for that of the Institution.

In *Free Associations*, Jones claimed that Dr Harry Campbell, his superior at the hospital, had asked him to examine the ten-year-old Rebecca Levi, 'a girl with an hysterical paralysis of the left arm'. Campbell, he wrote, 'challenged me to see if I could discover any sexual basis for the symptom, as according to Freud's theory of hysteria there should be'. It is doubtful that Campbell made such a request; it is equally doubtful that at that time Jones had anything more than a passing acquaintance with Freudian theory or practice. The parents of a second child also complained, and there is reasonable evidence that a *third* child went to the matron. Jones wisely resigned: he guessed that he might not be so lucky a second time, or that the London medical establishment would rally to his aid again. In *Free Associations*, he insisted that he *did* discover a sexual aetiology for Rebecca Levi's paralysis, and that Campbell had spread 'disreputable stories' about him. In his biography of Freud, Jones claimed that his dismissal was part of a wider persecution at the time of Freudian sympathisers.

Jones had 'less of the usual difficulty' in accepting Freud's theories of childhood sexuality. He was candid about his own very early sexual experiences: 'The practice of coitus was familiar to me at the age of six and seven, after which I suspended it and did not resume it till I was twenty-four; it was a common enough practice among the village children.' Margaret Mead might well have gone to South Wales instead of Samoa had she known about sexual customs there:

> A boy of nine, rolling on the floor with acute bellyache, groaned aloud: 'Oh God, it hurts so much I don't think I could f--k a girl if she was under me at this minute.' The same youngster asked me once if I believed that men ever thought of anything other than their c--k when they were alone. He was the son of a prominent minister.

Jones recalled a 'nurse', a family servant who taught him that the Welsh language had 'two words to designate the male organ, one for it in a flaccid state, the other in an erect. It was an opulence of vocabulary I have not encountered since.' His boarding school, Llandovery, also prepared Jones for his future career, learning there 'the depths of cruelty and obscenity to which human beings can descend'. Years later, when he came across the Austrian anthropologist F. S. Krauss's 1906 book *Anthropophyteia*, a scholarly compendium of obscene jokes and anecdotes, Jones found nothing shocking: 'I failed to find any topic in the field of sexology, recondite sexual perversions, *et hoc genus omne*, on which any Balkan peasant could have enlightened the boys of Llandovery.'

Jones's decision at the age of fifteen to study medicine was partly inspired by the local GP in Gowerton, 'a handsome dare-devil fellow', who lodged for a time with the Jones family: 'It was a lucky decision, for I cannot imagine myself happy at any other work.' Jones was impressed by this doctor's sexual charisma: 'He was loved by all the women of the neighbour-hood, a fact confirmed by the enormous crowd of weeping women I saw at his funeral, when I was about twelve.' (This magnetic physician died of a morphine overdose.) Jones recalled that as a child, he had been 'in love' with the doctor: 'Now, I well remember, when about ?7 years old, being examined by the doctor who used a single, wooden stethoscope, and it is easy to recall the erotic sensation I got, during the rhythmic chest movements, from the pressure of the instrument. I must at that time have unconsciously symbolized it as his penis.'

In a letter to Freud, Jones confessed that he had 'always been conscious of sexual attractions to patients'. Over the next decade, Jones would be attracted to many patients, and they to him.

3

At 8 a.m. on 27 April 1908, at the Hotel Bristol in Salzburg, Sigmund Freud began his keynote address, scheduled to last for one hour, and the highlight of the first ever international psychoanalytic congress. The event was organised by the young Swiss psychiatrist Carl Gustav Jung, who, acknowledging the star attraction, gave it the title of *Zusammenkunft für Freud'sche Psychologie* (Meeting for Freudian Psychology). Over the previous decade, Freud had gathered around him a small circle of Viennese disciples, all of whom were Jewish. But it was Jung, the Swiss gentile, who became his chosen *dauphin*; Freud had a strong conviction that if psychoanalysis was to develop and become respectable, it would have to break out of its Austrian ghetto.

Among the forty or so delegates were Ernest Jones and Wilfred Trotter. Jones had been sacked from his post at the West End Hospital just over a month before – his trip to Salzburg was typical of his matter-of-fact approach to setbacks. He had also decided to emigrate to Canada, having been offered a post in Toronto, partly through the recommendation of the great

Canadian physician Sir William Osler, then Regius Professor of Physic at Oxford. Over the previous couple of years, Jones had flirted with psychology; he had used hypnosis to treat a patient called Tom Ellen, a man with hysterical blindness and 'allochiria' – the sensation that his body was folded over on itself. Jones had also developed a taste for conferences; in September 1907, he attended the First International Congress of Psychiatry and Neurology in Amsterdam, where he first met Jung; in November of that year, he spent a month in Munich attending a postgraduate course run by the famous psychiatrist Emil Kraepelin. On the way home, Jones stopped off in Zurich to visit Jung; they spent several days in intense conversation about Freud's revolutionary ideas. All these trips were paid for by Jones's wealthy new mistress, a Dutch woman called Louisa ('Loe') Kann. He was engaged to a girl called Maude Hill when Loe came to see him as a patient. Having broken off this engagement, Jones was soon sharing Loe's elegant apartment; not surprisingly, this led to a cooling of his friendship with Trotter – they travelled separately to Salzburg.

Freud was then fifty-one; all the other attendees were in their twenties or thirties. He sat at the end of a long table, with the delegates arranged on either side. He spoke without notes, quietly, conversationally. At 11 a.m., after exceeding his allotted time by two hours, he suggested that perhaps it was time to conclude. His rapt audience *begged* him to continue, which he did, for another two hours. Freud's five-hour talk was about a single case, that of a Viennese lawyer and army reserve officer called Ernst Lanzer, now immortalised as the Rat Man. He was one of only five cases fully written up by Freud, published in

1909 as 'Notes upon a Case of Obsessional Neurosis'; the Rat Man is the only case of Freud's for which 'process' notes (his own informal jottings taken during the analysis) exist. In the decades following Freud's talk, the Rat Man became the subject of a large academic commentary, his fame as Freud's most famous patient eclipsed only by the Wolf Man.*

Lanzer first came to see Freud in 1907. He was then twenty-nine and had experienced disturbing obsessional thoughts for several years; lately, these thoughts had prevented him from working as a lawyer. 'The chief features of this disorder', wrote Freud, 'were fears that something might happen to two people of whom he was very fond – his father and a lady who he admired [Gisela, who later became his wife]. Besides this he was aware of *compulsive impulses* – such as an impulse for instance to cut his own throat with a razor.' Lanzer had consulted several doctors, most notably Julius Wagner-Jauregg, professor of psychiatry at Vienna, a contemporary and friend of Freud's.† The fact that the Rat Man had been treated by Wagner-Jauregg was important to Freud: he was desperate to prove that psychoanalysis could cure where conventional psychiatry had failed.

---

* The Wolf Man was Sergei Pankejeff, a Russian aristocrat who spent most of his long life (he died aged ninety-two) in analysis. Freud, with whom he was in analysis from 1910 to 1914, wrote up his case, calling him 'The Wolf Man' after a particularly vivid dream Pankejeff described of white wolves sitting on a tree.

† Wagner-Jauregg went on to win the Nobel Prize in Medicine in 1927 for his treatment of tertiary syphilis ('general paralysis of the insane', or 'dementia paralytica') by inoculating patients with malaria, a 'therapy' that carried a one in seven risk of death.

Lanzer's neurosis reached a crisis in August 1907 when he was on military manoeuvres in Galicia (Poland) while on national service. First, he lost his spectacles, a minor inconvenience that triggered a domino-like sequence of events. Then, a particularly sadistic captain called Nemeczek told him – with some relish – about a brutal punishment he had come across in a novel, Octave Mirbeau's best-selling 1899 shocker, *The Torture Garden*:

[A Chinese professional torturer describes the technique:] You take a man, as young and strong as possible, whose muscles are very resistant. You strip him, you make him kneel down on the ground and bend over his back and secure him in chains which are fixed onto iron collars that fit tightly on his wrists, ankles, and the back of his neck and knees. Then in a big pot you put a very big rat that's been deprived of food for a couple of days in order to stimulate his ferocity. And this pot with the rat inside you apply hermetically like an enormous cupping glass onto the prisoner's buttocks, with the help of strong straps attached to a leather belt going around the loins. You introduce into the hole of the pot an iron rod, reddened at the fire of a forge. The rat wants to flee the burning of the rod and its dazzling light. It panics, scrambles about, jumps and leaps, circles the wall of the pot, crawls and gallops on the man's buttocks, which it first tickles and then tears with its feet and bites with its sharp teeth, looking for an exit through the rummaged bleeding skin. The great merit in this is that one must know how to prolong this initial operation as long as possible.

22

It can even happen that the sufferer become crazy. The rat penetrates, and it dies, suffocated, at the same time as the victim, who, after a half-hour of unutterable, incomparable tortures, ends, he too, by succumbing to haemorrhage. It's extremely beautiful!

Lanzer was horrified and fascinated. He began to harbour the bizarre conviction that his father (long dead) and his fiancée (very much alive) were undergoing this torture. He would snap himself out of this delusion by regularly saying to himself: 'But whatever are you thinking of?' But still he was assailed by all kinds of rat-related obsessional thoughts: that subterranean rats were causing the ground beneath him to heave; that a rat was feeding off his father's buried corpse.

Still on manoeuvres, Lanzer ordered new spectacles, which were delivered to his regiment's post office. Captain Nemeczek gave Lanzer the spectacles and told him that he must pay three crowns eighty to a Lieutenant David, who had already paid this charge on his behalf. In Lanzer's mind, this order to pay transformed into a command from his father. Lanzer *wanted* to pay the debt, but at the same time, he did *not want* to pay it, believing that if he did so, his waking nightmare about the rats eating his father and his fiancée would come true.* Ever

---

* In 1953, the French psychoanalyst Jacques Lacan, influenced by the anthropologist Claude Lévi-Strauss's idea of 'mythic construction', built an entire new theory of 'The Neurotic's Individual Myth' on this unpaid debt: 'I think that this difference between the Oedipal triangulation and the quaternary of the obsessional's economy ought to lead us to question the general anthropology derived from analytic doctrine as it has been taught up to the present.'

since his father's death, Lanzer had suffered from intense guilt. As a child, his father had punished him with a severe beating; this beating prompted fantasies of killing his father. On his deathbed, the old man had called for him, but Lanzer refused to see him. This guilt was exacerbated by Lanzer's having *wished* for his father's death, which would give him a large inheritance, thus allowing him to marry the dowerless Gisela.

The key to solving the Rat Man's problem, according to Freud, was *transference*: the phenomenon where the patient's feelings about parents and authority figures are projected – or *transferred* – on to the analyst. During the analysis, Lanzer subconsciously equated Freud with *all* authority figures: his own father; the father of a wealthy cousin his parents had encouraged him to marry instead of Gisela; the sadistic Captain Nemeczek; even his boyhood governess. In one 'difficult' session, Lanzer shouted abuse at Freud, and even tried to hit him: 'he began heaping the grossest and filthiest abuse upon me and my family.' The analysis, nevertheless, was conducted in 'a warm atmosphere': Freud, who had an obsessional personality himself, empathised with this neurosis. Lanzer's exchanges with Freud were often witty and aphoristic, and he was an obliging patient: he loved free-associating, and his dreams were vivid and dramatic. Lanzer recounted a dream in which a dentist mistakenly pulled out a large healthy tooth adjacent to the diseased one; Freud interpreted this as symbolising Lanzer's youthful masturbation *and* his 'vengeful castration of his father'; a dream about Japanese swords represented his father's prohibition against Lanzer marrying Gisela, and so on.

Freud saw the case of the Rat Man partly as a linguistic puzzle: Lanzer's father, for example, was a gambler who regularly lost money at a game called *spielratte* (gambling rat); rats symbolised money: when discussing his fee with Freud, Lanzer thought to himself, 'so many florins, so many rats'. The German language lent itself to this game: 'guessing' is *raten*, 'marrying' *heiraten*. When the Rat Man spoke about his governess, one Fräulein Rudolf, Freud deduced that he *must* be homosexual, because he had referred to her by her *surname* – a common male *first* name. Freud presented psychoanalysis to his Salzburg audience as the interpretation of riddles, the solving of puzzles, a skill that required both deep knowledge and intuition. Freud liked to compare himself to Sherlock Holmes,* once boasting to Jung: 'I made it appear as though the most tenuous of clues had enabled me, Sherlock Holmes-like, to guess the situation.' Just like Holmes, Freud got to the core of the Rat Man's problem by treating as deeply significant the most trivial of clues.

The analysis lasted from 1 October 1907 to sometime in September 1908, so the Rat Man was still in treatment at the time of the Salzburg congress. Freud, however, gave the impression that the analysis had been completed, that the Rat Man was

---

* Arthur Conan Doyle and Freud were near contemporaries, the latter being three years older. In *Sherlock Holmes and the Case of Dr Freud* (1985), the eminent English psychiatrist Michel Shepherd drew a parallel between the intuitive deductions made by Holmes from the smallest clues and Freud's overestimation of the significance of word similarities, dreams and slips of the tongue. He called their common approach – which he saw as pseudoscientific and embedded in myth – a 'mythod'. In Nicholas Meyer's 1974 Holmes pastiche *The Seven-Per-Cent Solution*, Dr Watson tells Freud: 'you are the greatest detective of them all.'

cured. In his 1982 'entertainment', *The End of the World News* (not the finest of his thirty-three novels), Anthony Burgess fictionalised the five-hour talk, giving Freud these concluding words: 'After eleven months of daily sessions he was able to look squarely at the elements of the fantasising that had been locked in his unconscious. He saw that he had no occasion to feel guilt towards his father. Once the rat obsession was dissolved, I was able to pronounce him cured. He is now practising law with vigour and success. He is also happily married.' In Burgess's novel, the rat phobic Hungarian analyst Sándor Ferenczi faints several times during the talk and is eventually persuaded by Freud to leave the room, 'to save himself from further distress'.

In *Freud and the Rat Man* (1986), the Canadian Freudian scholar Patrick J. Mahony (no relation) indulgently writes that 'in those instances where Freud's published case histories did not factually conform to his process notes, we notice he retained his role as effective storyteller, aesthetically guiding his fabled reconstruction by narrative principles' – in other words, Freud was perfectly happy to embellish and fib if it made for a better story. According to Mahony, the Rat Man's cure was

> in large measure a transference cure, owing greatly to the imposing Freud's accepting attitude and his reassuring technique of reconstructing the infantile as well as the recent past. The Rat Man 'had to be forced into remembering what he had forgotten and into finding out what he had overlooked'. Within the first seven sessions, Freud declared

that the Rat Man's illness had arisen mainly from unresolved mourning for his father's death, a pathological mourning traceable to parricidal wishes from the patient's sixth year.

Freud must have been a hypnotic speaker to hold his audience's attention for so long; then again, this was a highly selected group of psychoanalytic pioneers, who regarded him as a visionary. Listening to the five-hour lecture might even have been a test: if you could endure it, you were *one of us*. 'I have never before been so oblivious of the passage of time,' recalled Ernest Jones:

> As is well known, Freud was no orator, and all the arts of rhetoric were alien to him. He spoke as in a conversation, but then his ordinary conversation was so distinctive as to be worthy of literary recording. His ease of expression, his masterly ordering of complex material, his perspicuous lucidity, and his intense earnestness made a lecture by him – and I was to hear many – both an intellectual and artistic feat.

Freud's lecturing style was influenced by his hero Jean-Martin Charcot (1825–93), the French neurologist, best known for his work on hysteria* and hypnosis. When he was a young doctor, Freud spent four months during the winter of 1885–6 training with Charcot at the Salpêtrière hospital

---

* Now called 'conversion disorder', as 'hysteria' is thought to be misogynistic. Patients typically present with 'medically unexplained' neurological symptoms, such as paralysis, blindness and seizures.

in Paris. Freud translated Charcot's 'Tuesday Lectures' into German; in the introduction, he wrote: 'These lectures owe a particular charm to the fact that they are entirely, or for the most part, improvisations. Charcot is obliged to behave before his audience as he ordinarily does only in medical practice, with the exception that he thinks aloud and allows his audience to take part in the course of his conjectures and investigations.' Freud too, improvised, speaking to find out where his thoughts would lead him. The five-hour lecture was not, however, entirely unrehearsed: he had already spoken about the Rat Man on no less than *six* occasions at the Wednesday evening Vienna psychoanalytic meetings held at his apartment. Freud had quite a bit of practice in all things rat-related by the time he stood up to speak at the Hotel Bristol in Salzburg.

When he finally wound up his talk, Freud's audience was both exhausted and ecstatic. Otto Gross, the Austrian bad boy of psychoanalysis, was the first on his feet to lead the standing ovation and sustained applause. He toasted Freud as a scientific revolutionary, a Nietzschean destroyer of old prejudices, an enlarger of psychological horizons. Gross, a bohemian drug addict, was *not* the kind of follower Freud wanted to attract, and sternly admonished him: 'We are doctors, and doctors it is our intention to remain.'

Freud disliked any debate or discussion after his 'scientific' presentations; 'it was in deference to this attitude', wrote Jones piously, 'that papers read at psychoanalytic congresses have never been followed by discussion of them'. The other speakers, now four hours behind schedule, had each been allocated a paltry thirty minutes. Jones, presenting a paper on 'rationalisation* in everyday life', had to follow Freud. Although he was almost completely unknown, had been dismissed from his last job, and had no expertise in psychoanalysis, Jones had the combination of courage and neck to follow the great man. 'No one will admit', he told his audience, 'that he ever deliberately performed an irrational act, and any act that might appear so is immediately justified by distorting the mental processes concerned and providing a false explanation that has a plausible ring of rationality.'† Jones might have been laying down here the template for the rest of his life.

Trotter missed Freud's address; he told Jones that his German wasn't up to following a long lecture. It is odd that having travelled from London to Salzburg, Trotter did not bother, even out of curiosity alone, to see what all the fuss about this Viennese doctor was about. He did, however, attend the congress dinner, and found himself seated between Jones and Fritz Wittels, who, according to Jones, 'tried to entertain him [Trotter] with jejunely facetious remarks about the hysteria of some Greek goddess'. Trotter turned to Jones and muttered revealingly: 'I console myself with the thought that I can cut a leg off, and no one else here can.' Wittels, 'the *enfant terrible* of the group', according to Jones, was then a baby-faced twenty-seven-year-old, a curious mix of braggart and lickspittle. Freud, he later wrote, 'accepted me as a naughty

---

* Jones coined the neologism 'rationalisation' for this talk.
† Four years before, in 1904, Trotter had written a long essay on 'The Herd Instinct', which was eventually published by the *Sociological Review* in two parts in 1908 and 1909; Jones's paper on rationalisation was remarkably similar to parts of Trotter's essay.

boy'.* Around the time of this congress, Wittels was involved in a typically Viennese erotic triangle with the journalist Karl Kraus and a teenage actress called Irma Karczewska. Kraus, six years older than Wittels, was a sort of Austrian H. L. Mencken who repeatedly mocked Freud. It was he who coined the memorable phrase: 'Psychoanalysis is the disease for which it pretends to be the cure.'† Kraus had published some pieces by Wittels in his magazine *The Torch* and introduced him to the seventeen-year-old Irma, the daughter of an immigrant janitor. Wittels fell in love with Irma, 'a miracle of a Dionysian girl born several thousand years too late'. She inspired his concept of the *child-woman*: 'a girl of great sexual attraction, which breaks out so early in her life that she is forced to begin her sex life while still, in all other respects, a child. All her life long she remains what she is: oversexed and incapable of understanding the civilised world of adults.' In *Freud and the Child Woman*, his posthumously published memoir, Wittels proudly called this 'one of my more important contributions to analytical psychology'. Unable to earn a living as a GP, Wittels decided to give psychoanalysis a shot, and joined Freud's Wednesday evening discussion group. (Freud later remarked that in the early days, he wasn't too choosy about the calibre of disciple and took whoever turned up.) Wittels brazenly admitted to his opportunism: 'I swam elatedly in the psychoanalytic current. I was one of the few who clearly foresaw the world "craze" it was to become.'

* Freud once referred to him as a '*Lausbub*' [little rascal].
† Although Freud commonly dismissed any criticism of psychoanalysis as motivated by anti-Semitism, Kraus was a Jew.

Such was the man telling jokes to the profoundly unimpressed Wilfred Trotter. Many years later, Jones lamented:
'After a couple of days in what was evidently an atmosphere
uncongenial to him, he abruptly left for home, and so ended
one of his two or three brief visits to the Continent. Trotter's
conduct in Salzburg was characteristic of him. An outstanding
difference between us was that, whereas I could be happy in
any strange assembly, whether I was playing a personal part
or simply enjoying myself as an onlooker, Trotter was at ease
only on his own ground and on his own conditions.' Trotter's
son Robert wrote fifty years later: 'My father's interest in
the subject thereafter lapsed. I think he found Freud's earlier
followers somewhat odd.' While Trotter was unpersuaded,
Jones was enthralled: he had found his master and his cause.

The Rat Man was not cured, as Freud had claimed. His analysis
continued long after Freud's triumphant lecture, well into 1909,
when Freud admitted to Jung that Lanzer's 'father-complex
and transference still gives him trouble'. Ernst Lanzer, the Rat
Man, died on 25 November 1914, having been taken prisoner
by the Russian army only four days before. We don't know if
he was executed, or died of injuries, exposure or disease. His
mother died in Vienna the same day.

4

What a busy little man Jones was. After the Salzburg congress, and with the unpleasantness at the West End Hospital now behind him, he paired off with Abraham Brill, the American-based, Austrian-born psychiatrist who, like Jones, had been recently converted to Freud's ideas. Jones had now decided to throw in his lot with psychoanalysis, an entirely pragmatic decision; all doors in London medicine were now closed to him – he had nothing to lose. He and Brill travelled on to Vienna, where they were entertained by Freud, who saw them as valuable new recruits. Jones and Freud enjoyed long intimate conversations; Brill offered his services as Freud's English translator. From Vienna, Jones travelled on to Munich, where he had arranged to spend two months as an observer in Emil Kraepelin's department. Jones looked forward also to renewing his acquaintance with the charismatic Otto Gross, whom he had first encountered the previous November. It was on that visit that he also first met Gross's wife, the irresistible Frieda Schloffer.

Gross, born in Gniebing, near Feldbach in the south-eastern Austrian province of Styria, and who had qualified as a doctor in

1899, was then Kraepelin's 'assistant'. He was indulged by both Kraepelin and Freud because his father, Hans, was a distinguished – indeed, famous – criminologist and forensic scientist. Although Hans Gross was in all other respects a disciplinarian, he regarded Otto as an intellectual prodigy, and the boy grew up without any boundaries imposed on his behaviour. He became that rare bird, a bohemian doctor, and Jones's 'first instructor in the practice of psychoanalysis'. Gross did not spend very much time assisting Kraepelin, preferring to spend most of his time in the Schwabing district of Munich. Here, he conducted his 'practice' at a table in a café that was open twenty-four hours a day, spending his fees on morphine and cocaine.

Gross, then thirty-one, was in bad shape, drug addled and manic, in the weeks leading up to the Salzburg congress. His father and colleagues arranged for his involuntary admission to the Burghölzli clinic in Zurich under the care of Carl Gustav Jung on 11 May, two weeks after the Salzburg congress; it was not his first admission there. Jung diagnosed schizophrenia; Freud thought he had 'paranoia'. Jung, who had far more experience with psychosis, was probably correct. While Otto was in Zurich with Jung, Jones was in Munich with Frieda. She was beautiful and captivating, 'one of the few Teutonic women I have ever liked', wrote Freud. Otto had asked Jones at the Salzburg congress if he would consider analysing Frieda; Jones discussed this with Freud, who wrote to Jung:* 'Jones wants to

---

* This was the golden age of letter writing, when people sent letters as easily and frequently as we might text. Freud was a diligent (and fabulously indiscreet) letter writer; his huge correspondence has been the main source of material for his biographers.

go to Munich to help the Grosses. The little woman seems to be seriously smitten with him. He should not accede to Gross's insistence that he treat his wife but try to gain influence over him. It looks as if this were going to end badly.'

Jones, staying at 9 Glückstrasse, Munich, wrote to Freud on 13 May 1908; it was the first letter in a correspondence that lasted thirty-one years:

As to Gross: you know, no doubt, that he has entered the Burghölzli, so he is probably having a bad time in the early drugless days. My relation to his wife is of course difficult. Gross is obsessed with the idea of my treating her and is expecting reports from both of us as to complexes etc. Her hate against him is not at all so strong as I expected. Also, her feeling for me is not so strong as you and I expected. She has a whole series of nervous symptoms. For the past few months, she has been deeply in love with another man, and has had to conceal this from Gross, as the two men dislike each other. Gross gets delight in getting other men to love her – no doubt a perverse development of his free love ideas. This she doesn't like, as she says it is her own business; in addition, she has been very jealous about his relations with other women. All this I know you will treat as strictly private.

Jones would soon learn that Freud could not treat *any* news as 'strictly private'.

Captivated by Frieda, Jones was ostensibly attached to Kraepelin's clinic, but admitted that 'work was subordinated to enjoyment', coyly adding that 'I began to understand why Germany was the land of youth, of romanticism, of wine, women and song'. In *Free Associations*, Jones mentions 'a lady from Styria'* to whom he gave a slim volume of poetry inscribed: 'And May and June'. By 9 June, their relationship now clearly sexual, he wrote to Frieda: 'We who glory in the New Love must be strong', signing the letter: 'Your lover, Ernest'. Not content with cuckolding Otto, he was even nicking his slogans about sexual freedom being the road to enlightenment.

Meanwhile, Jung confessed to Freud that Gross's treatment was not going well, that Gross was 'like a six-year-old boy'. He refused to wash or shave, and despite the warm weather, he wore several layers of clothing; he would only eat vegetables cooked to his precise specifications; although he was supposed to be withdrawing from morphine and cocaine, he continued to use opium; he wandered the corridors of the clinic day and night, scribbling drawings on the walls and floors. By now, Jung and Gross were in *mutual* analysis. This therapy was draining; one session went on for twenty-four hours until both their heads were 'nodding like china mandarins'. His willingness to be analysed by his *analysand* might have had something to do with the fact that Gross was encouraging Jung – who was in love with his patient Sabina Spielrein – to shed his inhibitions, persuading him that to sleep with her would be liberating.† In late May 1908, Jung told Spielrein that Gross had inspired in

* Frieda was a native of Graz, in Styria.
† In *A Dangerous Method*, David Cronenberg's 2011 film based on this relationship, Jung (Michael Fassbender), in a sado-masochistic scene, canes Spielrein (Keira Knightley).

him 'the great insight' about polygamy and the 'New Love'. (For a certified madman, Gross seems to have been remarkably persuasive.) Some years later, Spielrein recalled: 'Dr Jung was my doctor, then he became my friend and finally my "poet", my beloved. Eventually he came to me and things went as they usually do with "poetry".' Sabina Spielrein was an early couch-jumper – a *analysand* who became an *analyst*. She worked in this capacity in Vienna, Berlin, Geneva and Moscow. Along with her two daughters, she was murdered by the SS in Rostov-on-Don in 1942.

When Frieda visited Otto on 14 June, he begged her to get Jung to discharge him, but she refused. Three days later, Otto escaped. He wrote to Jung:

Dear Jung

I climbed over the asylum wall and am now in the Hotel —. This is a begging letter. Please send me money for the hotel expenses and also for the train fare to Munich.

Yours sincerely.

Gross turned up in Munich a week later, much to Jones's consternation. Otto, he wrote to Freud, 'seems much worse, quite paranoiac – shut off from the outside world – and has already started taking cocaine again'. Fearful that he might discover their affair, Jones – to explain his constant presence and intimate knowledge of the couple's business – fibbed to Otto that he was analysing Frieda. Frieda discovered she was pregnant sometime later that summer but miscarried in late August. She was convinced that the father was neither Jones nor Otto, but the Swiss painter Ernst Frick. She told Jones (but not Gross) about Frick; he naturally relayed all of this to Freud. This pregnancy was very convenient for Jones, who was soon back with Loe Kann in London, planning his move to Canada. In July 1908, Jones wrote to Frieda; it was a break-up letter, of sorts: 'I agree with you about the advantage of not being too much together, much as I long for you.'

Somehow, Gross managed to publish, in 1909, a book on antisocial personality disorder,* a diagnosis that might well have been bestowed on its author. He underwent several more involuntary hospital admissions before he died on a Berlin street in 1920 from a combination of starvation, hypothermia and pneumonia. His many conquests included both Else Jaffé and her sister, Frieda von Richthofen (later Mrs D.H. Lawrence),† the writer Regina Ullmann, and the three sisters Marianne, Nina and Margarethe Kuh. He fathered several children, two of whom were confusingly named Peter. He established an anarchist commune in Ascona, Switzerland, but was expelled for 'inciting orgies'. His charisma was baffling – he was once hired, for example, as a staff psychiatrist by an Austrian mental hospital where he had been forcibly admitted as a *patient*. Franz Kafka was among several writers and artists who were entranced by him, writing that Gross 'made me

---

* *Über psychopathische Minderwertigkeiten.*
† Some years later, Frieda and D.H. Lawrence were both, quite briefly, Jones's patients. 'They were impelled', recalled Jones, 'by mischievous demons to goad each other to a frenzy.' One evening in 1915, Frieda turned up at Jones's flat asking for refuge from her husband, who was threatening to kill her. 'From the way you treat him,' Jones told the startled Mrs Lawrence, 'I wonder he has not done so long ago.'

think of the consternation of Christ's disciples at the foot of the cross'. Gross's personal credo 'Repress nothing!' and his espousal of 'free love' inspired the many counter-cultural libertines who followed him. The French psychoanalyst Janine Chasseguet-Smirgel wrote that 'Gross's paradise was the wish of every pervert: to free himself from the paternal universe and the constraints of the law'.

Many years after his death, the 'psycho-anarchist' Gross was rediscovered and lionised by the radical left, who saw him as the forerunner to figures like R. D. Laing and Wilhelm Reich, and the inspiration for the 'Freudo-Marxists'. Gross's admirers claim that he anticipated both the gay rights and anti-psychiatry movements, even the campaign for voluntary euthanasia – on the grounds that he had actively facilitated the death of a suicidal patient. He was among the first to advance the anti-psychiatry thesis that madness was the only possible response to a crazy world, that the mad were possessed of transcendental insight. Gross had once believed that psychoanalysis would be a tool of revolutionary anarchism: instead, as he saw it, it had become a form of patriarchal oppression. The way to challenge this oppression, he wrote, was 'to eradicate the authority that has infiltrated one's own inner being'.

The International Otto Gross Society (founded in 1999) was formally dissolved at a meeting in Dresden in 2017 and replaced by 'a working group without formal membership' as, no doubt, the anarchist Gross would have approved. Ernest Jones, who could cuckold a man without afterwards bearing him the slightest ill feeling, admired Gross to his dying day. He was, he wrote, 'the nearest approach to the romantic ideal of a genius I have ever met'.

Otto Gross: 'Repress nothing!'

5

When Jones arrived in Canada in August 1908, he
swiftly acquired several part-time posts, just as he had
in London. He became a demonstrator in physiology and
psychiatry at the University of Toronto, part-time pathologist
and clinical neurologist at the local asylum, and an assistant
in the Department of Psychiatry at Toronto General Hospital.
Somehow, he also found time to see private patients in
his home.

Early in 1909, Jones and his 'harem' (Loe Kann along with
his two sisters, Bessie and Sybil) moved into a new house.
Unpacking his old wooden stethoscope, he felt 'impelled' to
place it on his desk in such a position that it stood exactly
between his chair and the one reserved for his patients. In his
1913 collection *Papers on Psycho-Analysis*, Jones confessed that
'the instrument in question had in some way or other become
invested with a greater psychical significance than normally
belongs to it. The physical appearance of the instrument – a
straight, rigid, hollow tube, having a small bulbous summit at
one extremity, and a broad base at the other – was not unlike

a phallus.'* Self-analysis revealed to Jones (who referred to himself in the third person, as if somebody else was peddling all this phallic symbolism) that 'he':

> had placed his wooden stethoscope between him and his patients, just as Sigurd had placed his sword (an equivalent symbol) between him and the maiden he was not to touch. The act was a compromise-formation; it served both to gratify in his imagination the repressed wish to enter into nearer relations with an attractive patient (interposition of phallus), and at the same time to remind him that this wish was not to become a reality (interposition of sword). It was, so to speak, a charm against yielding to temptation.

Jones published many papers during his time in Canada, most notably 'Psycho-Analytic Notes on a Case of Hypomania' (1909) in the wonderfully titled *American Journal of Insanity*. The patient, who, had she read the article, would have immediately recognised herself, was, according to Jones, a woman whose 'sexual demands reached nymphomaniac proportions far exceeding her husband's capacity to satisfy them'. She believed that the eucharist was a form of oral sex:

> When speaking of religious observances, particularly Holy Communion, the patient broke off, and slowly and reverently, went through a perfect pantomime of the whole ceremony. This culminated in her taking a glass of water,

---

* Jones later coined the word 'phallocentric'.

which she had placed on a Bible, and gradually raising it to her lips, where she beatifically sucked the rim, slowly revolving the glass as she did so. During the latter part of the performance a complete and exhausting orgasm took place.

Jones described the event in detail in a letter to Freud: 'The patient, who of course did not touch me, would close her eyes, get flushed cheeks, breathe rapidly, make movements of coitus (this was on her back in bed), and come to a climax just as in an orgasm. It was curious, wasn't it?' He added (rather unnecessarily): 'She did not use her hands for masturbation.' Jones's use of the phrase 'complete and exhausting orgasm' was unusual in a medical journal – even the *American Journal of Insanity*. And it was not the only time 'a complete and exhausting orgasm' was witnessed by Jones while analysing patients. Jones's son Mervyn recalled (in his autobiography *Chances*): 'The couch in his consulting-room, originally corduroy, had to be recovered because a lordly patient had an orgasm when he reclined on it – "something to do with a stable-groom", my father explained.' (Astonishingly, Mervyn, who claimed to have 'no memory' of his prolonged analysis as a child by Melanie Klein, could recall that this couch, prior to the soiling by his father's aristocratic patient, was covered with *corduroy*.)

Jones wrote to Freud about several other patients with sexual neuroses, including a boy whose 'main complexes were concerning the oral and anal zones, and his chief obsession that Christ was sucking his penis all the time. It was a beautiful case, and he was an excellent subject.' Another patient believed that 'sexual relations consisted in blowing flatus into the partner's anus'. Freud replied with a quotation from Genesis about God inflating Adam with his '*Odem*' [breath] and suggested to Jones that 'some good work' could be done on 'the Mystery and Mythology of Flatus'.

Jones made many enemies in Toronto, including a surgeon called Herbert Bruce. In 1962, the ninety-four-year-old Bruce was contacted by Cyril Greenland, a historian of psychiatry who was interested in Jones's Canadian period (1908–13) and was especially intrigued by his paper in the *American Journal of Insanity*, which was reprinted in 1910 by the local *Asylum Bulletin*, edited, naturally, by Jones. Greenland discovered that the publication of Jones's article in the *Bulletin* had caused something of a local scandal,* and he was anxious to talk to anyone who remembered it. Bruce was reticent about the whole business and declined an invitation to be interviewed by Greenland, but was persuaded by his wife to write to him:

> My memory of the reason Jones left England was that he faced a prison sentence if he did not. As for the claim that he was unpopular because he was an Englishman – that is not a fact. It was because of his behaviour. I have talked to one of Jones's students who told me that in his first year he was able to get in to two of his classes only as he and the other

---

* The chief minister (premier) of Ontario called in the Professor of Psychiatry Dr C.K. Clarke, demanding to know why such 'filthy stuff' was being published by university staff.

80 students were crowded out by students of the previous years who went to be entertained and perhaps sexually excited by the uninhibited lectures. This doctor, a very able physician, was of the opinion that these classes were not held to give instruction as much as to satisfy Jones's own sexual impulses. Two other students likened him to the case of the Yoga teacher who has recently been sent to prison for six months because of his method of 'teaching' the cult to young girls. Jones was dismissed from the Faculty for good reasons – not because the city was Toronto the Good but because he was a pervert.

After two years in Canada, Jones faced yet another accusation of sexual misconduct. On 13 January 1911, he wrote a remarkably candid letter to his new friend James Jackson Putnam:*

A woman whom I saw four times last September (medically) has accused me of having sexual intercourse with her then, has gone to the president of the University to denounce me, is threatening legal proceedings, and has attempted

---

* Putnam, then sixty-four, was just the kind of eminent doctor Jones liked to cultivate: a Boston Brahmin (even his wife was a Cabot), and professor of neurology at the Harvard Medical School. Jones had first met Putnam in December 1908, when he gave a seminar at Harvard on Freudian psychoanalysis; Jones was deeply impressed by the older man, who in turn, was receptive to Freud's ideas. Putnam, recalled Jones, was 'the only man I have ever known, in a vast experience of scientific discussions, to admit publicly that he had been mistaken'. Such candour is very rare in academic medicine.

to shoot me. At present I am being guarded by an armed detective. I foolishly paid the woman $500 blackmail to prevent a scandal.

Less than a month later (8 February), he wrote to Freud:

The atmosphere is very unhealthy here for psychoanalysis, owing chiefly to an incredibly developed prudery, a total ignorance of and misunderstanding of your writings, and perhaps partly to some jealousy of me in certain circles. Stupid rumours keep spreading about my mode of treatment. I recommend masturbation, and advise debauchery to young women. I stimulate sexual feeling by showing patients obscene postcards! But most annoying is some trouble that has been going on for over a month. A severe hysteric woman whom I saw only a couple of times last September declared that I had sexual relations with her 'to do her good'. She is a divorcée, a morphine-maniac, has attempted suicide, and in all probability she will be deported from the country as an 'undesirable character'.

Loe, appalled by the arrival of this gun-toting woman at their house, paid the blackmail and the hire of the armed detective. His accuser's friend, Dr Emma Gordon, a doctor and member of the Women's Christian Temperance Union, tried to get Jones sacked from the University of Toronto, but the president, Robert Falconer, refused. Meanwhile, Jones was being stalked by two irate husbands, whose wives, having been analysed by him, had demanded divorce; one of them, a Dr Joseph Collins, regularly disrupted Jones's lectures. A rumour also did the rounds that Jones had been arrested by the Toronto police after exposing himself. Jones dismissed all of this as a prudish reaction to his revolutionary new ideas on the psychosexual origin of the neuroses, writing to Freud: 'the attitude in Canada towards sexual topics I should think has hardly been equalled in the world's history: slime, loathing and disgust are the only terms to express it.' Jung, now Jones's rival, cannily observed in a letter to Freud from 7 March 1909: 'the interior of Africa is better known to me than Jones's sexuality.'

Jones's stalker eventually ceased and desisted. He wrote to Freud on 8 March 1911: 'I still keep a detective, but that silly couple of female doctor and patient have done nothing more of late. They applied to a magistrate for a warrant to arrest me, but he sent them about their business. My wife is very upset and urges me, as she has done for a long time, to retire from private practice on account of its being "such dangerous work". If I refuse I think she will leave me.'

Jones did not spend all his time in Canada embroiled in sexual scandals. With his inexhaustible energy and ability to compartmentalise his life, he travelled regularly to meetings in New York, Boston and Detroit, where he met many prominent neurologists and psychologists, such as Putnam, Morton Prince and William James. Jones was part of the delegation that welcomed Freud on his only visit to the US in September 1909; he seized this opportunity to ingratiate himself with the master, pledging his life to 'die Sache' [the cause], and in a bare-faced attempt to supplant the *dauphin*, advised Freud to be wary of Jung.* Freud hated this trip and vowed he would never return. He found the food too rich, complaining of severe flatulence throughout.† He did, however, get his first inkling of his growing fame on this visit, when he noticed that his cabin steward was reading *The Psychopathology of Everyday Life*.

Wilfred Trotter wrote to Jones on 26 May 1909, having returned from South Wales, where he had witnessed the final hours of Ernest's mother, Mary-Ann Jones, who died of a brain haemorrhage at the age of fifty-one:

> I got back from Gowerton this morning. It was quite clear that there was nothing to be done. I saw her about 24 hours after the onset which had been absolutely abrupt. She was in a coma of the profoundest depth, pinpoint pupils, temperature 105 – which had been 108 – high tension pulse and frequent vomiting; mucus was already accumulating in the chest and there was cyanosis of the extremities. It was

---

* Jung was equally suspicious of Jones, writing – with great perspicacity – to Freud the year before: 'Jones is an enigma to me. He is so incomprehensible that it's quite uncanny. Is there more in him than meets the eye, or nothing at all? At any rate, he is far from simple; an intellectual liar hammered by the vicissitudes of fate and circumstance into many facets. But the result? Too much adulation on one side, too much opportunism on the other?'
† He wrote to Ferenczi: 'Whoever is not master of his *Konrad* [the name Freud gave his body when he became ill] should not set out on travels.' Freud suffered throughout his life from irritable bowel syndrome but was uncharacteristically silent on the psychological origins of this condition.

obvious that the largest decompression would be no good with the haemorrhage there.

Still, I am glad I went down as there would always have been the little thought that perhaps...

Your father was taking it in his usual dogged matter of fact way with occasional heart-breaking little lapses. How helpless I felt and was I leave you to imagine. It is to be supposed he will get through the first days fairly but I am afraid for him – as you of course will have been – in the long weeks later on. I am glad that Bessie is to be over so soon.

'Die Sache': Clark University, Worcester, Massachusetts, 1909. Sitting: Sigmund Freud, G. Stanley Hall (President, Clark University), Carl Gustav Jung; standing: Abraham Brill, Ernest Jones, Sándor Ferenczi.

The medical details finished with, Trotter continued, as if to a lover:

> You may suppose how much I thought of you going down there to your country. I had to reconstruct you on the spot and among the people. I think I saw you among them; the train journeys to school; all the odd scrapes you have told me at one time or another – and the dreams beyond it all. Does it sound cheeky to say I got a deeper look into your mind than I've had before?
>
> My love to Loe.

6

Loe was very unhappy. She hated Canada – deranged patients turning up at the house with a gun can't have helped; Jones presented her as his 'wife', but had no intention of regularising the relationship by marrying her; she had miscarried; she had been dependent on morphine for several years, having first used the drug for the pain of kidney stones; she had developed chronic abdominal pain and arthritis; she and Jones no longer slept together – he attributed this to her 'frigidity' or 'sexual anaesthesia': Jones, who prided himself on his attractiveness to women, could not conceive of any other explanation. He also confided in Freud that he had got himself 'in fresh difficulties with a woman'. Inevitably, and predictably, and despite Loe's clearly expressed 'hostility' to this therapy, Jones decided the answer to all these problems was psychoanalysis, and who better to analyse Loe than Freud himself?

Jones and Loe arrived in Vienna in June 1912; Freud hit it off with 'Frau' Jones, 'a precious creature of the highest value'. Loe, he told Ferenczi, 'is a highly intelligent, deeply neurotic Jewess, whose disease history is easy to read. I will be pleased to expend much Libido [mental energy] on her.' Jones, who had been advised by Freud that it would be best if he left Vienna for the duration of the analysis, went off on a tour of Italy for several months,* while Loe moved into an apartment with her maid, Lina, and her dog, Trottie (named in honour of Wilfred). Jones had been sleeping intermittently with Lina for some time; he confessed to Freud that 'some devil of desire made me yield to temptation'.

Freud wrote often to Jones about Loe's analysis, while Jones wrote regularly to both Freud and to Loe, who showed his letters to Freud. Jones wrote to Freud from Florence, relaying that Loe 'complains bitterly about you, that you do not trust her. She is beginning to feel the treatment as an attack on her personality.' Freud replied that this was 'a purely hysterical attack', and that 'she is splendid and charming since'. They speculated on Loe's sex drive, Freud warning 'perhaps she will be eager to begin intercourse and feel highly disappointed when anaesthesia has not subsided', while Jones anticipated that 'she will desire intercourse', but that he would 'not make any overtures'. When Jones confessed to succumbing to another 'lapse' with Lina, Freud warned him that Loe had discovered his infidelity. (I wonder how?) Jones, who viewed this 'lapse' through a forgiving psychoanalytic lens, told Freud that it was 'dictated', not by goatishness, but 'by a repressed spirit of hostility against my dear wife'. This discovery caused Loe to have an attack of severe abdominal pain, which in turn triggered in Lina two

---

* While staying at a *pensione* in Florence, Jones somehow managed to take on a new patient, who was, he told Freud, 'a great bore'.

episodes of pain identical to that experienced by her mistress: 'the nicest case', wrote Freud, 'of *Übertragung* [transference] I have ever seen.'

Jones returned to Canada early in 1913 to give a series of lectures in Toronto. Freud wrote almost daily with details of Loe's analysis; the only item he did not share with Jones was that Loe had met and fallen in love with a young American called Herbert ('Davy') Jones, who, at twenty-five, was six years her junior. This Jones (later dubbed 'Jones the Second' by Ernest) was a fabulously wealthy Princeton graduate (the family wealth derived from zinc mines in Wisconsin), who had arrived in Vienna on a 'cultural' tour of Europe. Freud wrote to Sándor Ferenczi: 'I still do not know how Jones will take it when he finds out that his wife, in consequence of the analysis, does not want to remain his wife anymore.' (Freud was still unaware that Jones and Loe were not married.)

Jones arrived back in Vienna in May 1913; he was devastated by the news of Loe's new attachment. 'It will cost me pretty severe depression', he told Freud, 'before getting over the blow of seeing her love given to another.' He had been determined to leave Canada for some time, complaining to Freud that the President of the University of Toronto had reneged on a promise to promote him to professor, 'owing to strenuous opposition from various people'; maybe, as Herbert Bruce asserted, he had been fired. What with the gun-toting, blackmailing patient, the stalking, heckling husbands and the accusations of pornography and sexual perversion, Jones concluded that he had no future there. Freud encouraged him to return to London, to be the pioneer and leader of psychoanalysis in England. By this time,

Freud's relationship with Jung had broken down, mainly because of the latter's scepticism about the sexual origin of neurosis. Jones capitalised on Jung's banishment by setting up – with Freud's blessing and deep satisfaction – the 'Central Psychoanalytic Committee', with himself as chairman. This committee would be a secret body, with a small group of 'Paladins'* who would protect Freud and promote his work. The chosen six were Jones, Ferenczi, Otto Rank, Hanns Sachs, Max Eitingon, and Karl Abraham. Freud presented each of them with an antique Greek intaglio, which they had mounted on rings.†

Having manoeuvred himself into such a position of influence and indispensability, Jones spent the months of June and July 1913 in Budapest, undergoing a brief but intensive analysis with Ferenczi. Naturally, he reported his progress regularly to Freud, who had instructed Ferenczi to 'put some stuffing in the clown, so we can make him a king'. During the two hours of daily analysis, they discussed Jones's not being breast-fed – his mother fed him with a 'quack' milk substitute, which Jones believed caused his short stature. 'The premature weaning and early ill-health', he recalled, 'had combined with internal factors to induce a deep feeling of insecurity and inferiority.' Ferenczi concluded that Jones had developed 'an omnipotence complex' resulting from 'the rejecting breast, his small stature, and lower-class origins'. Jones found the analysis 'highly

---

* The Paladins were twelve legendary knights, the trusted inner circle of Charlemagne's court in the eighth century, who guarded, according to Jones, 'the kingdom and policy of their master'.
† Jones was the only Paladin to lose his ring; the box containing it was stolen from his car boot in London.

constructive'. He wrote to Freud: 'As you no doubt suspect, my unconscious, with the logic peculiar to itself, had been blaming you for the loss of my greatest friend (Trotter), then of my wife, i.e., the man and woman who were dearest to me. However, there isn't any doubt that this is only a passing phenomenon.'

Loe visited him in Budapest; Jones had the enviable ability to extract himself from relationships with the minimum of mess, and nearly always remained on good terms with his ex-lovers. 'We have both worked off our infantile sexuality,' he wrote to Freud. 'I will do all in my power to further her happiness.' Although he was secretly relieved that another man (and how wonderful that he too was Jones!) had taken this barren, morphine-dependent, neurotic woman off his hands, he and Loe remained on such good terms that when Ernest Jones moved back to London in August 1913, she went with him, briefly suspending her analysis. She supervised the redecoration of a flat in Portland Place, and even offered to cover his expenses for three years while he established himself. Jones wrote (with considerable relief) to Freud: 'I rejoice now to think we are parting, for with all her magnificent character and many charms she has as well a devouring and all-absorbing personality, so that life with her is at the best a strenuous performance, and at the worst, when she does not love, a painfully disagreeable and racking experience.'*

---

* A few weeks later, he described to Freud an episode illustrating Loe's neurotic personality: 'She brought home a stray kitten when I was away, overfed it, and then late last night gave it an overdose of purge as well as an enema. The cat got a little twitching and because I took this at first lightly she flew into a most violent temper and outburst of hate. Then

Loe returned to Vienna in November 1913; Jones destroyed 'masses of old letters, documents, etc', confiding in Freud that this exercise unrolled 'a story of much turmoil and turbulence; an unhappy childhood followed by ten years of uninterrupted success, then a series of foolishness and failures'. By the following March, Freud reckoned he had finally got to the root of Loe's problem: when she was a child, Loe wanted to give her father a baby, and simulated the appearance of pregnancy by holding on to the contents of her bowels; her mother made her 'miscarry' by giving her daily enemas. Jones had become her husband-father; when Loe *really* miscarried in Canada, she 'became' her own mother. Now, Loe and her 'mother' *imago* were battling for her soul, and it was this battle that had torn her apart. Naturally, Freud conveyed all of this to Ernest Jones. Following this dazzling insight, Loe married Herbert 'Davy' Jones in Budapest on 1 June 1914. Freud, Rank and Ferenczi were witnesses; it was one of only two weddings outside his family that Freud attended. Herbert's family, who were opposed to this union, did not attend. There was no honeymoon, as Loe returned immediately to analysis; she 'completed' her treatment on 11 July 1914, having lain on Freud's couch for 392 hours. It all worked out for Ernest Jones: the woman who had caused him such 'intolerable suffering' was off his hands; his psychoanalytic practice in London was growing; Lina kept house and shared his bed.

she kept me for three hours running "urgent messages" as a punishment. Bromide had to be fetched and a special syringe procured to administer it. She certainly has the power of gratifying and developing the masochistic side of a man.'

By the time war broke out in August 1914, Loe and Davy had also relocated to London; Loe had to smuggle Trottie (her dog)* through Holland. She purchased huge quantities of morphine (then perfectly legal), which she planned to distribute to the needy soldiers. Ernest Jones wrote to Freud: 'Isn't she wonderful?' Anticipating a bombing of London, she and Davy purchased a Rolls-Royce, which they had converted into an armour-plated ambulance, so that Davy could collect wounded soldiers arriving by boat at the southern ports.

After the completion of her analysis, Loe stayed in contact with Freud. She even offered him the gift of her family's house in the Hague, now empty since her brother Kobus had emigrated to Palestine. Although she regarded him as a liar and an opportunist, Loe followed Ernest Jones's life with bemused interest and continued to meet him intermittently. Her kidney stones recurred, she remained dependent on morphine (as Ernest Jones predicted), and she grew corpulent; Davy developed 'chronic ill-health', a psychosomatic reaction, Ernest thought, 'centred round his jealousy of me'. In the early 1920s, Loe and Davy moved, 'for Davy's health', to a country house near Dorking in Surrey, where they kept a large collection of animals, including, according to Loe, 'two dogs, one pet cock, chickens, one donkey, one cat, two kittens and heaps of mosquitos and bumble bees'. Writing to Freud on 30 November 1921, Ernest Jones described the domestic arrangements of the Herbert Joneses:

---

* In 1915, anticipating poison gas attacks by German Zeppelins, Loe had a miniature respirator made for Trottie.

I must tell you the latest story of Loe. She replaced Trottie by a more obvious symbol, a cock, who always slept in her bedroom. A time came when she had to go away for a while, so that he had to take his place with the hens in the fowl-coop. Lest, however, he should suffer from fear or loneliness in this unaccustomed environment she had her bed moved there also and slept there with him for the first two nights until he no longer found it strange. Of her health I have no news.

The Herbert Joneses soon tired of country life, moving back to London in 1923. Ernest Jones wrote gleefully to Freud: 'I hear indirectly that Loe has returned to London, for Herbert Jones did not obtain the hoped-for benefit by living in the country. He still suffers from obscure abdominal symptoms and has just produced another book of poor verse.'* As well as writing poetry, Davy occupied himself with painting (he was good enough to exhibit at the Royal Academy), sailing and horse-riding. Loe remained addicted to morphine and continued to be plagued by kidney stones. Sometime in the 1930s, Wilfred Trotter operated on Loe for these stones; after the operation, she was cared for at home by a team of private nurses, including one Mary Pritchard-Jones. When Loe had fully recovered, she threw a small party for the nurses, which was attended by Olwyn Pritchard-Jones, the younger sister of Mary. Davy fell in love with Olwyn (fourteen years his junior)

* *Finlay* (1923); he had published three collections before this: *The Well of Being* (1920); *The Blue Ship* (1921), and *Romanel* (1922).

and begged Loe for a divorce, telling her that he wanted to have children. She agreed: Davy married Olwyn in New York on 20 May 1938. Their first son (also Herbert) was born on 14 May 1940, when Davy was fifty-two. He fathered two more sons: Tim (b. 1942) and Bill (b. 1945). Davy died in 1957, aged sixty-nine. Herbert junior was killed in action in 1982 at the battle of Goose Green during the Falklands War; he was awarded the Victoria Cross posthumously.

Loe died in February 1944; Anna Freud wrote to inform Ernest Jones. 'A momentary flash of the past hit me so vividly,' he replied to Anna. 'I saw her face and heard her speak as if she were alive again. It was disturbing.'

'None of the Committee was well-favoured in looks.'
From left: Otto Rank, Freud, Karl Abraham, Max Eitingon, Sándor Ferenczi, Ernest Jones, Hanns Sachs.

7

On 2 July 1910, Wilfred Batten Lewis Trotter married Elizabeth Jones, Ernest's elder sister. Elizabeth, or Bessie, as she was known, had kept house for Jones and Trotter in Harley Street; during this period, Trotter operated on her for a thyroid problem – probably thyrotoxicosis (overactivity of the gland), in which he was now an acknowledged expert. When Jones moved to Canada in 1908, Bessie went with him, along with their younger sister Sybil, to keep his house.

Early in 1910, Bessie returned to Britain to visit a 'suitor'; Trotter got wind of her plans – presumably from the fabulously indiscreet Jones – and met her at Victoria station when she alighted from the boat train. In the only romantic gesture of his entire life – he would have regarded the performance as irredeemably vulgar in anyone else – he proposed to Bessie, who accepted immediately. On 22 June 1910, less than two weeks before their marriage, Trotter wrote to Bessie before she left Canada for good: 'Telegraph to me the time of your train and look out for my ancient and venerable figure on the platform. Tremendous excitement reigns here at your approach, especially in the soul.'

Although Trotter's marriage to his best friend's sister (not to mention his operating on her) later prompted some feverish psychosexual speculation, the union was happy and lasting. 'I doubt if they had ever been alone together,' wrote Ernest Jones. 'They had certainly never written to each other and the only intimate passage between them had been an operation he had performed on her thyroid gland. Theirs was as successful a marriage as I have known.' Their only child, a son called Wilfred Robert (known as Robert), was born on 14 May 1911. He too became a doctor, and followed his father to UCH, where – neatly and predictably – he became a specialist in thyroid disease.

Trotter had been passed over for promotion to UCH's permanent staff in 1901; the much coveted post of staff surgeon went instead to the dashing and brilliant Rupert Bucknall.* Trotter stayed on at UCH as surgical registrar until 1904, when he took up a post as demonstrator in anatomy at the medical school. Over the next two years, this undemanding

---

* Bucknall (1874–1913), according to the Royal College of Surgeons' *Plarr's Lives of the Fellows*, was 'a man of singular brilliance with a genius for friendship, who met with a severe motor accident in 1910'. He was forced to retire, aged just thirty-six, and died three years later. Jones, however, claimed he was 'the first to recognise that the poor fellow showed the beginnings of general paralysis of the insane [tertiary syphilis]. Three years later this became manifest when he declared that he was the German Kaiser, and I remember Trotter remarking that if he ever fell a victim to the same disease, he would not develop such a banal delusion.'

appointment allowed him the leisure to indulge his intellectual interests, writing the essays that would later form the basis for his best-selling book on social psychology, *Instincts of the Herd in Peace and War* (1916). 'Another young surgeon', wrote the surgeon and author R. Scott Stevenson, 'would probably have been turning out contributions on surgical literature designed to catch the favourable eyes of his seniors.'

This prolonged immersion in anatomy would prove to be the foundation of his meticulous surgical technique, and it gave his mind, he said, 'something of the trained athlete's sinewy hardness'. Trotter combined his anatomy demonstratorship with a part-time appointment at the East London Hospital for Children, where he pioneered new operations for torticollis (wry neck) and talipes equinovarus (club foot). In 1906, at the age of thirty-four, Trotter was finally appointed to the permanent staff at UCH; a vacancy arose after the sudden and unexpected resignation of Victor Horsley, who had quarrelled with the hospital's governing committee over specialisation – he had no interest in 'general' surgery and refused to do it. Trotter had no such Olympian fastidiousness; although he became pre-eminent in the surgery of head and neck cancer, he made major contributions also in neurosurgery, abdominal surgery and thyroid disease.

The Trotter legend began to grow at UCH: the bone-dry wit; the self-effacing modesty; the technical brilliance; the antique courtesy shown to patients, colleagues and students; the intellectual hinterland. Junior doctors and medical students like to create such legends; this mythologising creates a camaraderie, and the hope that one day, these trainees will themselves be the subject of the indulgent, flattering anecdote. Was it so with Trotter? We will never know; all his contemporaries, trainees and students are dead. There is no one left to ask.

Elizabeth ('Bessie') Trotter.

At the time of the 1911 census, Wilfred and Elizabeth Trotter were living at 19 Harley Street, along with their 'boarder', the thirty-one-year-old surgeon Hugh Morriston Davies. In 1909, Trotter and Morriston Davies published a now famous paper in the *Journal of Physiology* – 'Experimental Studies in the Innervation of the Skin'. Trotter was prompted to take on this laborious and personally hazardous study when he came across a 1905 paper – 'The Afferent Nervous System from a New Aspect'– in the neurology journal *Brain*, by the neurologist Henry Head and the psychiatrist-anthropologist W. H. R. Rivers, and muttered to himself, 'that can't be right'. Head was fascinated by the neurology of sensation – particularly pain – and wanted to determine how nerves regenerated after injury. The sincerest form of science being self-experimentation, Head persuaded a surgeon to cut two nerves in his left arm (the radial and lateral cutaneous), and over the next five years, he travelled every weekend from London to St John's College, Cambridge, where Rivers carefully mapped the slow recovery of sensation.* Head, his eyes closed, willed himself to enter a trance-like state or 'reverie', which he called 'a negative attitude of attention', as Rivers tested the sensation in his arm. They reported two separate stages in the return of sensation: the first they called the 'protopathic' phase, where 'the sensations are vague and crude in character, with absence of any exactness in discrimination or localisation'; the second, or 'epicritic' phase, 'is characterised by the return of those

---

* Head and Rivers also carried out a lesser-known experiment, testing the sensation of Head's penis. (This is a rare example of *double* nominative determinism: could there be a better name than 'Head' for a neurologist who carried out experiments on the sensation of the penis?) Rivers tested sensation separately in the glans, corona, neck and foreskin, dipping the penis into glasses of different water temperatures. The sensation of pain in his *glans penis*, reported Head – with a wonderful grasp of the obvious – was 'more unpleasant than over normal parts'.

features of normal cutaneous sensibility'. They elaborated a dualist concept of cutaneous sensation: *epicritic* sensibility related to temperature discrimination, light touch and localisation of stimuli, while the more evolutionary primitive *protopathic* sensations were those of pain and extremes of temperature. Head and Rivers's model was widely accepted: it was simple, elegant, and seemed to explain so much. The words 'protopathic' and 'epicritic' swiftly became part of the neurological vocabulary.

Trotter, who was confronted with the problem of pain every day in his work, had long before decided to study the phenomenon. He thought that the findings of Head and Rivers were implausibly neat and had major doubts about their methodology. While most sceptical readers of this paper – particularly if they happened to be busy surgeons – might have tut-tutted and thought no more, Trotter, rather remarkably, decided that he would *have* to interrogate these claims. The only true means of doing so would be a bigger, better study:

We propose therefore to publish here such observations only as we have made upon ourselves. The chief bulk of the material has been obtained through the division by operation of seven cutaneous nerves in one or other of us. The cutaneous nerves we divided were the following: first the internal saphenous at the knee; six weeks later the great auricular [in the neck]; three months later the posterior division of the internal cutaneous of the arm just below the elbow; a month later the anterior division of the same nerve; and after a similar interval a branch of the same nerve.

A month after the division of the last-named, a branch of the middle cutaneous nerve of the thigh was divided in one of us. Finally, after an interval of seven months the corresponding nerve was divided in the other.

Over a year, Trotter and Morriston Davies recorded the stages and pattern of recovery. 'The analysis', wrote the UCH physiologist T.R. Elliott, 'was as laborious as that of an astronomer compiling a map of the smallest stars, for it involved the registration on each skin area of the thousands of minute points at which alone the sensations of touch or temperature or pain can be evoked.' Trotter eliminated some of the biases he had detected in Head's experiment by having *two* observers, and by cutting the nerves sequentially. Trotter was alert to the slightest of methodological flaws, writing with bleak understatement: 'at a certain stage of the work we were led to make and record in detail a series of 50,000 separate touches only to discover that the solution we had sought was not to be obtained by that method.' Trotter found no evidence of Head's dual 'protopathic' and 'epicritic' process. What happened when severed nerves regenerated was far more complex than Head had suggested, and this process of recovery was not *physiological*, but *pathological*: for example, nerve fibres sprouted into the denervated skin from adjacent, undamaged healthy nerves. No conclusions about normal nerve physiology could be drawn from data derived from surgically severed nerves.

This paper is of little interest outside the narrow world of neurophysiology, but it was widely lauded as a model of experimental *method*; the neurologist Sir Francis Walshe wrote that it bore 'the hallmark of scientific genius'. Trotter showed that a single, methodologically flawed experiment does not constitute scientific 'truth', that any novel finding – particularly if that finding is then the basis for a new *model* – can only be accepted if the original experimental result can be reproduced, or replicated. The vast bulk of novel scientific 'findings' are never subjected to the harsh judgement of reproducibility, and the 'replication crisis' is a blight on science and medicine to this day.

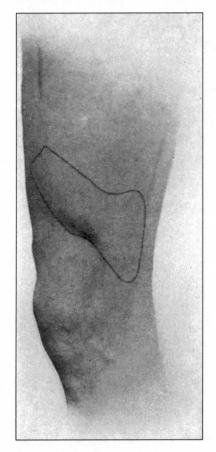

Illustration from Trotter and Morriston Davies's 'Experimental Studies in the Innervation of the Skin'. But whose leg is this?

Almost uniquely, Trotter combined scientific rigour with generosity of spirit. In 1921, Sir Francis Walshe wrote a devastating critique of Head's experiment; Trotter, aware that Head (who had developed Parkinson's disease) was now a sick man, persuaded Walshe to defer publication of this paper until after Head's death. Walshe reluctantly agreed; it eventually appeared in *Brain* in 1942, more than a year after Head had died. Trotter, so solicitous of his feelings, was outlived by Head. Walshe's essay is a relic of the days when medical journals published articles written in plain English, often expressing robust opinions – even if Walshe called these journals 'repositories of obsolete lumber'. 'The notion of pathways for localization or for discrimination', he wrote, 'are in the same category as that for pathways for truth or beauty, and are but figments of the observer's mind.' Head's conclusions were 'incredible', his formulation a 'fatal embarrassment', his general theory succumbed 'to the danger that always besets abstract thinking: that of confusing thoughts with things'.

Head's collaborator, Rivers, always more interested in psychology than neurology, was inaccurately and lazily known as 'the English Freud'. The title of Pat Barker's 1991 novel *Regeneration* – with its themes of trauma and healing – was inspired by Head and Rivers's experiment. To some a dilettante, to others a brilliant polymath, Rivers was a neurologist, experimental psychologist, clinical psychiatrist, anthropologist and ethnologist. He hadn't practised medicine for some years when he began treating shell-shocked soldiers at Moss Side Military Hospital in Maghull near Liverpool in 1915, and then at Edinburgh's Craiglockhart Hospital after 1916. Although

Rivers was influenced by Freud, his psychotherapeutic approach ('talk therapy' and *autognosis*, or self-knowledge) had as much in common with cognitive behaviour therapy as psychoanalysis. The *perception* that psychoanalysis was an effective treatment for shell shock did much to raise its profile during and after the war. Rivers's treatment of Siegfried Sassoon was the basis for *Regeneration.*

Trotter's pupil, the cardiac surgeon Robin Pilcher, speculated that 'the only man I met who might have been a close friend of Trotter's was Morriston Davies'. I wonder how Morriston Davies (his trainee *and* lodger) reacted when Trotter first told him about his plans for 'self-experimentation' – the protocol for this study would never get past a clinical ethics committee now. Morriston Davies was nearly as able and ambitious as Trotter, going on to become one of the first specialist chest (thoracic) surgeons in Britain. Overcoming the antagonism of the senior medical staff, he installed the first X-ray machine in UCH; he performed the first ever resection (lobectomy) for lung cancer in 1912. This brilliant progress came to a sudden halt in 1917, when Morriston Davies developed septicaemia with severe infection of his right hand and forearm after pricking his finger on a sliver of glass from a catgut tube.* This being long before the arrival of antibiotics, the infection worsened,

---

* Before he met Trotter, Ernest Jones's closest friend was his fellow medical student Bertie Ward. Ward died in 1902 from a finger infection that turned to septicaemia. This was a regular risk for medical students at the time; in an 1892 entry in *A Writer's Notebook*, Somerset Maugham described the death of a fellow St Thomas's student from septicaemia after cutting himself during a post-mortem.

and the great surgeon Sir Rickman Godlee told Morriston Davies that his arm would have to be amputated. When he refused, Godlee washed his hands of him, and Trotter took over his care. Morriston Davies eventually recovered, but his hand was now so deformed that he had to abandon his surgical career. He busied himself by buying and running a tuberculosis sanatorium in North Wales, while slowly retraining – by painting watercolours – his crippled right hand. By 1920, he was back in the operating theatre, and eventually became the first director of chest surgery in Liverpool. When he died in 1965, the *British Journal of Surgery* called him 'the Doyen of Thoracic Surgery in this country'.

The nerve study would be Trotter's only experimental investigation. I wonder why a young surgeon would do such a foolhardy thing as having a nerve in his arm severed, when his hands were his livelihood. Perhaps it was just something he *had* to do. 'Experimental Studies in the Innervation of the Skin' later persuaded the Royal Society to make Trotter a fellow – a rare distinction for a surgeon; near the end of his life, he successfully lobbied the society to similarly honour Freud.

Having made his point so definitively, Trotter dedicated himself thereafter to his craft. His theatre book for 1909 lists operations for breast abscess, laryngeal cancer, inguinal hernia, varicose veins, thyroid cyst and brain tumour. He made his reputation in the surgery of head and neck (tongue, pharynx) cancer, applying his scrupulous technique and magical feel for anatomical detail. He proved comprehensively that the brutal, mutilating operations then in vogue were quite unnecessary, that a careful, 'conservative' local dissection gave better results.

In this pre-antibiotic era, he found that he could dramatically reduce post-operative infection – which was usually fatal – by removing all the teeth before surgery.

Still only in his thirties, Trotter was – if only in UCH – a star. But he missed his old friend and surmised that Freud had taken his place. Six months after the Salzburg congress, he wrote to Jones:

> As to Freud. I think you write greatly about this business, and I have read and reread your letter with much joy. I get as I have often got before in our talks about Freud a certain sense that you are letting me down easily, a 'therapeutic' flavour which gives me an uneasy feeling that the distance between us has a quality of the indefinite and certain ominous hints that it is large. As regards the facts, as far as I know them, I do not think I am resistive, but I do not get the sense of illumination, the sense of splendour that you do.

Jones recalled the contrast between Trotter's 'fluency of speech' in conversation and the 'turgidity' of his letters. Although they corresponded regularly, Trotter found it a poor substitute for personal contact: 'Do you understand how difficult this letter business tells against me? I can't exaggerate how difficult it is to me: the harshness and falsity of it vex me continually – I really must talk *with* you.' Trotter predicted that Jones's evangelical zeal for Freud would end in 'a parting of the ways'; Jones replied that he had 'no pangs of doubt' about psychoanalysis or Freud, but that he would 'feel lonely' if there were such a parting. Trotter, the empiricist, the man who had seven of his own cutaneous nerves severed just to prove that Henry Head was *wrong*, who knew that science is measurement, could not accept Sigmund Freud's speculative theories.

If Trotter feared Jones was lost to this strange new religion of psychoanalysis, Jones too noticed 'a distinct change' in his friend around the time of the marriage to his sister: 'In the earlier years he was the most extreme, and even blood-thirsty, revolutionary in thought and phantasy that one could imagine, though there was never any likelihood of this being expressed outwardly. After the change he shut down this side of his nature completely; as he somewhat cynically put it to me, shocking me by the words, he decided to put security first.' Trotter, who was now supporting a wife, a baby and an unemployed younger brother, was faced with the age-old problem of *sustenance*; his decision to 'put security first' is one that countless young men, growing out of the fantasies of youth, have reluctantly, and sadly, made. Jones's son, Mervyn, was more forgiving:

Having encountered Trotter's cynical wisdom, I could hardly believe my father's assertion that in earlier days my uncle had been an ardent and impatient revolutionary. It would have been logical for him to approve of Trotter's progress into realism, good sense and maturity – instead of deploring Trotter's cautious (the implication is almost 'cowardly') abandonment of idealism. One feels that the change in Trotter had robbed Jones of something of himself – something of his youth.

8

The eighteen-year-old Anna Freud, accompanied by Anna Hammerschlag Lichtheim (a family friend) arrived in Southampton on 17 July 1914, having sailed from Hamburg. Waiting for her on the dock, with a bouquet of flowers, was Ernest Jones. A regular visitor to the Freuds' Berggasse apartment, he had known Anna – the youngest of the six children – since she was twelve. She had just finished school and embarked on this holiday hoping to improve her English before starting teacher training. Jones was now thirty-five and had thoughts of marriage. Lina, of course, was out of the question – his ambition was much higher. The prospect of becoming Sigmund Freud's son-in-law was so intoxicating that he talked about it to Edith Eder, his patient (and probable lover), wife of his close friend and fellow psychoanalyst, David Eder.* Jones also foolishly confessed his interest to

---

* Jones confided mainly in women, creating an intimacy that only increased his appeal. Edith was in analysis with Jones, and clearly in love with him, writing to him in 1914: 'I'm going to be equally frank about myself. So, suppose a woman of pretty vigorous sexuality is pretty strongly

Loe, who wrote immediately to warn Freud. He recognised Jones's usefulness to the cause of psychoanalysis and to him personally, but the thought of this now middle-aged seducer taking his beloved daughter was more than he could bear. Freud wrote to Anna on 17 July in a state of panic: 'I know from the best sources that Dr Jones has serious intentions of marrying you.' He described Jones as 'a very valuable co-worker', before pointing out his age, his 'very simple family' background, his lack of tact and consideration, his 'need of moral support'. She should not even consider marriage, he advised, for at least five years, and she should look to Loe for guidance in 'feminine matters'.

The agitated Freud wrote again five days later, warning Anna not to allow herself to be alone with Jones: 'When left to himself, Jones shows a tendency to put himself into precarious situations and then to gamble everything, which for me would not guarantee your security.' He also sent a warning salvo to Jones: 'She does not claim to be treated as a woman, being still far away from sexual longings and rather refusing man. There is an unspoken understanding between me and her that she should not consider marriage or the preliminaries before she gets two or three years older. I don't think she will break the treaty.' Freud suspected that Jones was using Anna to get back at him for his part in the break-up with Loe, writing to

---

attracted to a man...' Five years later, in 1919, during the interval between Jones's two marriages, and while her impotent husband was in Palestine, Edith spent at least one weekend alone with Jones at his country house. She wrote to him afterwards: 'Is this rather like a love letter, Ernest? Well, of course I do love you – you know that.'

76

Ferenczi that he did not want 'to lose the dear child as an act of revenge'.

Freud needn't have worried: Jones behaved impeccably, taking Anna on day trips to the countryside, to the theatre, to restaurants. Loe came along to chaperone, keeping watch 'like a dragon'. When war appeared imminent, Jones (with the help of Jones the Second) arranged for Anna's safe passage back to Vienna. He wrote – rather pointedly – to Freud on 27 July: 'She has a beautiful character and will surely be a remarkable woman later on provided that her sexual repression does not injure her. She is of course tremendously bound to you, and it is one of those rare cases where the actual father corresponds to the father-image.' Freud's panic over Jones's interest in Anna was misplaced. She wasn't interested in him, or indeed, any man. Freud had hoped that she might marry one of his Viennese Jewish disciples, but Anna's sexual orientation was to women; throughout the four years of the war, she fantasised about being reunited with Loe Kann.

Anna Freud was one of the few women wooed by Jones who was impervious to his charisma. In 1974, Anna – now in her late seventies – wrote about this episode: 'Naturally I was flattered and impressed, though not without a lurking suspicion that his interest was directed more to my father than to myself.' What could be more off-putting in a suitor? They maintained superficially cordial but distant relations until Jones's death. Although Jones was instrumental in rescuing the Freuds after the Nazi occupation of Austria in 1938, Anna felt that he had betrayed her when he later sided with Melanie Klein in the bitter English psychoanalytic civil war in the mid-1940s. Jones, for his part, protested that he was neutral in this dispute, and treated Anna with the utmost courtesy and respect; he needed her cooperation for the great work of his old age – his three-volume biography of her father. In the early 1950s, while researching this biography, he read Freud's letters to Anna warning her about him; Jones was aggrieved that Sigmund Freud thought he was motivated by revenge, and that Anna Freud thought he was using her to get closer to her father. He wrote to Anna: 'I found you (and still do) most attractive. It is true I wanted to replace Loe, but felt no resentment against her for her departure, it was a relief from a burden. In any case, I have always loved you, and in quite an honest fashion.'

In 1918, Anna began analysis with her own father; it was supposedly a 'training' analysis. Anna had now decided on a career as a psychoanalyst, which Freud approved of, even though he forbade her to study medicine – she would be a 'lay' analyst. Patrick J. Mahony called this analysis – with some justification – 'impossible and incestuous, an iatrogenic seduction and abuse of his own daughter'. Anna's adolescence had been difficult, with periods of depression and an eating disorder; in his analysis, her father explored these problems, along with her masturbation fantasies of beating. Freudian apologists explained this violation away with the phrase *Quod licet Jovi, non licet bovi* – 'What is permitted to Jupiter is not permitted to an ox' or, more prosaically, in the Yiddish '*Der Reb meg*' – 'The Rabbi is allowed'.

After three years, Freud was disappointed with the progress of the analysis, and asked Lou Andreas-Salomé to 'assist' him. Andreas-Salomé, now in her late fifties, was a Russian-born collector of great men, famous for her intimacies with Nietzsche (whom she drove to distraction) and Rilke (it was she who persuaded him that 'Rainer' was a more stylish name for a poet than 'René'). She came to Freud for analysis in 1912; he encouraged her to jump the couch and become an analyst herself, which she did, despite her admission that she lacked 'interest in ordinary people', and Freud's shrewd assessment that she was 'a narcissistic cat'. Although she refused to sleep with her husband (the hapless Friedrich Carl Andreas) for the entire duration of their forty-three-year marriage, Lou had numerous lovers, including the analyst Victor Tausk, eighteen years her junior.* Freud was entranced by this fabulous creature, his muse until she was displaced by the even more fabulous Princess Marie Bonaparte. Although he was uxorious and sexually unadventurous, Freud basked in the admiration of these flattering and flirtatious women.

Lou Andreas-Salomé and Anna shared interests in beating fantasies, anal sexuality and masochism. Lou, according to Anna, helped her in a 'strange and occult way'. She went back into analysis with her father in 1924. After years of intimate access to the most secret and hidden thoughts of his daughter, it finally dawned on Freud, after a thousand hours of analysis, that Anna was not the marrying kind. This suited him just

* Tausk committed suicide in 1919; before his death he had written numerous impassioned, but unanswered, letters to Lou. Leaving nothing to chance, he managed to simultaneously hang and shoot himself.

fine. After his first operation for cancer of the palate in 1923, she became his main carer, closest confidante, professional colleague and defender of the psychoanalytic faith.

Anna had first attended the Vienna Psychoanalytic Society in 1919 as a visitor; in 1922, she presented her first paper on beating fantasies, following which she was admitted as a member. Having trained as a teacher, Anna decided she would like to work with children. She was influenced by the work of Hermine Hug-Hellmuth (acknowledged to be the first child analyst); she was not diverted from this ambition when, in 1924, Hug-Hellmuth was murdered by her eighteen-year-old nephew Rolf, whom she had been analysing for several years. By 1925, Anna was *teaching* at the Vienna Psychoanalytic Training Institute.

Anna's life partner was Dorothy Tiffany Burlingham, an American heiress who arrived in Vienna with her four children in 1925. Dorothy, the daughter of the artist Louis Comfort Tiffany, was fleeing from her marriage to the surgeon Robert Burlingham. Robert, the scion of a wealthy New York family, had bipolar disorder, with episodes of severe mania. As the marriage floundered, Bob, their eldest child, developed asthma and eczema, and became 'difficult' with temper tantrums and petty thieving. The boy's problems began early on, when his mother handed over his rearing to a nanny, who regularly locked him in a closet. Dorothy, who had heard about Anna Freud's work with children, decided to move to Vienna so Bob could be analysed; it was also a useful pretext to get away from her husband. Robert objected, but Dorothy was determined; on 1 May 1925, she and Bob (ten), Mabbie (eight), Tinky (six) and Mikey (four) arrived in Europe. Their father was heartbroken; his friend Constance Buffin wrote that taking the children away was 'like refusing water to a man dying of thirst'.

En route to Vienna, they stopped in Geneva, where Dorothy engaged the psychologist Émile Coué, who 'treated' Bob by having him stand facing a wall and endlessly repeat: 'Every day in every way I am getting better and better.' At the start of his analysis, Anna Freud described Bob as 'a boy of ten with an obscure mixture of many anxieties, nervous states, insincerities, and infantile perverse habits'. Bob initially refused to cooperate, but Anna won him over by her willingness to do small favours and to excuse him from punishment. As the analysis progressed, Anna 'discovered' homosexual tendencies in the boy, tendencies that (whatever her own inclinations) she decided must be nipped in the bud. His superego, she deduced, had detached itself from parental influence; if she could reinstate the Oedipal rivalry with his father for Dorothy, 'normal heterosexual development' could proceed. Anna next turned her attention to Mabbie. While Bob had reacted to the breakdown of his parents' marriage by becoming an asthmatic delinquent, Mabbie instead became a tearful, sensitive, clingy girl, desperate to please her analyst.

Anna became a surrogate parent to the four Burlingham children and Dorothy's closest friend; in 1927, she told her father that she and Dorothy shared 'the most agreeable and unalloyed comradeship'. Dorothy, naturally, had gone into analysis herself, going first to Theodor Reik (one of the first lay analysts), then to Freud himself; just as naturally, she jumped the couch and began psychoanalytic training. The annexation of the Burlinghams was complete when Dorothy moved into an apartment two floors above the Freuds in the same building on Berggasse; Dorothy installed a private telephone line connecting the two households. The Burlinghams were tended to by two maids, a governess and a driver.

Robert Burlingham, nursing vain hopes of a reconciliation, came to Vienna in 1929, where he had a frosty meeting with Anna; an even more hostile exchange took place the next day between Sigmund Freud and Robert's father, Charles Culp Burlingham. In his biography of Dorothy, *The Last Tiffany*, Bob's son Michael John Burlingham wrote: 'The cornerstone of Sigmund Freud's self-mastery program for Dorothy, then, was an intellectual preoccupation so engrossing as to reroute her sexual drive. Desexualisation is not an attractive concept, but that was nevertheless Freud's intent. His denials to Robert aside, he was raising an absolute barrier between husband and wife.'

Anna combined the roles of psychoanalyst, teacher and co-parent for the Burlingham children; she believed that the analysis of children could only succeed with such an all-encompassing approach. By 1935, Bob was twenty and had undergone 2,000 hours of analysis. Mabbie, who had also been in analysis for ten years, she proclaimed 'the most successful' of her early cases. Tinky – who resisted psychoanalysis – endured a mere three years of Anna's attentions; Mikey, who was born after his parents' separation, appears to have escaped completely. Anna steadfastly opposed any contact between Robert Burlingham and his children. On 27 May 1938, he obligingly committed suicide by throwing himself from the window of his fourteenth-floor New York apartment. Sigmund Freud wrote to Dorothy, 'to remind you how little guilt, in the ordinary sense, there was in your relationship with your husband'.

Despite – or because of – the thousands of hours of analysis, Bob and Mabbie continued to have 'problems', unable to divest themselves of their dependence on Anna. Bob inherited his father's bipolar disorder, but Anna opposed the drug therapy (lithium) that might have stabilised this condition. Instead, he self-medicated with alcohol, and experienced regular episodes of mania and *delirium tremens*. A heavy smoker, he developed emphysema and angina, and died of a heart attack in January 1970, aged just fifty-four. Mabbie, a frustrated artist, returned frequently to Anna for an analytic top-up whenever any problems arose with her marriage or her children. In late 1974, she flew from the US to London and moved into the Hampstead home shared by Dorothy and Anna, where in July 1975, she took an overdose of sleeping tablets and died a week later in hospital. Michael John Burlingham – with heart-breaking understatement – wrote:

Bob and Mabbie's children particularly found it hard to see Dorothy and Anna Freud in a positive light. When the turbulence subsided, what remained was a nagging image: that instead of, or perhaps in addition to, having received a golden key, Bob and Mabbie had been loaded with an enormously heavy cross, and bear it they did, to the very altar of psychoanalysis. There remains the ironic conclusion that psychoanalysis had been foisted on them unnecessarily, and when dependent upon it, had not helped them. Then, when they had really needed help, Freudian ideology had discouraged them from seeking it, for example, in the realm of pharmacology.

～

The Burlingham children were not Anna's only victims; their tragedy would be re-enacted in thousands of American families. When divorce rates rose dramatically in the US during the 1960s and 70s, the family courts looked to psychologists for guidance on child custody. Anna Freud teamed up with the child psychiatrist Albert Solnit and the legal academic Joseph Goldstein.* They came up with the idea that every child has *one* 'psychological parent' to whom the child looks for security and affection. The psychiatrists and psychologists who were now routinely called in as experts by the divorce courts generally took the Goldstein-Freud-Solnit line, and these courts saw their role as the identification of the 'psychological parent', who would be granted full custody; in the great majority of cases, this was the mother. Freud and her collaborators recommended that the parent granted custody should have the right to 'control' (i.e. prevent) visitation by the noncustodial parent. Post-divorce contact between parents was discouraged as being inherently dangerous, and fathers

---

* Goldstein had trained first as a psychoanalyst and continued to see patients in his office at Yale Law School.

commonly disappeared from their children's lives. Although Goldstein, Freud and Solnit* elaborated their ideas in a series of books,† the evidential basis for their claims was shaky. Anna's beliefs about the role of fathers were formed by her experience with the Burlingham children; the fate of two of these children – Bob and Mabbie – was a closely guarded secret until Michael Burlingham's biography of his grandmother appeared in 1989, seven years after Anna's death.

The Burlingham children – like many psychoanalytic experiments – led tragic lives, but the relationship between Dorothy and Anna was sunny and cloudless as a summer's day. Dorothy ran their various households in Hampstead, Suffolk and West Cork; they enjoyed knitting and weaving together, and steadfastly refused to identify as homosexuals. Sigmund Freud once remarked that he stood 'for a much freer sexual life', but that he had 'made little use of such freedom'. His daughter was similarly lukewarm; one analysand referred to her 'spinsterish holiness'. Their secretary, Gina Bon, wrote an affectionate memoir for *American Imago* in 1996: 'I felt there

---

* Goldstein, Freud and Solnit invented a persona they called 'Judge Baltimore' when they wanted to speak with one voice. Baltimore, recalled Dorothy, was 'the benevolent figure of an enlightened judge who in his person combined the knowledge and personal characteristics of the three authors'. (Baltimore was the West Cork village where Anna and Dorothy had a holiday home, where Goldstein and Solnit were regular visitors.)
† *Beyond the Best Interests of the Child* (1973); *Before the Best Interests of the Child* (1979); *In the Best Interests of the Child* (1986).

was a kind of unfraught companionship, free of tensions or the kind of conflicts born of power struggles or jealousies that can prove so destructive in some marriages.'

Suffer little children: Dorothy Burlingham (left) and Anna Freud (right).

9

When Jones resettled in London, he was thirty-four; Trotter was now forty. While Jones was witnessing orgasms in Canada and being analysed in Budapest, Trotter was quietly becoming the finest British surgeon of the inter-war years. Although they were now brothers-in-law, Jones and Trotter had grown apart. Jones recalled:

> With Trotter the situation was complex. Although I had paid him brief annual visits since we separated five years before, there had been little opportunity for real talks, and I now remarked a decided change in him, both towards myself and in general. He welcomed me cordially, talked freely and as interestingly as ever on all sorts of topics, but nevertheless made me feel that a new barrier had grown up between us which I was not to transgress; we were no longer to share our lives, our hopes, and aspirations. He did not invite me to visit him, nor did he ever visit me except occasionally for medical purposes. That was, it is true, a general attitude of his, but still it was new towards me.

It naturally caused me some pain, or rather a sense of deprivation, and yet it became intelligible to me. In the first place, he was now on the staff of University College Hospital, with a rapidly growing consulting practice, and he had a wife and child. He certainly had none of the bourgeois ambitions that these words might imply, and they relate to something more subtle. He himself said rather brutally to me once that he had 'decided to choose security in life', but what he meant to convey, I think, was his perception that he could accomplish more in life, and give of what he had to give to his fellow-man, by functioning in the world of reality as he found it, rather than by indulging in revolutionary and impracticable phantasies. His coolness towards me really betokened his repudiation of that part of himself. Years later, when my increasing maturity reassured him that I was not likely to commit myself to any sort of wildness, he drew closer to me, but it was never 'glad confident morning' again. Another more personal motive was perhaps an even stronger ground for his attitude. He was possessive and very jealous indeed; he opened his heart only to those he considered his disciples. When I became interested in psychoanalysis he confessed to me that his jealousy of my interest in Freud's work was coming between us. Having little or no propensity to jealousy myself, I laughed at the notion of taking such a matter in a personal sense, but I am sure he was deeply affected by it. So he adapted himself to his environment; but unfortunately he was not able to accomplish the change except at the cost of considerable inhibition. Great as was his value in his surgical teaching and in his occasional inimitable addresses, the world lost much when he exchanged freedom for security.

Trotter's 'coolness' towards Jones is hardly surprising: he was distancing himself from a man whom he knew was lucky to be acquitted of charges of 'gross indecency' only a few years before; he would also have heard all about Jones's Canadian adventures from Bessie. Many of us, as young men, have had friends like Ernest Jones; when we get to early middle age, we wonder what we saw in them.

Although Trotter had chosen the life of the respectable surgeon over that of the bohemian intellectual, he made one lasting, major contribution to social psychology, with his book *Instincts of the Herd in Peace and War*, published in February 1916 at the height of the Great War. Trotter was persuaded by a government official – who thought it might be useful anti-German propaganda – to expand two essays, published in 1908 and 1909 in *The Sociological Review*, into a book. The core of *Instincts of the Herd* is a mere thirty-five pages (the original 1908–9 essays) followed by a new ninety-three-page section, 'Speculations upon the human mind in 1915', and in later editions, a twenty-nine-page 'post-script of 1919'. The book was a bestseller, going through several print runs and new editions from 1916 to 1963. The phrase 'herd instinct' became as familiar as the 'inferiority complex'. (Even Boris Johnson used the phrase in his resignation speech.)

Admitting that his thesis was 'frankly speculative', Trotter argued that human beings are essentially irrational and suggestible, 'always, everywhere, and under any circumstances'. The key to understanding their behaviour was *gregariousness*, which 'is of a biological significance approaching in importance that of the other instincts' (self-preservation, sex and food), and the foundation of the 'stupendous success' of the human species. He directly challenged Freud, arguing that 'all human psychology must be the psychology of associated man, since man as a solitary animal is unknown to us'. The herd, wrote Trotter, 'is the only medium in which man's mind can function satisfactorily. It is not only the source of his opinions, his credulities, his disbeliefs, and his weaknesses, but of his altruism, his charity, his enthusiasms, and his power.' While Trotter accepted the eugenicist Karl Pearson's argument that altruism is not a religiously inspired moral quality but a product of gregariousness, he observed – in a typical vinegary aside – 'how constantly the dungeon, the scaffold, and the cross have been the reward of the altruist'. Gregariousness, he argued, comes with a cost:

> The individual is more sensitive to the voice of the herd than to any other influence. It can inhibit or stimulate his thought and conduct. It is the source of his moral codes, of the sanctions of his ethics and philosophy. It can endow him with energy, courage, and endurance, and can as easily take these away. It can make him acquiesce in his own punishment and embrace his executioner, submit to poverty, bow to tyranny, and sink without complaint under starvation. Not merely can it make him accept hardship and suffering unresistingly, but it can make him accept as truth the

explanation that his perfectly preventable afflictions are sublimely just and gentle.

Trotter was one of the first empiricists 'from the bracing atmosphere of the biological sciences' to express doubts about Freud, confessing to 'a certain uneasiness as to the validity, if not of his doctrines, at any rate of the forms in which they are expounded'. Several passages in *Instincts of the Herd* could be read as an apophatic commentary on psychoanalysis:

> Every doctrine that makes disciples freely must contain in it some embodiment of psychological reality, however exiguous; but where it has been arrived at by the methods of the prophet, there is no reason that stress will be laid on the true more than on the false elements of the doctrinal scheme, and experience shows that the inessential falsity has for the expositor as many, if not more, attractions than the essential truth.

Trotter had an ambivalent attitude to Freud: he admired his intellect and prose style, even referring to his 'rich genius'; he accepted the validity of *some* of his ideas, such as the concept of the unconscious and the importance of early childhood experience. He noted, however, 'a certain harshness in Freud's grasp of the facts and even a trace of narrowness in his outlook' and was alarmed by his 'inclination for the enumeration of absolute rules, a confidence in his hypotheses which might be called superb if that were not in science a term of reproach, and a tendency to state his least acceptable propositions with the heaviest emphasis'.

In a review of the book for the *New Republic,* Walter Lippmann wrote: 'It is a dramatic episode in the history of thought, for Trotter is an Englishman and Freud is an alien enemy.' This did not go down well in Vienna. Freud's only comment (naturally, in a letter to Jones) was: 'Psychoanalysis stands rather isolated in this book.' In his 1921 book *Group Psychology and the Analysis of the Ego,* Freud grudgingly acknowledged the importance of the herd instinct, but grumbled that 'Trotter's exposition takes too little account of the leader's part in the group'. Although he would never admit it, Freud was influenced by Trotter: the cultural historian Gillian Swanson argued that *Instincts of the Herd* informed Freud's 'collective psychology', and the Dutch social psychologist Jaap van Ginneken suggested that Freud's concept of the superego was inspired by Trotter. In 1920, he confessed to Jones that he had 'devoted a thorough study to Trotter's clever book'.

Trotter should have published the thirty-five pages of his original 1908–9 essays and left it at that; the remainder of the book is jingoistic and repetitive. He elaborated an argument about the herd taking three forms – the protective, the socialised and the aggressive, represented respectively by the sheep, the bee and the wolf. English society was akin to the beehive, and Germany to the wolf pack: 'This conflict is between socialised gregariousness and aggressive gregariousness. It is a war not so much of contending nations as contending species.' Trotter predicted that Germany would lose the war because its lupine society was ruled by the whip, because its people had 'swallowed the doctrine of the biological necessity of war'. Meanwhile, his idealised England would 'continue on her road unconscious of herself and her greatness'. This went down a treat with the British public when it appeared in 1916. In his 1919 postscript, Trotter, now faintly embarrassed, admitted that he was 'not immune to prejudice'. He did, however, among all this stuff about the brutality of German society and the inevitability of a British victory, manage to sneak in an anti-war argument, writing that pacificists might be regarded, mid-war, as cranks, but 'legal and religious torture were doubtless first attacked by cranks; slavery was abolished by them'. He was withering, too, on the strange combination of religiosity and bellicosity at the time, pointing out the 'deep inconsistency between war for whatever object and the Sermon on the Mount'.

While he wrote *Instincts of the Herd*, Trotter watched with horror 'the growing river of blood which bathes the feet of advancing mankind'. The First World War was a terrible validation of his ideas on suggestibility; the entire nation had behaved like a herd – what exactly did all those young men give their lives *for*? They died, he concluded, because of *conformity*: 'Physical courage is admired by everyone, hence it is universal (soldiers are by definition "brave" even in a conscripted army); moral courage is admired by few, so it is rare; intellectual courage is admired by no one, consequently it does not exist.'

He deplored the British class system, and the conviction of the ruling class 'that its interests are identical with those of the nation'. He correctly predicted that the war would lead to an appetite for social change, but was horrified by communism, which was 'deeply tainted by the belief in an inverted class segregation of its own, and by a horror of knowledge'. Trotter, however, didn't hold out any great hopes for progress:

We seem almost forced to accept the dreadful hypothesis that in the very structure and substance of all human constructive social efforts there is embodied a principle of death,* that there is no progressive impulse but must become fatigued, that the intellect can provide no permanent defence against a vigorous barbarism, that social complexity is necessarily weaker than social simplicity, and that fineness of moral fibre must in the long run succumb to the primitive and the coarse.

Trotter pessimistically concluded, in a sentence that could have been written by John Gray: 'Material development had far exceeded social development; mankind, so to say, had become clever without becoming wise.'

Despite the success of *Instincts of the Herd*, Trotter was never tempted to write another book, or to become a public intellectual. 'Wilfred Trotter, the most perceptive social psychologist before 1914,' wrote the historian Reba Soffer, 'yielded after 1914 to Wilfred Trotter, distinguished surgeon and Fellow of the Royal Society, a sceptic who had overcome his sense of obligation.' Soffer interviewed Bessie Trotter in 1960, more than twenty years after her husband's death; she told her that Trotter, motivated by a sense of social responsibility, finished the book late at night after long days in the operating theatre.

* Trotter anticipates here Freud's concept of the 'death drive', which he elaborated in his 1920 essay *Beyond the Pleasure Principle*.

94

Ernest Jones recalled that Trotter was 'endowed with a strong Saviour complex. He yearned to do great things, and felt he was destined to redeem mankind from at least some of its follies and stupidities. In later years this love of mankind changed to a considerable scepticism.'

10

Freud may have been lukewarm about *Instincts of the Herd*, but his nephew Edward Bernays was mightily impressed. Bernays (1891–1995) was Freud's *double* nephew: his father, Ely, was Martha Freud's brother; his mother, Anna, was Sigmund Freud's sister. Bernays was born in Vienna, but his father moved the family to New York when he was still an infant. Over his very long life, he became the self-styled 'father of public relations'.* He lived long enough (he died at the age of 103) to be present at the peace talks at Versailles and to witness the digital revolution. When he saw Woodrow Wilson

---

* Public relations is as much the Freud family business as psychoanalysis. Sigmund Freud's great-grandson Matthew Freud (b.1963) is head of Freud Communications, an international public relations firm. In an article for *GQ* magazine, he wrote: 'My eldest sister once asked who Sigmund Freud was. My dad [the posthumously disgraced Clement] said he had invented a new kind of toilet and she was not to mention him again.' (The toilet reference is *very* Freudian.) Matthew complained that he was forever being asked: 'any relation?' He once landed a major new client in the 1980s who asked the 'any relation?' question, and when told 'yes', hired Freud on the basis that his 'shrink' had been 'out of town for three weeks'. Matthew, however, admitted in this essay that he 'gravitated towards Jung'.

being mobbed by cheering French crowds, Bernays, who had been fascinated by how the Committee on Public Information persuaded Americans to support the nation's entry into the First World War, realised that 'propaganda' – thought of then only as an instrument of war – could be used just as successfully for peace, and more importantly – for business.

In his 2002 documentary *The Century of the Self*, Adam Curtis argued that Bernays was mainly influenced by Freud, but in his 1923 manual *Crystallizing Public Opinion*, it was Trotter (although he lazily referred to him throughout as 'William') Bernays quoted – *not* his uncle Sigi. Bernays, struck by Trotter's assertion that 'the bulk of the opinions of the average man' were 'without rational basis', realised that the herd instinct could be exploited. He was so impressed by this sentence from *Instincts of the Herd* that he quoted it in italics: '*Man is not, therefore, suggestible by fits and starts, not merely in panics and mobs, under hypnosis, and so forth, but always, everywhere, and under any circumstances.*' Human suggestibility, Bernays decided, would be the foundation of a whole new industry: 'The only difference between "propaganda" and "education", really, is in the point of view. The advocacy of what we believe in is education. The advocacy of what we don't believe in is propaganda. Political, economic and moral judgments, as we have seen, are more often expressions of crowd psychology and herd reaction than of the calm exercise of judgment. The only way for new ideas to gain currency is through the acceptance of them by groups.' Bernays sent Freud a copy of *Crystallizing Public Opinion*, but his uncle's response was cool: 'I have received your book. As a truly American production it interested me greatly.'

Bernays's most famous publicity stunt – although he preferred the term 'the creation of circumstances' – took place in New York on Easter Sunday 1929, when a group of ten young women walked up and down Fifth Avenue, all smoking. The *New York Times* front page carried the headline 'Group of Girls Puff at Cigarettes as a Gesture of Freedom'. Bernays had been hired by George W. Hill, President of the American Tobacco Company, who asked him: 'How can we get women to smoke on the street? They're smoking indoors. But damn it, they spend half the time outdoors and if we can get 'em to smoke outdoors, we'll damn near double our female market.' Bernays sought advice from the psychoanalyst A. A. Brill, who advised him that cigarettes could be sold as a symbol of female emancipation. Bernays came up with the brilliant ruse of calling cigarettes 'torches of freedom'. He persuaded his secretary to pose as a women's rights advocate; she recruited a group of young feminists to march in the city's Easter Parade, ostentatiously puffing on their 'torches of freedom'. In private, Bernays was vehemently opposed to smoking; he flushed his wife's freedom torches down the toilet.

In 1920, Freud wrote to Bernays to sound him out on the possibility of writing some articles 'for a good magazine' in New York; in the same year, Bernays had arranged the US publication of *Introductory Lectures on Psychoanalysis*.* He approached

* Jones told Freud that 'the translation is loose and rapidly done, full of vulgar Americanisms'.

the editors of *Cosmopolitan*, who offered Freud $1,000 a piece for articles on 'The Wife's Mental Place in the Home' and 'The Husband's Mental Place in the Home'. Freud was appalled and rebuked his nephew: 'This absolute submission of your editors to the rotten taste of an uncultivated public is the cause of the low level of American literature and to be sure the anxiousness to make money is at the root of this submission.' Undaunted, Bernays wrote a month later to his uncle with an offer of $10,000 for six months' work in New York, seeing patients in the morning and lecturing in the afternoon. Freud considered the offer carefully; he declined, having calculated that with expenses and taxes, it wouldn't be worth his while. Freud appointed 'my queer nephew' as his agent in America in 1923. Bernays fared no better with his proposal to his uncle in 1925 that he might write an autobiography. Freud replied: 'Let's just say that your publisher shows American naivety in imagining that a man, honest until now, could stoop to so low for five thousand dollars. The temptation would begin at one hundred times that sum, but even then, I would renounce it after half an hour.'*

If Trotter influenced *Crystallizing Public Opinion*, Bernays's book, in a bizarre twist, influenced Josef Goebbels's campaign against the German Jews and the creation of the personality cult of Hitler. Bernays was shocked (but also, I suspect, secretly

---

* He later turned down an offer of $100,000 from Samuel Goldwyn to collaborate on a film about Antony and Cleopatra. Freud, according to the disappointed producer, was 'the greatest love specialist in the world'.

flattered) by this revelation. He certainly approved of the creation of another personality cult – that of his uncle. It was almost as if the persona of the great man, with his 'penetrating gaze' and 'trademark cigar', was an invention of an advertising agency. This much photographed gaze was such a strong image that people who have never read anything about psychoanalysis could identify Freud, just as they could identify Einstein, with his unruly hair and bushy moustache. Freud's penetrating gaze appeared on the certificate of membership awarded by the New York Psychoanalytic Society & Institute and was reproduced in thousands of stern busts and book covers.

Bernays, who was loathed by many within the public relations industry, saw himself as a figure of comparable importance to his uncle. This high self-estimation was partly justified; although he was an assiduous self-mythologiser, Bernays *did* almost single-handedly establish public relations as a profession. He pioneered the tactic of using 'front groups' to indirectly advertise the product; he promoted disposable 'Dixie' cups, for example, by founding the bogus Committee for the Study of the Sanitary Dispensing of Food and Drink, which promoted the idea that *only* disposable cups were safe. (This indirect approach to marketing has been successfully deployed by the pharmaceutical industry through its funding of patient advocacy groups, medical conferences and 'research'.) Bernays was using influencers before this word was used to describe what they did: he paid an army of women to promote cigarettes as slimming, encouraging their friends to 'reach for a Lucky instead of a sweet'.

Bernays believed that 'special pleaders' like him were a force for good: 'The conscious and intelligent manipulation of the organized habits and opinions of the masses is an important element in democratic society.' He saw himself as a pioneer, much like his uncle, overcoming the forces of reaction and prejudice: 'My uncle, Sigmund Freud, encountered almost insurmountable obstacles in gaining acceptance for psychoanalysis. I decided to try to establish public acceptance for the work I was doing and have made this an avocation of the years since.' Some have argued that Bernays's influence was as great as Freud's: he persuaded the world that needs and wants were the very same.

New York, Easter Sunday, 1929: women
smoking 'torches of freedom'.

11

On 31 October 1916, Jones wrote to Freud: 'I have been three years in England now, and am glad to be able to reassure you finally about any fears you may have had concerning my sexual life. I am a "reformed character", as they say.' A few weeks later, Jones (now thirty-seven) attended a party in London where he met the twenty-five-year-old Morfydd Owen, a Welsh musician, singer and composer. This was a welcome respite from the attentions of his patient Dr Ethel Vaughan-Sawyer (surgeon, widow, Fabian, feminist), who at the time was writing him gushing letters, often several a day: 'I hug myself for having found you.'* After a short courtship, he proposed to Morfydd on 18 January 1917, and they were married at Marylebone Register Office on 6 February, with Bessie Trotter and David Eder† as witnesses.

---

* 'Tottie', as Ethel was affectionately known, was then forty-eight; her husband Henry Vaughan-Sawyer had been killed in action in 1914.
† Jones and Eder had clashed over the latter's support for Jung; only Ernest Jones could invite a man he had quarrelled with (and probably cuckolded), to act as witness to his marriage. Jones, the recipient of passionate letters

Morfydd lied about her age on her marriage certificate, stating that she was twenty-three; she was, in fact, twenty-five, then regarded as relatively old for a bride. The atheist Jones insisted that they marry at the Register Office – even though Morfydd was a regular worshipper at the Welsh chapel on Charing Cross Road – and then, at the last minute, moved the date a day forward, thus ensuring that her parents would miss the event. It was an inauspicious start to their marriage.

Writing to Freud with news of his wedding, Jones described his bride: 'She is Welsh, young (23), very pretty, intelligent and musical. After taking her degree in music, she studied at the Academy and sang at her first and last concert the week I captured her.' Morfydd Owen was a musical prodigy born in Treforest, Pontypridd, to a nonconformist family who ran a drapery. In 1912 she won a scholarship to study advanced composition at the Royal Academy of Music. During her four years there, she won more prizes and medals than any student before or since. 'It was the unanimous verdict of her generation', wrote the music scholar Rhian Davies, 'that Morfydd Owen was the most supremely gifted and diversely talented musician Wales had yet produced.' She was a great beauty, having famously received fifteen proposals of marriage by the age of twenty-one; her olive skin and black hair were rumoured to be of Spanish heritage. Gifted and beautiful, Morfydd was also spirited and witty. Her many admirers view her as a genius, a once-in-a-generation phenomenon; their

---

from Edith Eder, had also treated Eder's first wife, Florence, who killed herself when Eder left her for Edith.

opinion of Jones ranges from indifference to a suspicion that he was culpable, directly or indirectly, for her death in 1918.

When she met Ernest Jones, Morfydd was in love with the old Etonian Eliot Crawshay-Williams – MP, poet, novelist, soldier, explorer, parliamentary private secretary to Lloyd George when he was Chancellor of the Exchequer. They met when she was a teenager; he was in his early thirties and married. Morfydd set some of his poems to music when she was just nineteen; he persuaded her to apply for the scholarship at the Royal Academy. In 1913, his fellow Liberal MP Hubert Carr-Gomm named Crawshay-Williams as co-respondent in divorce proceedings against his wife Kathleen; Eliot in turn was forced to divorce his wife and marry Kathleen. His political career was finished. Eliot and Morfydd conducted an intimate correspondence: she wrote to him that she longed for 'the title of Mrs Crawshay-Williams'. It was an unconsummated passion.*

Morfydd was an unlikely victim of Ernest Jones's magnetism. He was still a vaguely scandalous figure; psychoanalysis was tainted in the public mind with an unhealthy preoccupation with sex, and his 1906 court case had not been forgotten. Sir John Herbert Lewis (Liberal MP for Flintshire) and his wife Ruth, who had been surrogate parents to Morfydd when she first came to London, disowned her after her marriage. Jones

---

* In 2015, Sweetshop Revolution staged the dance drama *I Loved You and I Loved You* at the Edinburgh Fringe. The play has three characters: Morfydd Owen, Ernest Jones and Eliot Crawshay-Williams. Donald Hutera, reviewing for the *Times*, wrote: 'His quirkily detailed dance, executed as Jones delivers a paper on the erotic possibilities of the anus, could be the most unselfconscious nude solo I've ever seen.'

and Owen had little in common, apart from their nationality and modest backgrounds. 'It was irrational,' he recalled, 'but something in me strove against marrying an Englishwoman; it seemed so commonplace.' Jones was looking for a housekeeper, mother and secretary, and found instead a beautiful young woman of uncommon talent, but, as he recalled in old age, 'genius of such an order does not go hand-in-hand with a completely harmonious personality'. He had no interest in music or her milieu; she cared little for Freud or psychoanalysis and was bored by Jones's political manoeuvrings and his solemn, humourless friends. Almost from the start, the union of this ill-matched couple was a disaster. Jones forbade her to play the piano in their flat and mocked her 'very simple-minded religious beliefs'. Her career stalled, while his – despite the hostility he encountered on his return to London – forged ahead. She composed only twelve of her one hundred and fifty works after her marriage; these few pieces were mediocre.

In the late summer of 1918, Jones and Morfydd travelled to Oystermouth, near Swansea, to visit Ernest's father and stepmother. On 31 August, Morfydd fell ill with severe abdominal pain and fever. Jones suspected appendicitis; this is now not an alarming diagnosis, but in 1918, it was often fatal – the first successful appendectomy was carried out in 1887, only thirty years before. Jones's immediate instinct was to contact Trotter, but it took four hours to get through by telephone. He agreed with Jones's diagnosis but advised him that because it would take too long for him to get there from London, he should call a local Swansea surgeon, William Frederick Brook. A few days after the operation – which was carried out at the home of Jones's father – Morfydd became delirious with a high fever. Trotter hurried from London, arriving at 4 a.m., and diagnosed 'delayed chloroform poisoning' – liver failure caused by the anaesthetic. He told Jones (who administered the anaesthetic) that he should have used ether instead. This was both spectacularly unhelpful and incorrect. There was nothing Trotter could do; Morfydd slipped into a coma and died at 2 a.m. on 7 September.

Morfydd's death has been the subject of much speculation and rumour. Why did Brook operate in the house when the local hospital was only four miles away? Did wartime sugar shortage put Morfydd at risk of this chloroform poisoning? Why was she buried before a death certificate was written? Why did Jones act as anaesthetist? Did he give too much chloroform? Was Morfydd pregnant when she died? Surgeons often carried out operations in patients' homes, routinely so in the case of the wealthy. As regards Jones giving the chloroform, the speciality of anaesthetics had not yet properly developed; GPs were often part-time anaesthetists. Delayed chloroform poisoning is an acute hepatitis, an 'idiosyncratic' reaction – i.e., it is not dose-related – so Jones could not have given 'too much'. A widespread myth at the time was that 'sugar depletion' was a risk factor for chloroform poisoning – if only Morfydd had accepted the box of chocolates Jones had bought for her! This poisoning was certainly more common in alcoholics and the severely malnourished, but Morfydd did not die for the want of sugar. Many cases of supposed chloroform poisoning were almost certainly due to other causes, such as sepsis, kidney failure and surgical complications like bowel leakage. A paper published in the *British Journal of Anaesthesia* in 1997 reviewed seventy-four cases of supposed delayed chloroform poisoning published in the medical literature up to 1912. The authors concluded that only eighteen (24 per cent) of these cases stood up to scrutiny as episodes of chloroform-related liver failure.

We don't know why Morfydd died. Her death was registered a fortnight after the event, listing 'Appendicitis Abscess' as the principal cause of death, with 'Operation Acidosis' as a contributory cause. Although it is tempting to blame him – the marriage was troubled, and he was, after all, a practised liar who had narrowly escaped jail just twelve years before – Jones didn't kill Morfydd. Many years later, he blamed himself:

> We thought there was blood poisoning till I got Trotter from London. He at once recognised delayed chloroform poisoning. It had recently been discovered, which neither the local doctor nor I had known, that this is the likelihood with a patient who is young, has suppuration in any part of the body, and has been deprived of sugar (as war conditions had then imposed); in such circumstances only ether is permissible as an anaesthetic. This simple piece of ignorance cost a valuable and promising life. We fought hard, and there were moments when we seemed to have succeeded, but it was too late.

Trotter, for once, was almost certainly incorrect. Even if he *was* right, he landed Jones with a permanent burden of guilt over his supposed ignorance of the particular dangers of chloroform in Morfydd's case.

Morfydd was buried on 11 September 1918, at Oystermouth Cemetery. The Reverend Enoch Lewis Mendus, who conducted the brief funeral service, wrote to Lady Herbert Lewis: 'She was buried in a beautiful corner at the top of a rising cemetery overlooking the sea. There was no singing – we were too few to sing; but she was buried mid bright coloured roses and other flowers which she loved and in a grave with laurel-leaves. You will be glad to know that she was not afraid of death. It seems tragic, but God knows best.' Morfydd's headstone was engraved with a quotation from Goethe's *Faust*: '*Das Unbeschreibliche, hier ist's getan*' – 'Here the indescribable is done'. Her year of birth on the headstone is given as 1893, but she was born in 1891: Jones was still unaware of the fib on the marriage certificate. Twenty-five was too old to marry; twenty-six was too young to die. Two days after the funeral, Jones visited Trotter in London; what did they say to each other?

Just two months (5 July) before her death, Jones, in a letter to Freud that was lost in transit, mentioned 'the best personal news'; Jones referred to this letter after Morfydd's death. Was 'the best personal news' a reference to Morfydd's pregnancy? In *Free Associations*, Jones hinted that the marriage was difficult; his son, Mervyn, put it more succinctly: 'had she lived the marriage would not have lasted.' For the rest of his life, a photograph of Morfydd hung in Jones's dressing room – a space his second wife, Kitty, rarely entered. When Mervyn married in 1948, Ernest gave Morfydd's wedding ring to his bride, Jeanne.

For the first time in years, Jones had no one to share his bed. Lina, who wrote to him in December 1916 during his courtship of Morfydd Owen, 'Oh but I have loved you my dear Ernest', had been dumped (by letter) on New Year's Day 1917. On 18 January – the day after Morfydd accepted his proposal of marriage – Jones found her a job in Worthing. 'I have recently parted company with Lina,' he told Freud, 'and set her up in a little flat and found work for her. She has been with me for over three years, which is long enough time to spend with such a character. It has been very difficult lately and altogether I feel I have paid heavily for my sin against her and Loe. I now have a housekeeper of fifty who shines with respectability.'

'Here the indescribable is done': Morfydd Owen.

12

Jones was distraught after Morfydd's death; 'an indescribably terrible experience', he told Freud. He couldn't bear to be alone at night – how he must have longed for Lina's homely embrace – so he stayed with various friends for a few days at a time. Some of his clients were irritated by the fact that the grief-stricken Jones took some time off work. He bitterly recalled: 'Patients naturally expressed their resentment at the interruption by finding opportunities to flick my still unbearably raw wound; psycho-analytic treatment does not bring out the most charming aspects of human nature.' On 30 October 1918 – just six weeks after Morfydd's death – one of these patients, Mrs Joan Riviere, wrote to him:

The state of mind into which you were thrown on your wife's death would be to the most casual observer unnatural and abnormal. Your need for self-analysis is urgent and extreme. If you now want me to attempt some such analysis for you, I will do the best I can. I regard it as absolutely unquestionable that your wife was to you a substitute for me. Your sorrow at her death is inordinate – why? Is it some form of a resistance to a satisfaction at her death? When you married and I left London you discovered that as a substitute she would not work, in fact that she was *not* me – your love for me was then really repressed.

The thirty-five-year-old author of this letter was one of the great monsters thrown up by psychoanalysis in England. Born Joan Verrall to a well-off 'county' family in 1883, she married the barrister Evelyn Riviere* at the age of twenty-three; their only child, a daughter named Diana, was born in 1908. Joan had artistic and intellectual interests, and although her uncle A. W. Verrall was a classics professor at Cambridge (and the first occupant of the King Edward VII Professorship of English Literature†), she was not sent to university. Joan spent a year with a family in Gotha, becoming fluent in German; she then worked briefly as a dressmaker. Following the death of her father in 1909, she had a 'breakdown' – probably a depressive episode caused by pathological grief, which makes her dismissal of Jones's 'inordinate' sorrow all the crueller. Joan suffered from a variety of physical ailments – thought to be psychosomatic – for which she consulted numerous doctors. Like many in England at the time, she first became aware of psychoanalysis through the Society for Psychical Research, then a highly respectable organisation.‡

* Joan pronounced it 'Rivear', which she regarded as more stylish and aristocratic.
† Later occupied by Trotter's grandson, David.
‡ Founded in 1882, early members included the philosopher Henry

Jones was not really Joan Riviere's *type*, nor she his ('she does not attract me erotically,' he told Freud, 'though I certainly have the admiration for her intelligence that I would have for a man'), but as so often before, his mysterious charisma overcame any snobbish reservations she might have had. She was tall, beautiful, well-born; the Bloomsbury psychoanalyst James Strachey described her as 'strikingly handsome, distinguished-looking, and somehow impressive'. Throughout her fractious analysis, she bombarded Jones with letters.* In one of these, she is positively skittish: 'you irresponsible puck! Irresistible to women, meeting them on their own ground. The emotions.' Freud would have regarded this simply as a nuisance, a troublesome manifestation of transference, but Jones, who prided himself on his appeal to women, was flattered. He led her on somewhat, allowing her, for example, to use his newly acquired country residence, a Jacobean farmhouse in Sussex called 'the Plat'. When Jones became engaged to Morfydd Owen in January 1918, Riviere was enraged, and reacted by taking herself off to a sanatorium in East Anglia for treatment of 'nervous exhaustion'. She stayed there for several months, returning to London in June. Jones refused to see her, possibly because she hadn't paid his fees. (Although Evelyn Riviere was a Chancery barrister, he was not rich, and the couple had to take in lodgers.) At any rate, Riviere was back in analysis shortly after Morfydd's death. Her letters displayed the classic

---

Sidgwick, the psychologist William James, and the Nobel-laureate physiologist Charles Richet. Freud himself contributed a paper to its journal.
* There were five postal deliveries a day in London at the time. A letter sent at midnight would be read by the recipient over breakfast.

stalker's mixture of adulation, invective and threats. In one, she tells Jones that 'one can't take you seriously' *and* 'I shall always love you'.

A contemporary psychiatrist might diagnose Joan Riviere as having narcissistic personality disorder; this makes Jones's decision, early in 1919, to encourage her to become a psycho-analyst herself – he even referred patients to her – puzzling. It was probably the only ruse he could think of to distract her from tormenting him; she was terrifying. 'I was afraid of her,' confessed James Strachey, 'a lot of people were. I often felt sure, for instance, that Ernest Jones was.' Her biographer Marion Bower described Joan's entry into psychoanalytic practice: 'Modern psychoanalysts usually have an initial training such as psychology or psychotherapy which gives them experience of working with patients. Joan had plunged in the deep end. It is possible that Jones gave her some support or supervision.' Riviere was one of the many prominent couch-jumpers during the early years of psychoanalysis. With her upper middle-class insouciance, and blithe disregard for her own lack of any formal instruction, she later became a prominent member of the *training* committee of the British Psychoanalytical Society and took on several trainees herself. One of these, Hannah Segal, recalled: 'She was very tall. And superego incarnate!'

Jones's strategy seems to have worked; Riviere's obsession with him gradually abated. In late 1921, she announced to Jones that she would like to go into analysis with Freud himself and insisted that he refer her. Jones agreed with an alacrity that betrayed his palpable relief. On 22 January 1922, he wrote a long referral letter to Freud:

Dear Professor

I thought it might interest you if I told you a few words about your new patient Mrs Riviere, who is going to Vienna next week. It is a case of typical hysteria, almost the only symptoms being sexual anaesthesia and unorganised Angst. Most of her neurosis goes into marked character reactions, which is one reason why I was not able to cure her. I am especially interested in the case, for as it is the worst failure I have ever had I have naturally learnt very much from her analysis. Seeing that she was unusually intelligent I hoped to win her for the cause, a mistake I shall never repeat. I underestimated the uncontrollability of her emotional reactions and in the first year made the serious error of lending her my country cottage for a week when I was not there, she having nowhere to go for a holiday. This led to a declaration of love (she has been the mistress of a number of men) and to the heartbroken cry that she had never been rejected before. From that time on she devoted herself to torturing me without any intermission and with considerable success and ingenuity, being a fiendish sadist; my two marriages gave her ample opportunity for this which she exploited to the full. The treatment finally broke down over my inability to master this negative transference, though I tried by all means in my power. She has the most colossal narcissism imaginable; to a great extent secondary to the refusal of her father to give her a baby and her subsequent masculine identification with him. Incidentally she has a strong complex about being a well-born lady (county family) and despises the rest of us, especially the women.

In February 1922, when Riviere had her first session with Freud, she was uncharacteristically dumbstruck, lying on his couch, unable to speak. But she soon found her voice. Riviere was just his type: Freud's preferred analysands were beautiful, cultured and wealthy women; there was no shortage of them in the post-war years. In old age, Anna Freud admitted to being 'very jealous' of her. Naturally, Freud wrote regularly to Jones as the analysis progressed. He was charmed by Joan, rebuking Jones: 'Mrs Riviere does not appear to me half so black as you have painted her. I am very glad you had no sexual relations with her as your hints made me suspect.' Jones, clearly stung, replied: 'I am not surprised that she is showing her best qualities at present. To satisfy her vanity she has always maintained the theory that I was in love with her but was not honest enough to confess it. It is over twelve years since I experienced any temptation in such ways, and then in special circumstances.'

In May 1922, Jones, who had received several 'heated letters' from her, complained to Freud that he had quoted 'passages from my letters' to Joan, and warned him of the special challenge she presented: 'The saying here is that her visit to Vienna will be the final and most severe test of psychoanalysis and people are most curious to see if her disdainful way of treating other people like dirt beneath her feet will undergo any modification.' Freud rose to this taunt, criticising Jones for his handling of this patient: 'I cannot praise the way you handled her. You seem to have soon lost the analytical superiority especially required in such a case. You seem to have treated her as a bad character in life but you never got behind her surface to master her wickedness.' He also, however, sheepishly confessed that Riviere had revealed the cloven hoof:

> She soon became harsh, unpleasant, critical even with me, tried to provoke me as she had done with you. I made it a rule never to get angry with her. She cannot tolerate praise, triumph, or success. Not any better than failure, blame or repudiation. Whenever she has got a recognition, a favour, or a present she is sure to become aggressive and unpleasant. It is an infallible sign of a deep sense of guilt, of a conflict between Ego and Ideal. She projects her self-criticism to other people, turns her pangs of conscience into sadistic behaviour, tries to render other people unhappy because she feels so herself. Her sexual freedom may be an appearance, the keeping up of which required those conspicuous compensatory attitudes as haughtiness and majestic behaviour.

Freud was always on the lookout for talent, and thought that Riviere, with her intelligence and her fluent German, would make an excellent translator of his work. He was right: she transformed Freud's sometimes very technical German prose into fluent, elegant and readable English. 'She is', he observed, 'an uncommon combination of male intelligence with female love for detailed work.' Her analysis, however, was, he conceded, a failure: 'I fear she will require special care indefinitely.' Characteristically, he blamed Jones, whose 'serious errors in handling her' had 'fearfully constrained my position'.

Riviere, like many of her class at the time, was casually anti-Semitic, writing with disdain to a friend about a rail journey in September 1922 to the Psychoanalytic Congress in Berlin, when she had to share a compartment with a 'Maida Vale Jew' and his wife, 'a common little actress in a fur coat, very much made up and covered in scent'. She made an exception for Freud, remarking that his appearance was 'not particularly Jewish'.* Freud was aware of her anti-Semitism and told her that a longer analysis might have revealed 'the connection between neurosis and national or social prejudice'.

Riviere's relationship with Freud later cooled when she sided with Melanie Klein in her doctrinal dispute with Anna Freud.† She and Klein were unlikely allies, given that Klein was blowsy, plump, Jewish, and what Riviere (had it been anyone else)

---

* Jones wrote that Freud 'had a strikingly well shaped head. The circumference of his head was fifty-five and a half centimetres, the diameters measuring eighteen and fifteen and a half centimetres respectively. So with a cephalic index of eighty-six he was decidedly dolichocephalic.' Dolichocephaly (where the skull is long and narrow) was unusual among European Jews, who were far more commonly brachycephalic (where the skull is rounder). How did Jones know the precise details of Freud's head circumference? Did he carry out the measurements himself? Did he document these details to suggest that Freud's appearance was 'not particularly Jewish'? Freud in turn had talked to Jung about Jones's head when he first met him in Salzburg in 1908, remarking that 'the shape of his head suggested he was not English – wasn't he Welsh?' Thereafter, he often referred to Jones as 'der Celt'.

† A fuming Sigmund Freud wrote to Jones in October 1927: 'Here I must reproach you for having carried tolerance too far. If a member of any of our groups expresses such mistaken and misleading basic views, that is a good reason for the group's leader to give that person a private lecture.'

would have called *common*. 'Klein', recalled Joan's daughter, Diana, 'was a dowdy bundle, *very* unsophisticated.' As she grew older, Riviere mellowed a little, but only a little; Jones wrote to Freud in 1932: 'she has shown unmistakable signs of reverting to her earlier troubles; nothing can please her.' Psychoanalysis had given this aimless, intellectually frustrated, bitterly angry woman a purpose, status within an elite community, and an income. It allowed her to become herself, to drop the 'masquerade of womanliness' that she railed against. Although she stayed with her husband, Evelyn, she had one last passionate attachment – to a woman, Lella Secor Florence. Miraculously, she and Jones became friends – she even organised the annual Ernest Jones lecture of the British Psychoanalytical Society in 1959, the year after his death.

Jones remained wary and somewhat frightened of Joan: 'It is not easy for anyone to get on well with her,' he told Freud, 'unless either he is in a position of acknowledged supremacy, as you are, or else is effeminate like Strachey.' Riviere may have been in the vanguard of a decidedly modern movement, but 'in spite of everything,' wrote James Strachey, 'she still kept much of her Victorian attitude to life. She disapproved of many things in the modern world.' The analyst Paula Heimann wrote: 'She could not appreciate the social revolution that took place during the war, ending the class of domestic servants, and felt it was a bitter personal blow that "nowadays there are only bad servants". Her life would have been easier had she been able to relax her traditional standards.' I wonder how this snobbish misanthrope managed to work for so many years as an analyst, listening for hours, day after day, year after year, to the tedious woes of other people. She shocked her trainee Hannah Segal by referring to some patients as 'pot-boilers' – of interest only because of the fees they paid. (Then again, many psychoanalysts were misanthropes, most notably Freud himself, who admitted that 'my dear fellow creatures – with individual exceptions – are rabble'.) I wonder too, how a woman who despised the modern world could devote her life to this most modernist – and modish – of movements. It must have taken its toll, for in her final years she was haunted by the old melancholy. Every day, she wrote in her diary the same single word: 'nothing'.

Joan Riviere: 'strikingly handsome, distinguished-looking, and somehow impressive.'

Ernest Jones married Katharina (Kitty) Jokl at a Zurich registry office on 9 October 1919, thirteen months after Morfydd's death: 'great and unexpected happiness,' he told Freud. The groom was forty, the bride thirty. She was introduced to Jones by his fellow committee member and Paladin Hanns Sachs, who was living with Kitty's sister, the divorced actress Gretl Ilm.

Jones had mentioned to Sachs that he needed a secretary fluent in English and German. Kitty, who, like Freud, came from a Moravian Jewish background,* and had a PhD in economics, was perhaps over-qualified for this post, but after lunch with Jones, she accepted both the job offer and his proposal of marriage. Kitty, despite her intellectual *Mitteleuropa* hinterland, was content to be what Ernest Jones was looking for: mother, housekeeper and secretary.

---

* Loe Kann called Jones 'an incorrigible fibber' because he told his family and friends that Kitty was a close friend of the Freuds, when she had never met them.

13

When the thirty-year-old James Strachey approached him for guidance on a career in psychoanalysis, Ernest Jones told him – as he told everyone who asked this question – that he should first qualify in medicine. This was *not* the advice Strachey wanted to hear, but he thought he'd better give it a go. He enrolled at St Thomas's, but lasted just three weeks, telling his wife, Alix, that he had 'had enough of dissecting frogs' legs'. He informed the medical school that he had 'influenza', and never returned. His short career as a medical student was entirely consistent with his life to that point as a drifting dilettante, forever in the shadow of his brilliant older brother, Lytton. 'What chiefly dismayed and maddened him', wrote Lytton's biographer Michael Holroyd, 'was the sight of his brother James, a preposterous caricature of his past self, sitting there, silent, contemptuous, utterly ineffectual, impotent and dull – a mere reflection of a reflection.' At Cambridge, James was dubbed 'the Little Strachey'; he fell in love with Rupert Brook, who didn't reciprocate, and later had an affair with John Maynard Keynes. A conscientious objector during the First

World War, he strolled into a job at the *Spectator*, where his uncle was editor; he toyed with the idea of opening a theatre, but nothing came of it. Although he was bisexual and in love with another woman (Noël Olivier), he somehow drifted into marriage with Alix Sargant-Florence; he admitted that her ownership of a flat in Gordon Square (prime Bloomsbury real estate) was the clincher.

Bloomsbury and Cambridge, its twin town in the Fens, were the spiritual homes of psychoanalysis in England. Freudianism appealed to the Bloomsberries because it was simultaneously *avant-garde* and elitist, and because it legitimised their unorthodox sexual behaviour. The Russian literary historian Prince Mirsky wrote of them in 1935:

> Being theoreticians of the passive, dividend-drawing and consuming section of the bourgeoisie, they are extremely intrigued by their own minutest inner experiences and count them an inexhaustible treasure store of further more mutinous inner experiences. They have a high opinion of Dostoievsky and of Freud. They believe that reason plus education will someday bring an age in which people will be enlightened ladies and gentlemen much like themselves, and there will be no more wars or revolutions.

They were, wrote W. H. Auden, 'accustomed to efficient servants, first-rate meals, good silver and linen, and weekends in country houses'. They freely used words like 'fuck', 'bugger' and 'semen', enunciated loudly in that notoriously exaggerated accent. Their estimation of themselves was such that Virginia

Woolf could famously claim: 'On or about December 1910 human character changed.'

In November 1918, Virginia wrote in her diary: 'Poor James Strachey was soft as moss, lethargic as an earthworm. James, billed at the 17 Club to lecture on "Onanism", proposes to earn his living as an exponent of Freud in Harley Street. For one thing, you can dispense with a medical degree.' In 1920, James Strachey, now aged thirty-two, with (in his own words) 'the barest of B.A. degrees, no medical qualifications, no knowledge of physical sciences, no experience of anything except third-rate journalism', decided he would *have* to go to Vienna to be analysed by Freud. The deal was brokered by Jones, who wrote to Freud on his behalf. Strachey wrote to Freud on 31 May 1920:

Dear Sir,

I believe that Dr Ernest Jones has mentioned to you that I am anxious if possible, to arrange to go to Vienna to be analysed by you. He will, I expect, have explained that my object in doing so is to try to obtain the essential empirical basis for such theoretical knowledge of psychoanalysis as I have been able to derive from reading. For this purpose, I should be prepared to remain in Vienna for at least a year. In face of the possibility and (from my point of view) the desirability of a prolonged analysis, allow me to afford a fee of more than one guinea an hour in English currency.

Freud, who had struggled during the war years, at one stage down to 'only two or three patients, all Hungarian aristocrats', replied: 'As long as the English pound continues to be equivalent to 600 Kr or about so, I am ready to take you on as you propose.'

James Strachey started his analysis in October 1920, and Alix, after an episode of palpitations at the opera (a performance of *Götterdämmerung*) also went into analysis with Freud. The palpitations might have been a symptom of panic attack, or agoraphobia, or even (heaven forfend) a *cardiac* problem, but no matter – no symptom was too trivial to justify full psychoanalysis for English people paying in sterling. In one of their first sessions, Freud retrieved Jones's referral letter and read it verbatim to James: 'He is a man of 30, well-educated and of a well-known literary family (I hope he may assist with translation of your works), I think a good fellow, but weak and perhaps lacking in tenacity.'

Freud was at first unimpressed by his new patient, writing to Jones: 'I have taken Mr. Strachey at one guinea the hour, do not regret it but for his speech being so indistinct and strange to my ear, that he is a torture to my attention.' The psychoanalyst Donald Winnicott* wrote that 'something halfway between an analysis and a conversation broke out between Strachey and Freud'. After this unpromising start, Freud slowly warmed to the Stracheys, and wrote to Jones: 'They are exceptionally nice and cultured people though somewhat queer. They are rather sensitive and critical.' With Alix, Freud focused on her chronic constipation, telling her to stop taking laxatives 'for the purpose of releasing material into the analysis'.

---

* Winnicott (1896–1971), who became an eminent child psychoanalyst, had trained initially as a paediatrician. He underwent a ten-year 'training' analysis with James; he was later in analysis with Joan Riviere.

In June 1922, Freud wrote to Jones: 'I propose the Stracheys should become full members of the [British Psychoanalytical] Society as they have gone through 1½ years of serious analysis, are theoretically well informed and people of a high order.' James returned to London, 'puny and languid', according to Virginia Woolf: 'such is the effect of 10 months psychoanalysis.' In a speech given forty-two years later, Strachey, with typical Bloomsbury candour and nonchalance, reflected on the ease of his professional progress:

I got back to London in the summer of 1922, and in October, without any further ado, I was elected an associate member of the Society. I can only suppose that Ernest Jones had received instructions from an even higher authority, and that he had passed them on to the unfortunate Council. A year later, I was made a full member. So there I was, launched on the treatment of patients, with no experience, with no supervision, with nothing to help me but two years of analysis with Freud.

Strachey later admitted to 'blood-curdling feelings of anxiety and remorse' about the unfairness of his admission as a member of the British Psychoanalytical Society (BPS).

By 1927, James was seeing eight patients a day, many of them sent on by Ernest Jones, who could not take on all the people requesting analysis with him. Jones, who at this point had been president of the BPS for several years, effectively controlled the London market in psychoanalytic patients; or at least he convinced his fellow psychoanalysts that he *did*. At any one time, the average analyst had eight patients undergoing the full Freudian (one hour four or five times a week), so the loss of even a single patient was financially significant. Jones held on to power in the BPS through his perceived monopoly on patient supply. The Scottish analyst William Gillespie recalled in 1979: 'Jones was always in the chair, with Glover* at his left hand. I had the strong impression that everyone was in awe of Jones and that it was important not to say the wrong thing, for Jones could on occasion be very cutting. He was also, of course, a very important potential source of patients. Jones initiated me into the source of analytic patients. Virtually, the sources were himself and Edward Glover, he told me. I think this was widely believed, however little truth there may have been in it.'

Strachey made few original contributions to the psycho-analytic literature; he wrote a paper on 'Some unconscious factors in reading', in which he argued that 'a coprophagic [shit-eating] tendency lies at the root of all reading. The author excretes his thoughts and embodies them in the printed book; the reader takes them, and after chewing over them, incorporates them into himself.' James – in collaboration with Alix – found his true métier in translation. Jones, who was appalled by A. A. Brill's early translations of Freud, had spotted Strachey's potential as a translator; he wrote to Freud in November 1921:

The average doctor writes worse English than a poor trades-man writes German in Austria. Last week, for instance, I

* Edward Glover, secretary of the BPS.

had the occasion to read for the first time Brill's translation of your Leonardo,* and I was deeply shocked time and again to see punctuation as illiterate as that of a servant girl's, with expressions of a similar order. Men of sensitive feeling, taste and education like Strachey rightly shudder at such things.

Strachey's great achievement, the translation of Freud known as *The Standard Edition*, was the work of his old age. It was James, recalling the half-forgotten Greek and Latin of his boyhood, who transmuted Freud's technical words and phrases into the pseudo-scientific vocabulary still used. Jones thought psychoanalysis might be taken more seriously if it sounded *sciencey*: Strachey – who had the advantage over Riviere of a classical education – obliged, with neologisms like *cathexis* for Freud's original *Besetzung* (investment of libido, or mental energy). Joan Riviere's translations may have been more elegant, more in keeping with the spirit of the original, but it was Strachey's twenty-four-volume *Standard Edition* that became the canonical work, even if it has been the object of some criticism. (The secondary literature on English translations of Freud is now a recognised academic sub-discipline within psychoanalysis.) James started this great task when he was sixty and worked on it until his sudden death at the age of seventy-nine in 1967. Alix was supposedly his 'assistant', but her contribution was nearly as great, and her

* Freud's 1910 psychobiography, *Leonardo da Vinci and a Memory of His Childhood*.

German was better. They were so familiar with the minutiae of Freud's life that in old age, they would amuse themselves by picking a random date, and asking the other: 'what was Freud doing on that day?'

In the autumn of 1962, the twenty-seven-year-old writer Michael Holroyd visited James and Alix Strachey, now living in Marlow Common in Buckinghamshire. Holroyd had been given an advance of £50 by the publisher Heinemann to write a biography of Lytton Strachey, who had died of cancer in 1932 at the age of fifty-one; he was advised by the Bloomsbury writer Frances Partridge that the first person he should see was James Strachey, Lytton's literary executor. Holroyd described the Stracheys' domestic arrangements:

> I arrived at mid-day, prepared for practically anything – but not what I found. Though it was frosty outside, the temperature within the house seemed set at a steady eighty degrees Fahrenheit. No windows were open and, to prevent the suspicion of a draught, cellophane curtains were drawn against them. There was an odour of disinfectant about the rooms. I felt I had entered a specially treated capsule where some rare variety of *homo sapiens* was being exquisitely preserved.
>
> James Strachey was almost an exact replica of Freud himself, though with some traces of Lytton's physiognomy – the slightly bulbous nose in particular ... In a more subdued and somewhat less astringent form, he shared many of

Lytton's qualities – his humour, his depth and ambiguity of silence, his rational turn of mind, his shy emotionalism and something of his predisposition to vertigo.

Of all his Stracheyesque characteristics, it was his silence that I found most dismaying during the hour's 'interview', as he called it, before lunch. I could not tell whether he produced these silences spontaneously, or whether they were in some manner premeditated. Had he heard what I said? Or did he disapprove? Or again, was he pondering, indefinitely, upon some singular reply? It was impossible to tell. To fill the vacuum, I began jabbering nonsense.

His wife came in, austere and intellectual, very thin, with a deeply-lined parchment face and large expressive eyes. We all drank a little pale sherry and then moved in procession past Stephen Tomalin's bust of Lytton to the dining-room.

Lunch was a spartan affair. Though generous in spirit, my hosts were by temperament ascetic and lived frugally. We ate spam, a cold potato each, and lettuce leaves. In our glasses there showed a faint blush of red wine from the Wine Society, but I was the only one who supped any. After the spam, some cheese was quarried out from the cold storage, and some biscuits extracted from a long row of numbered tins ranged like files along a shelf in the kitchen. Everything, spam, potato, lettuce, cheese and biscuits was, like the windows, swathed in protective cellophane.*

---

* A few years after Michael Holroyd's spartan repast, the Freudian scholar Paul Roazen visited the Stracheys, and was also offered lunch: they sat in the garden on ramshackle deckchairs, and the meal was served from tins.

Lytton Strachey: A Critical Biography was published in two parts in 1967 and 1968 to great acclaim. In return for allowing him access to Lytton's archive, Holroyd afforded James the unique privilege of a right of reply (in the footnotes) to anything in the text that he disagreed with. Many reviewers and readers, such as the *Times*'s Alan Ryan, particularly enjoyed these interjections: 'Not the least lively part of this never dull volume consists of pungent footnotes by Strachey's younger brother and literary executor, James, expressing racy disagreement with the biographer.'

In 1919, Adrian Stephen (younger brother of Virginia Woolf) and his wife, Karin, visited Ernest Jones to ask for advice on training in psychoanalysis. Naturally, Jones told them that they should first qualify as doctors. Virginia Woolf wrote in her diary: 'that strange couple just decided to become medical students. After 5 years' training, they will, being aged 35 and 41 or so, set up together in practice as psychoanalysts. Halfway through, I suppose, something will make it all impossible and then, having forgotten his law, he will take up what – farming or editing a newspaper, or keeping bees perhaps.'

Virginia's scepticism about Adrian's latest plan was not misplaced, for his ability to stick at anything for long was even less than James Strachey's. While still a young man, he had lost both parents and his much admired older brother, Thoby. He and Virginia set up home together in Fitzroy Square. 'Poor Virginia! And Adrian!' wrote Lytton Strachey. Poor Virginia fretted constantly about Adrian, who was crushed by the weight of family achievement: 'wilted, pale, under a stone of vivacious brothers and sisters,' she wrote sadly. After taking a third in history and law at Trinity College, Cambridge, he was called to the bar (but never practised), then flirted with acting,* before going to Oxford, where he assisted Sir Paul Vinogradoff (Professor of Roman Law) with the translation of manuscripts. He shared with James Strachey a passion for both Rupert Brook and Noël Olivier; when she failed to reciprocate, Adrian swiftly married Karin Costelloe in August 1914. The stepdaughter of the art historian Bernard Berenson, Karin was wealthy and brilliant, and had taken a double first at (of course) Cambridge. Like James Strachey, Adrian saw out the war as a conscientious objector.

To everyone's surprise, Adrian and Karin, who enrolled as medical students at UCH, stuck at it. Over several years, they failed and resat examinations, bickered, separated and reconciled; during one such temporary break-up in 1924, Adrian moved in with the Stracheys in Gordon Square. Contemporaries at UCH recalled this strange-looking couple turning up late for lectures, and then sitting in the front row:

---

* Adrian's most famous acting role was that of 'interpreter' for 'the King of Abyssinia', a hoax in which he, Horace de Vere Cole, Virginia Woolf, Duncan Grant (who was Adrian's lover), Guy Ridley and Anthony Buxton (the last four in blackface) 'inspected' the flagship HMS *Dreadnought* at Weymouth in 1910. (Bloomsberries loved dressing up nearly as much as sexual adventure and psychoanalysis.) To show their approval of any equipment demonstrated to them, the group appreciatively murmured 'Bunga! Bunga!' Admiral Sir William May, who had led the home fleet's welcoming party, was thereafter unable to go ashore without people shouting 'Bunga! Bunga!' at him.

he gaunt and over six feet five inches, she short and stout, already deaf, theatrically wielding an ear trumpet. Adrian loathed medical school, but eventually qualified in 1926, with Karin following shortly after. Having undergone long 'training' analyses, they set up in practice, their Gordon Square house 'full of lodgers and patients', their unconventional marriage a living proof of Kingsley Martin's much-quoted joke that Bloomsbury was 'demographically a place where the couples were triangles who lived in squares'. Adrian became a respected analyst, possessed, according to his anonymous obituarist, 'of a kind of patient tolerance or acceptance of pain'. He died in 1948, aged sixty-four; Karin took her own life in 1953, joining the ranks of early psychoanalysts who committed suicide.* 'Mother and father', wrote their daughter Ann, 'were so ill-assorted and so far away from us children that the only things we had in common were the house and the servants.'

In the shadow of their older, more talented siblings, from families where high achievement was expected, James Strachey and Adrian Stephen, both sensitive men with a fluid sexual identity, married to rich cultured women they didn't love, were saved by psychoanalysis. Dabblers who had failed at everything else, in early middle age they found something they could finally stick at. And so, psychoanalysis became a home for rich directionless strays, who analysed other rich directionless strays.

* They include Wilhelm Stekl, Victor Tausk and Max Kahane.

James and Alix Strachey: 'What was
Freud doing on that day?'

14

When Freud became famous after the First World War, the world was ready for him. No other great figure of modernism was so accessible: you couldn't pop over to Paris and enrol in a creative writing class with James Joyce, or have music lessons from Stravinsky, or attend Picasso for tuition in abstract technique. T. S. Eliot would have been dismayed if you turned up at Lloyd's Bank with a portfolio of your poems. But in 1922, if you had the money (minimum two guineas an hour), the leisure, and a referral from Ernest Jones, you could take yourself off to Vienna and enter analysis with Professor Freud – whether you 'needed' it or not. 'You are providing well for my medical income,' purred Freud to Jones, who, in January 1922 alone, referred Mr Barbour ('an Oxford man'), Mr Cuming ('from Egypt, half-English and half Greek, neurotic and homosexual, well-to-do and extravagant, could easily afford three guineas'), Captain Daly ('in the regular Indian army; foolish characteristics, conceit and inferiority, slightly hysterical, rather an ass but easy to manage, I told him you would charge two guineas') and Mr Armstrong ('an Oxford student who consulted me on account of his bad asthma').

Throughout the 1920s, Jones sent several high-profile English patients to Freud. He acted as his agent and broker – screening potential analysands and writing detailed letters about their social background and intellectual clout. This was far more important than any actual *indication* for analysis; ability to pay and membership of the English intellectual and social elite were the most important criteria when choosing which 'patients' to refer on. Apart from the money, Freud was keen to take on these intellectuals; he admired the English – he had, after all, named one of his sons after Oliver Cromwell – and he was convinced that the most effective means of advancing psychoanalysis in England would be the recruitment of such influential individuals.

Arthur Tansley had already been in analysis with Jones before he moved on to Freud in April 1922; he was then fifty. Tansley had pursued a highly successful career at University College London and Cambridge as a botanist and ecologist, becoming a Fellow of the Royal Society in 1915. Tansley's mid-life crisis was triggered in 1916 by a dream, which he self-analysed in the Freudian manner:

I dreamed I was in a sub-tropical country, separated from my friends, standing alone in a small shack or shed which was open on one side so that I looked out on a wide open space surrounded by bush or scrub. In the edge of the bush I could see a number of savages armed with spears and the long pointed shields used by some South African native tribes. They occupied the whole extent of the bush-edge abutting on the open space, but they showed no sign of active hostility. I myself had a loaded rifle, but realised that I was unable to escape in the face of the number of armed savages who blocked the way.

Then my wife appeared in the open space, dressed entirely in white, and advanced towards me quite unhindered by the savages, of whom she seemed unaware. Before she reached me the dream, which up to then had been singularly clear and vivid became confused, and though there was some suggestion that I fired a rifle, but with no knowledge of who or what I fired at, I awoke.

'Tell a dream and lose a reader' is a warning commonly attributed to Henry James; Tansley's rather banal dream (or the telling of it) nearly cost him his career and his marriage. It prompted him to read all of Freud's work, to write a book, *The New Psychology and its Relation to Life* (1920), and to enter analysis with Ernest Jones, who, at Tansley's request, referred him on to Freud: 'He has written a very good letter asking me to approach you.' Tansley, who had a private income, was free to indulge his new passion. Jones and Freud, who were very sensitive to accusations that psychoanalysis was 'unscientific', were delighted to have recruited such an eminent biologist; Tansley, wrote Freud, was 'a nice type of the English scientist. It might be a gain to win him over to our science at the loss of botany.' Jones, however, fretted over Tansley's unsoundness on certain core psychoanalytical principles, and wrote to Freud: 'he is not yet sure of the ontogenic side of the Oedipus complex, let alone the phylogenetic or prehistoric.' Tansley's eminence as a scientist, however, trumped Jones's misgivings, and in 1924 he was admitted as an Associate Member of the British Psychoanalytical Society. Freud – always encouraging to couch-jumpers – suggested that Tansley should take on a patient himself, 'to learn the technique', but nothing came of it.

Tansley's dream was, predictably, a mid-life cliché: he was torn between his duty to his wife and children and his erotic obsession with a much younger woman.* James Strachey described the Tansleys' home life in a letter to Alix in 1925:

> ... a well-off middle-class household. Blazing fire in the bedroom, perfect bed, five-course dinner, excellent cooking, claret and port at dinner, hock at lunch, good coffee – what more can one desire? But besides these essentials† Tansley himself is very nice and quite intelligent. Mrs T is not too tiresome, and the girls most inoffensive though unluckily

---

* Thought to be Margot Hume, who happened to be in Vienna during Tansley's analysis in 1922; her time there was more productive than his. Hume was part of a research team sent to the city by the Lister Institute of Preventive Medicine in London to study the causes and treatment of rickets. They established that the disease could be prevented by cod liver oil supplements, which contains vitamin D, deficiency of which was later identified as the cause of rickets. Tansley was unaware, as he lay on Freud's couch, talking, day after day, about his dream, that the object of his desire was in Vienna, making a major contribution to the eventual cure and prevention of a devastating childhood disease. This indifference to events occurring at one's own doorstep is a recurring theme in the history of psychoanalysis.

† What happened to James Strachey between 1925, when claret, port and hock were 'essentials', and 1962, when he served Michael Holroyd spam and a single potato for lunch?

far from beauties. – They were all most affable; and last night Tansley went rather further, I think than he'd intended, and poured out a good deal of his troubles: his life's interest hopelessly divided between his old love, botany, and his new one, psychoanalysis.

In the end, botany and the comforts of 'a well-off middle-class household' won out. In 1927, Tansley was appointed Sherardian Professor of Botany at Oxford, a position he held until he retired in 1937. His mid-life crisis was over. In old age, Tansley recalled his analysis with Freud: 'We never seemed to

Arthur Tansley: 'Then my wife appeared...'

penetrate at all deeply into my "unconscious", and I think the main cause of this failure was probably that I had no marked neurosis, but a fairly stable mental and emotional equilibrium which was difficult to upset or penetrate.' He loftily described his analysis with Freud as the meeting of 'two sovereigns', claiming that he had entered it as an intellectual exercise, and because of his admiration for Freud, who, in Tansley's estimation, was the most influential man since Jesus Christ.

When the London Clinic of the Institute of Psychoanalysis opened in 1926, Lionel Penrose was appointed clinical assistant, and began carrying out analyses under the supervision of Ernest Jones. Penrose, who came from a wealthy family, read Moral Sciences at St John's College; his Cambridge contemporary and fellow Quaker John Rickman sparked his interest in the new Freudian psychology. Penrose was elected to the Apostles* in 1921, but his fellow member Lytton Strachey was underwhelmed: 'a complete flibbertigibbet, but attractive in a childish way, and somehow, in spite of an absence of brain, quite suitable for the Society.'

In 1922, Penrose set off for Vienna, hoping to be analysed by Freud, who was too busy to take him on and sent him to Siegfried Bernfeld. Vienna was full of his Cambridge

* Founded in 1820 with twelve members (hence the nickname) as a discussion group for undergraduates, also known as the Conversazione Society. Membership was by invitation and highly sought after. Famous Apostles include Bertrand Russell, Ludwig Wittgenstein, John Maynard Keynes and Jonathan Miller.

contemporaries, including his brother Bernard ('Beakus'), Frank Ramsey, Roger Money-Kyrle, Sebastian Sprott and R. B. Braithwaite, most of them undergoing analysis with second- or even third-choice analysts, what with Freud being so in demand. In the years between Versailles and the General Strike, the young men of Cambridge took themselves off to Vienna to be analysed just as previous generations of gentry went to spa towns to take the waters or embarked on the Grand Tour to take the culture. Psychoanalysis was as influential in Cambridge in the 1920s as communism in the 1930s; if religion was the opium of the masses, psychoanalysis was the opium of the intellectuals. A typical Cambridge Freudian was Desmond Bernal (1901–71), the Anglo-Irish scientist who expansively predicted that psychoanalysis would transform 'Philosophy, Psychology, Metaphysics, Ethics, Anthropology, Sociology, Politics, Economics, Medicine, Religion'.

Cambridge intellectuals discovered that they liked nothing better than talking about themselves, and the weakness of the Austrian Krone allowed them to do just that, while living in some style in Vienna. The dressing up of this prolonged immersion in the self as a 'scientific' and 'therapeutic' process was intoxicating. Psychoanalysis held out to these young men the prospect of fine-tuning their already brilliant minds, with their unique collections of resistances, transferences and complexes. Those minds cleared of wasteful debris and childhood detritus, they could stride forward into their glittering futures, the ideal versions of their wonderful selves: surely that was worth a few hundred hours of structured conversation? Cambridge undergraduates also loved secret societies; it was inevitable, therefore, that in 1925 they would form one called 'the Psychoanalytic Discussion Group', the main requirement for prospective members being that they should have undergone analysis.

It is not clear if Penrose had a specific neurosis requiring analysis, although 'bedwetting' was mentioned many years later. He was certainly obsessed by the idea that chess might be explained psychoanalytically – Bernfeld told him that he 'projected his infantile family conflicts on to the chessboard'. While in Vienna, he met Arthur Tansley, who encouraged him to take a medical degree with the aim of working in 'the field of abnormal psychology'. Penrose shared a large apartment with another Cambridge man, the astonishingly gifted Frank Ramsey; when not being analysed, they attended the opera and dined out. Ramsey was unimpressed by Penrose, 'whose brains, if ever he had any, have been analysed away pretty completely, so that serious conversation is almost impossible'. Ramsey had decided to undergo analysis to get over an unhappy infatuation with an older woman,* *and* because he thought it would be 'likely to make me cleverer in the future'.

'You're the ugliest person I've ever seen,' remarked Frank Ramsey when he met his psychoanalyst, Theodor Reik, for the first time in 1924. 'Everyone has to say that before we can get started,' Reik replied equably. Freud, being fully booked with more eminent patients, could not take Ramsey on; neither could

---

* The object of Ramsey's infatuation was Margaret Pyke, wife of Geoffrey Pyke, the founder of the progressive Malting House School in Cambridge, which was run on 'psychoanalytic principles'. Discipline of the children (predominantly the offspring of modish dons) was so lax that one former pupil described it as 'like *Lord of the Flies*'.

Otto Rank, his second choice. Thus it was that Frank found himself facing the ugliest person he had ever seen, the thirty-six-year-old Theodor Reik. Photographs of the young Reik show a bald, bespectacled, unremarkable-looking man; it is not clear what it was about his analyst's appearance that Ramsey so objected to. Perhaps it was his ethnicity: 'So I went to Dr Reik,' he wrote to Sebastian Sprott,* 'an unpleasant-looking Jew, with whom I have had a fortnight. It is surprisingly exhausting and distinctly unpleasant.' He confessed to his mother that he liked Reik, 'though he is a Jew (but all the good ones are)'. Ramsey was a virgin when he arrived in Vienna. 'To my surprise,' he wrote to Sprott, 'the other day I went home with a whore and enjoyed it, though I shook all over with fear. She said I ought to go to a doctor. She was rather nice and after a little I lost my fear.' The unhappiness caused by his infatuation there-after evaporated. Reik confessed to Alix Strachey that 'there'd never been anything much wrong with Ramsey'. The prostitute probably contributed more to his 'cure' than Reik.

Frank Ramsey died aged just twenty-six, probably of Weil's disease (leptospirosis), an infectious disease spread by contami-nation of water with rats' urine – Frank had swum in the Cam during a spell of mild weather before he fell sick. His younger brother, Michael (the future Archbishop of Canterbury), ran screaming from the church after his funeral service. During his short life, Ramsey made major contributions to mathematics, logic, philosophy and economics. It is tempting to bestow the

---

* Sprott eventually became Professor of Philosophy at Nottingham Uni-versity – 'did you know there was such a place?' James Strachey asked Alix.

Frank Ramsey.

Theodor Reik: 'The ugliest
person I've ever seen.'

title of 'genius' on a very clever person who dies at twenty-six,
but in Ramsey's case, it was justified. The philosopher A. J. Ayer
remarked in 1980 that Cambridge philosophers had spent the
1930s 'chewing over Wittgenstein when they ought to have
been chewing over Ramsey'.

Lionel Penrose acted on Arthur Tansley's advice: he spent 1923
and 1924 commuting between Vienna and Cambridge, where
he commenced his medical course, going on to St Thomas's
Hospital Medical School for his clinical training. While he
was still a student at St Thomas's, he joined Ernest Jones at
the Institute of Psychoanalysis, where he was allocated two

'training' patients. One, a young Irish doctor with a severe stammer (which Penrose mockingly reproduced in his personal diary), simply stopped turning up for his sessions – he must have been unimpressed, as a doctor himself, to discover that his 'analyst' was still in medical school. The second, an older married woman, attended for only one session, complaining bitterly to the Institute about the cold of the consultation room: 'I mentioned the discomfort of the draught to Dr. Penrose, but he did not see his way to alter the conditions.'

Jones advised Penrose that he had 'too many non-psychoanalytic interests' and should consider another line of work. Penrose took this advice, abandoned psychoanalysis and went on to do pioneering work in genetics, proving that most forms of mental illness and intellectual disability were not directly transmissible. Although he held the title of Professor of Eugenics at University College London, he was an *anti*-eugenicist, and eventually succeeded in having his title changed to 'Professor of Human Genetics'. Penrose opposed eugenics for both scientific and moral reasons. Eugenicists, he argued, oversimplified and overestimated genetics, and, more perniciously, contributed to the dehumanisation of individuals with intellectual disability.

In 1968, the seventy-year-old Penrose, now a Fellow of the Royal Society, was back in Vienna to give a lecture. His friend Frances Partridge wrote in her diary:

After his lecture we went to look in vain for Freud's house in the Berggasse. Later, an enormous walk in the dark to places connected with Lionel's early life in Vienna, all around the old town through streets of portentously tall houses, under bridges, up steps. Lionel was being psychoanalysed at that time for bedwetting, so Margaret [Penrose's wife] told me later. Having heard this I naturally saw the course on which he led us in symbolical terms. Down a deep sunken street called Tief Graben (Deep Trench) under a bridge and towards the Hohe Markt. 'I'm always dreaming about Vienna,' he said as we walked along, 'and in my dream there's always somewhere I'm trying to get to. Now I realize that it's here.' When we found a large fountain in full operation in the middle of the marketplace, it seemed too good to be true.

15

In the now largely forgotten 1983 film *Lovesick*, the ghost of Sigmund Freud (Alec Guinness) tells the apostate New York analyst Saul Benjamin (Dudley Moore) that psychoanalysis 'was intended only as an experiment, never as an *industry*'. But that is exactly what it was: Freud's enduring legacy was a new profession. In a form of apostolic succession, all analysts could connect themselves, directly or indirectly, to him. Freud laid down the basic rules in his 1913 paper, 'On Beginning the Treatment'. The session should last an hour. The analyst and the analysand should agree on the fee before commencing: 'Nothing brings home to one so strongly the significance of the psycho-genic factor in the daily life of men, the frequency of malingering, and the non-existence of chance, as a few years' practice of psychoanalysis on the strict principle of leasing by the hour.' The patient should be charged for no-shows; the patient should take holidays *only* during the same time as the analyst and should be charged the full fee if away on holiday while the analyst was working. The analyst should collect payments regularly and should *always* charge:

'Free treatment enormously increases some of the neurotic's resistances. The absence of the regulating effect offered by the payment of a fee to the doctor makes itself very painfully felt; the whole relationship is removed from the real world, and the patient is deprived of a strong motive for endeavouring to bring the treatment to an end.'* (Freud famously sent a very late invoice to Gustav Mahler's widow for his four-hour walk-and-talk with the composer in Leiden in 1910.) Freud's only other requirement was that his patients should 'possess a reasonable degree of education and a fairly reliable character', which would bar both the poor and those with personality disorders.

Freud worried a great deal about money – not because he was greedy, but because he supported up to twelve people at any time; his dependents included his wife and six children, his two sisters and his sister-in-law Minna.† As a young married man, he was obliged to borrow occasionally, and deeply resented those who lent to him. Lack of money and lack of prospects (because he was a Jew) forced the young Freud out of academic life into work as a private neurologist, where most of his patients had symptoms that were psychosomatic in origin. Thus it was that economic necessity and anti-Semitism led to Sigmund Freud's third-choice career, ministering to a fee-paying clientele of 'hysterical' patients.

---

* Freud often broke this rule; he treated several patients for free, including Heinz Hartmann, Eva Rosenfeld and even, for a time, the Wolf Man.
† Whether Freud did or did not have an affair with Minna has exercised Freudian scholars for many decades.

'What is the use of Americans, if they bring no money?' Freud asked Jones. 'They are not good for anything else.' In the early 1920s, many of them came to Vienna to be analysed with the sole aim of setting themselves up in analytic practice on their return. Most of these pilgrims were not medically qualified, and so gravitated to Otto Rank, 'lay' analyst and Paladin. When Jones indignantly asked Rank 'how he could bring himself to send back to America as a practising analyst someone who had been with him barely six weeks', Rank shrugged his shoulders and replied: 'one must live.' Psychoanalysis had become a franchise.

Like Freud, Ernest Jones had to make his own way in the world. When he returned to London in 1913, he soon realised that psychoanalysis was, from an economic perspective, unlike any other branch of medicine. Because the appointments were so long (an hour) and so frequent (several times a week), and because therapy went on for years, or even decades, he needed only eight patients at any one time to make a good living. The downside of this model was that the departure of even one patient was a serious loss; this undoubtedly encouraged analysts to take a lenient and forgiving approach to patients with 'transference problems'. Around this time, an advertisement appeared in the London *Evening Standard* from the bogus English Psycho-Analytical Publishing Company: 'Would you like to make £1,000 a year as a psychoanalyst? Take eight postal lessons from us at four guineas a course.'

In the early years, patients were few and highly prized: in 1914, there were only thirty to forty analysands in the whole of London, eight of whom were with Jones. The pool of such patients was narrow and shallow; they came almost exclusively from the upper-middle-class elite who occupied the squares and terraces of Bloomsbury and the high tables at Cambridge. The historian Gordon Leff recalled that his mother, one of 'the bright young things of the 1920s', had been given 'a full analysis' as a wedding present.

Jones was a prodigious worker: he saw up to eleven patients a day, wrote numerous papers and books, and ran the British Psychoanalytical Society. When he started his London practice, Jones's standard fee was a guinea an hour; some wealthier patients (like Ethel Vaughan-Sawyer) paid *two* guineas. By 1928, his fee had risen to three guineas. His lucrative practice eventually funded a fine Nash house in York Terrace, a country house (renovated by Freud's architect son, Ernst), a cottage in Wales and a summer house in Menton on the French Riviera.

The Freudians made the occasional feeble claim to treat the less well-off, but this was generally done only by analysts in training, who charged a reduced rate. (This arrangement allowed the impecunious Samuel Beckett to be treated by the tyro analyst Wilfred Bion in the 1930s.) Psychoanalysts are very prickly about the perception that they cater only for the well-off. The psychoanalyst and author Adam Phillips claimed – rather unconvincingly – that psychoanalysis is 'a psychology of, and for, immigrants', but you can be sure that the hotel chambermaid and the Deliveroo cyclist aren't free-associating on an analyst's couch during their free time.

There was much bickering over fees. When Donald Winnicott, then a young paediatrician, was in analysis with James Strachey, he had a habit of 'forgetting' or delaying paying his fees; he also failed to pay Ernest Jones on several occasions. Dissatisfied with Strachey (with whom he had been in analysis for ten years), he moved on to Joan Riviere, whom he tried to convince that he could only afford *one* guinea per session. When she found out that Winnicott was very well-off – his father, Sir John, was a wealthy businessman – she wrote to him to point out that *two* guineas was a relatively low fee for a 'front rank' analyst such as herself: 'I am second to no one in ability.' She later decided that Winnicott's stinginess was down to transference-induced envy: 'It is because it has become clear that you undervalue my work that I think it is right to ask if you can pay my full fee.'

Janet Malcolm's 1981 book *Psychoanalysis: The Impossible Profession* is an amusing insight into the business side of the discipline. She told the story through the work of one analyst, whom she called 'Aaron Green'. He advised one patient that because he (Green) took holidays in August, she would have to pay for missed sessions when, one year, she took holidays in July. 'She found this intolerable,' wrote Malcolm; 'he wouldn't back down; and she left the analysis.' Green rationalised this psychoanalytically: 'My blunder was that I didn't understand and interpret the transference soon enough, I didn't point out to her that she was taking flight because she couldn't face her painful feeling of love towards me. I didn't convince her that the money she wouldn't part with was the phallus-child she wanted from me.'

It is not surprising that psychoanalysis attracted so many would-be practitioners, particularly in the 1920s, when several lay analysts set up in practice with no qualification

other than having been analysed themselves. Even Wilfred
Trotter admitted to Jones that he could not imagine a more
agreeable way of earning money than 'telling people what you
really thought about them'. (I think Trotter got this wrong –
analysts rarely told their patients what they 'really thought
about them'.) Psychoanalysis – particularly during its imperial
phase in America – was a much more attractive option than
mainstream hospital-based psychiatry, being well paid, with no
weekend or night work, and no frightening psychotic patients.
Janet Malcolm wrote enviously about the older New York
analysts' apartments on Fifth Avenue and Park Avenue.

Just as very long books tend to be overpraised, patients who have
undergone long and expensive psychoanalysis tend to claim
that it cured them. One of the most revealing expositions of the
economics of psychoanalysis from the analysand's perspective
is the American writer Francis Levy's account of his decades-
long therapy: 'Psychoanalysis: The Patient's Cure', published in
American Imago in 2010. Levy, a struggling writer, went into
analysis, it seems, because he couldn't reconcile himself to the
bleak truth that he wasn't as good as John Updike. Luckily,
however, he had inherited a lot of money, and he began analysis
in the late 1970s, paying $70 for a fifty-minute session, rising
to $250 in 2000.

Levy sees Dr S. four days a week: 'For some time we had
been working on what is technically known as narcissistic
grandiosity. We're not friends, but colleagues who've been
working on something together for years.' The average duration

of a full analysis steadily increased from two to four years in the 1930s and 40s, to four to six years in the 1950s and 60s, to six to eight years in the 1970s. 'The majority of analytic cases end', wrote Janet Malcolm, 'because the patient moves to another city, or runs out of money.' Freud admitted that if he found a patient who was 'interesting but not too troublesome', and could afford his fee, it was easier for him to continue analysis indefinitely.

Dr S., the son of Austrian immigrants, plays the violin, is a Harvard graduate, and 'sighs a lot'. When he raised his fee from $315 to $350, it prompted Levy to do some quick calculations: 'Let's say I've seen Dr S. approximately forty-two weeks of the year, four times a week for twenty-nine years, for a total of 4,872 visits. By my calculations, that's close to $1,000,000 in fees. I ignore my father's voice saying, *Sure he likes you, why wouldn't he, you've made him rich.*' Dr S.'s Carnegie brownstone, which he bought for $165,000 in 1962, is now worth $5 or $6 million; he takes eight weeks' holiday a year, staying at hotels like the Hotel du Cap, the Connaught and the Cipriani. 'My wife and I', wrote Levy mournfully, 'have often observed that during summer vacations, when our analysts were away, we were like two siblings left alone at home by their parents.'

There have been a few challenges to the Freudian hour. As Sándor Ferenczi grew older, his methods became ever wilder. He would analyse patients for hours on end, throughout the day and often into the night. He did, however, tell this good joke about fees:

The most characteristic example of the contrast between conscious generosity and concealed resentment was given by the patient who opened the conversation by saying: 'Doctor, if you help me, I'll give you every penny I possess!' 'I shall be satisfied with thirty kronen an hour,' the physician replied. 'But isn't that rather excessive?' the patient replied.

Jacques Lacan, the French neo-Freudian, had his own unique variation on the analytic hour. He questioned the sacrosanct fifty minutes, arguing that a shorter session turned 'the transference relationship into a dialectic'. Lacan was repeatedly cautioned about this by the International Psycho-analytical Association and was eventually expelled. He reduced the session over time to ten minutes but did not reduce his fee; during these mini analyses, he would often see his tailor, pedicurist and barber. This new business model allowed Lacan to see up to eighty patients a day; he died a multimillionaire, leaving a legacy of discarded lovers, several patients who died by their own hand, and a dozen or more psychoanalytic societies and associations, each claiming to be the true heir to his progressive and revolutionary ideas.

16

Four-year-old Mervyn Jones had his first appointment with Melanie Klein on 15 September 1926. Klein had emerged as a leading child psychoanalyst, a field where her chief rival was Anna Freud. The Viennese-born Klein was the first European analyst to join the British Psychoanalytical Society; she eventually became its most influential member. Klein – like so many lay analysts – had first come to the discipline as a patient, undergoing analysis in Budapest with Sándor Ferenczi for postnatal depression. Klein's relationship with her husband, Arthur, had broken down, and she was emotionally dependent to an extreme degree on her mother, Libussa. Ferenczi foolishly told Klein that she had 'a natural gift' for psychoanalysis, which prompted her to experiment on her youngest child, Erich. He must have been surprised to be the object of such intense scrutiny, as Klein had often left her three children with their maternal grandparents for weeks, or even months, at a time while she recuperated from her 'fits of weeping and despair' in a Swiss sanatorium or in the Adriatic resort of Abbazia.

During these depressions, Klein wrote a great deal of erotic poetry.*

Erich began analysis at the age of three with his mother, who allocated an hour to this every night before he went to sleep. Klein encouraged little Erich to talk openly about sex, telling him how animals mate, using toys as erotic symbols. She presented her work with Erich to the Hungarian Psychoanalytical Society in 1919, following which she was instantly given membership; this allowed Klein (untrained, unsupervised) to style herself thereafter as a psychoanalyst. She proudly told the society that this analysis transformed the boy from 'slightly backward' to 'almost precocious', and that his 'games and phantasies showed an extraordinary aggressiveness towards his father and also of course his clearly indicated passion for his mother'. Privately, however, she confessed to Ferenczi that Erich had resisted analysis, and that his 'nervous condition' had worsened.

Erich later suffered from 'a mild phobia' about walking to school because he was tormented by 'rough boys' on the streets. Klein saw great significance in the route little Erich walked to the school, particularly a *tree-lined* road, which she interpreted as a symbol of his repressed desire for coitus with his mother. She ignored more obvious reasons for the boy's anxiety, such as the taunting he encountered on his way to his new school (where he was bullied for being Jewish), the prolonged absence of his father on military service, and his parents' marital discord. When they eventually divorced, Erich was sent to a boarding

---

* 'My body firmly pressed against yours, my mouth sucked on to yours – we are one inseparable being.'

school in southern Germany, and then to Frankfurt, where he boarded with a schoolmaster while undergoing further analysis with Clara Happel.* Years later, Erich (now 'Eric Clyne') remarked: 'It must be nice to be part of a normal family.'

Klein now turned her attention to her other two children, Hans and Melitta, both in their teens. She analysed Hans, who had developed a neurotic tic, for 370 hours over three years. She forbade the boy from seeing an older (by one year) girl, because she thought this friendship represented a projection of his subconscious fantasy that his mother/analyst was a prostitute: 'the transference proved strong enough for me to impose a temporary break in this relation. It could now be seen that on turning away from the originally loved but forbidden mother had participated in the strengthening of the homosexual attitude and the phantasies about the dreaded castrating mother.' Convinced that a friendship with another boy was homosexual, Klein ordered Hans to end this relationship also. She analysed repeatedly, and in detail, his masturbation fantasies. Hans's father was appalled but too weak to put a stop to it. Klein spent rather less time on Melitta. She was concerned by the girl's lack of proficiency at mathematics and concluded that it was caused by a castration complex. She tried, but failed, to make Melitta as emotionally dependent on her as she had been on her own mother. All three children went on to experience emotional difficulties in their adult lives; all three went on to other analysts.

* Happel (1889–1945), a German psychoanalyst, wrote papers on pederasty, homosexuality and masturbation.

Klein moved with her children to Berlin in 1921, where Karl Abraham became her analyst and mentor. She formed an unlikely friendship with Alix Strachey, who had also moved to the city to be analysed by Abraham.* Alix (tall, patrician, Bloomsbury) and Melanie (short, Jewish and gauche) were an odd couple. They enjoyed the Berlin nightlife, particularly fancy-dress and 'masked' balls.† 'She was most elaborately got up as a kind of Cleopatra,' Alix wrote to James about one such event, 'terrifically décolleté – and covered in rouge and bangles, a sort of heterosexual Semiramis in slap-up fancy dress waiting to be pounced on.' However, she found Melanie 'rather tiresome as a person – a sort of ex-beauty and charmer'. James, having read one of Klein's papers, wrote to Alix: 'What an awful woman she must be. I pity the poor kiddies who fall into her clutches.' Alix replied: 'When she said that the parents were the only proper people to analyse the child a shudder ran down my spine. It seems to me to be the last stronghold of the desire of adults to have power over others.'

On 6 May 1925, Klein wrote to Ernest Jones, offering to give a series of lectures at the British Psychoanalytical Society; he accepted with alacrity. On 17 July, he reported enthusiastically to Freud: 'Melanie Klein has just given a course of lectures before our Society on "Frühanalyse" [early analysis]. She made such an extraordinarily deep impression on all of us and won

---

* Alix's analysis with Freud had been interrupted when she developed pneumonia (complicated by a lung abscess) in 1922; Freud recommended that she should continue analysis with Abraham.
† Alix (accompanied by her lover, Nancy Morris) remained an enthusiastic partygoer throughout the 1930s.

the highest praise both by her personality and her work.' Freud did not approve of Klein or her ideas: 'Melanie Klein's works have been received with much scepticism and opposition here in Vienna.' Jones replied, extravagantly proclaiming that 'prophylactic child analysis appears to me to be the logical outcome of psychoanalysis' – *all* children, neurotic and healthy alike, should undergo analysis. Jones was so taken with Klein that he encouraged her to move permanently to England and invited her to analyse his wife Kitty and two children, Mervyn and Gwenith. Kitty was not naturally maternal and found her two small children difficult and demanding. Klein accepted the invitation and arrived in London in September 1926. Jones ensured that she swiftly became a member of the British Psychoanalytical Society.

In his autobiography *Chances*, Mervyn Jones claimed to have no memory of his prolonged childhood analysis with Klein, although he did recall that she was 'someone you didn't contradict':

> I suspect that my father, who was championing Mrs Klein against the opposition of other analysts, seized the opportunity to demonstrate his faith in her by sending his son for treatment. In a letter to Freud (which I read many years later) he claimed that the analysis was a great success, but I have my doubts. I certainly had marked neurotic traits in adolescence, and those who knew me would probably say that they have persisted in adult life. Anyway, I have forgotten – or, I should presumably say, repressed – everything about my sessions with Mrs Klein except the journey to her house

and the look of her room. The analysts whom I know react to this confession with bewilderment, with disapproval, or sometimes with amusement.

Mervyn, according to his father, was 'very introverted, lived in a babyish dream world, and had an almost complete sexual inversion'; Mervyn recalled that his parents were distant and undemonstrative, and that he was raised mainly by his nanny. He admired his father, who 'was infinitely the most important person in my life', but actively disliked his mother. Mervyn was desperate for his father's approval, and felt he never measured up to his standards: 'I thought then, and I still think, that he was a better man than I could ever be.' It didn't occur to Jones that Mervyn might have benefited more from his father's attention than that of Melanie Klein. She 'completed' Mervyn's analysis in December 1928 after eighteen months, but seems to have resumed in October 1931, continuing through 1932, and possibly even into 1933. Did this prolonged (and mysteriously forgotten) analysis contribute to Mervyn's conviction that he was 'a bad and difficult child'?

Jones's patronage of Melanie Klein made his relationship with Freud awkward. The Master saw her as a heretic, in open conflict with Anna, who was now emerging as the custodian of psychoanalytic orthodoxy. On 16 May 1927, Jones wrote to Freud, telling him about Mervyn's marvellous analytic progress: 'The changes already brought about are so striking

The serenity of the truly wicked:
Melanie Klein in old age.

and so important as to fill me with thankfulness towards the one who made them possible, namely yourself.' Freud, unmoved by this grovelling, initially maintained 'an impartial position', but eventually made it clear to Jones that he was in error: 'Melanie Klein is on the wrong track and Anna is on the right one.'

Mervyn's sister, Gwenith, eighteen months older, also underwent analysis; according to Jones, she 'proved to have a severe castration complex, intense guilt and a definite obsessional neurosis'. Gwenith died a year and a half later in March 1928, aged just seven, not of a severe castration complex, but of pneumonia. Mervyn recalled her death as the most significant event of his childhood:

There was something strange about Gwenith – 'the word would be *fey*,' my mother said to me years later. She was sweet and affectionate, and certainly she was much loved, but she lived in a contented present that envisaged no future. Once, when someone began a sentence with: 'When you grow up...', Gwenith said calmly: 'I'm not going to grow up.'

During her illness, I came down with German measles or some other childhood ailment and was sent home to be looked after by my uncle and aunt [the Trotters]. Gwenith stayed at home; my parents must have felt, when there was no hope, that it was better for her to die in familiar surroundings. I was taken to her sickroom on my sixth birthday so that she could give me a present. That was the day she was expected to die, but she lingered on for another four days. I never saw her again. My parents came to my bedroom in my uncle's flat – it must have been evening, for I was in bed – and my father said: 'Gwenith is dead.' I smiled, and turned my face to the wall to hide my smile. My father said to my mother: 'He doesn't understand.' They went out.

I still ask myself: what was the meaning of my smile? Was it – to give the simplest and most shameful explanation – a smile of selfish triumph now that I was the only child? Throughout my childhood, I was convinced that my parents regarded me as a bad and difficult child. Life would have been much easier for them, surely, if I had died instead of Gwenith.

Jones described Gwenith's agonising death in some detail in a letter to Freud. 'I am finding it hard,' he wrote, 'and as yet impossible, to discover enough motive to go on living and to endure the present and future suffering that this blow has brought. I thought I had tasted ten years ago all that the suffering of grief could bring.'

Ernest and Kitty later had two more children: Nesta, born in 1930, and Lewis in 1933. On a visit to Vienna in 1935, Freud playfully pinched Nesta's nose with two fingers; Jones wondered if she had realised that this was 'a symbol of castration'. By 1937, Nesta was in analysis with Donald Winnicott for 'pathological jealousy of her little brother'. Lewis was 'an accident', born when Jones was fifty-four; Morfydd's ghost must have been amused when Lewis (who alone of Jones's children escaped analysis) became a composer.

17

Ernest Jones proudly called himself the *Shabbes-Goy** of the psychoanalytic movement, even dropping Yiddish words into conversation. He thought that the Welsh and the Jews had a natural kinship; he also believed that his imaginative empathy allowed him to become close to the Jewish analysts: 'my own unusual capacity for adaptation and sympathetic understanding led me to being admitted to their intimacy on practically equal terms.' In his first letter to his fellow Paladins (all of whom were Jewish), he began: 'We are all good Jews.' A good part of the attraction of Kitty Jokl for Jones was her Jewishness; when his daughter Gwenith was a baby, Jones proudly wrote to Freud: 'she has a wonderful Jewish smile with twinkling eyes', while Mervyn was 'a typical *Judenbub*, but with blond hair and blue eyes'.

Jones, for all his self-proclaimed kinship with the Jews, was accused by A. A. Brill in 1923 of calling Otto Rank 'a swindling

---

* A gentile who carried out tasks forbidden to Jews on the sabbath.

Jew'.* A decade later, he suggested that Isidor Sadger (who had written a critical book on Freud) 'should be sent to a concentration camp' – Sadger died in the Theresienstadt Ghetto in 1942. As president of the International Psychoanalytical Association, Jones allowed the Nazis to purge the German Psychoanalytic Society of Jews when he should have dissolved the organisation. 'Deplorable as it would be,' he unconvincingly explained to Anna Freud, 'I should still say that I prefer psychoanalysis to be practised by Gentiles in Germany than not at all.' The presidency of the German society was taken over by Matthias Goering, cousin of Hermann. Jones later redeemed himself by rescuing not only the Freuds, but many other Jewish analysts.

Freud was unimpressed by Jones's philo-Semitic posturing. While he recognised and valued Jones's usefulness and loyalty, he didn't like him: the prospect of Jones becoming his son-in-law, for example, was unthinkable. The voluminous Jones-Freud correspondence (1908–39) provides the best insight into their relationship. Jones's wretched obsequiousness is abject; responding to Freud's regular rebukes, he replied: 'Your

---

* This accusation was made when the Paladins had gathered in San Cristoforo in the Italian Dolomites; Freud was staying nearby in the town of Lavarone. Jones never used the phrase 'swindling Jew'; he had written to Brill complaining that Rank's way of conducting business was 'distinctly Oriental'. Jones wrote to Kitty: 'The whole committee, after hours of talking and shouting … thought I was in Bedlam, decided that I was in the wrong, in fact that I am neurotic. A Jewish family council sitting on one sinner must be a great affair, but picture it when the whole five insist on analysing him on the spot and all together!' Jones narrowly avoided being forced to resign from the committee; he was put on probation and ordered to resume his analysis with Ferenczi.

personal remarks to me were quite justified' (1909); 'You have checked wrong tendencies in me' (1912); 'As usual, you hit the nail on the head' (1922); 'As to your own repeated disapproval of me I need not tell you how grievous I find that, for you must know what part you play in my life and feelings' (1922); 'I want to thank you for your outspokenness to me' (1923) and 'you were right in reproaching me' (1932). Jones's letters are packed with embarrassing declarations such as: 'To me it is clear that I owe my career, my livelihood, my position, and my capacity for happiness in marriage – in short everything – to you and the work you have done' (1920) and 'what has made my life worth living, is my relationship to you and your work' (1929). Freud occasionally bestowed some faint, wintry praise: 'So, is it really twenty years since you joined the cause? You have really made the cause quite your own, for you have achieved everything that could be made of it. What you have meant to it may be left for historians to ascertain. We may well be satisfied with each other. I have the impression that you sometimes overestimate the importance of our disagreements' (1926).

Freud was bored by Jones's endless fussing over the translation of his work, and the politics of psychoanalytic societies. They heartily agreed, however, on who was the protagonist and who the deuteragonist in this drama. 'However enterprising I might be intellectually,' Jones told Freud, 'I was not intended for a pioneer's life.' Freud agreed: 'I am glad you are not one of those fellows who want to show themselves original and totally independent when they do something in writing, but you do not despise to show yourself as interpreter of another's thoughts.' Even after thirty years of association, they never progressed to the intimacy of calling each other 'Sigmund' or 'Ernest', sticking with 'Professor' and 'Jones' until the very end.*

Freud had ambivalent feelings for his disciples, telling a patient in the late 1920s: 'The goody-goodys are no good, and the naughty ones go away.' The 'naughty ones' included Jung, Adler and Rank; although Jones was the chief 'goody-goody', Freud valued his talent for dirty work: 'Your intention to purge the London society of the jungish [sic] members is excellent' (1919). Jones eventually saw off his rivals in the committee; Karl Abraham died in 1925, and Otto Rank broke with Freud in 1926. Jones and Rank had clashed repeatedly over the latter's running of the *Verlag*† and because of the rivalry between their respective journals – Jones edited the English language *International Journal of Psycho-Analysis*, while Rank ran the German language *Zeitschrift für Psychoanalyse*. Jones had written several letters before this rupture, warning Freud of Rank's 'neurosis' and unorthodox beliefs – 'especially denial of the Oedipus complex'.‡ Jones was a great snitch: 'His disparaging remarks about both your person and your work are the most painful, simply a regression of the hostility from

---

* In 1922, nearly ten years after the foundation of the Central Psycho-analytic Committee, the members took the belated decision to address each other by first names and to use the familiar *Du*. Freud continued to address them all by surname, using the formal *Sie*. Apart from his family, the only two people Freud ever addressed informally were Julius Wagner-Jauregg and the archaeologist Emanuel Löwy, both friends from his student days.

† The International Psychoanalytical Press (*Internationaler Psychoanalytischer Verlag*), founded by Freud.

‡ Rank's 1924 book on the birth trauma, *Das Trauma der Geburt*, openly challenged the concept of the Oedipus complex.

the brother (myself, who had been useful in this role for some years) to the father.'

Jones's only deviation from the goody-goody role was his championship of Melanie Klein, which almost ruptured their relationship in 1927. Freud rose above his usual mild irritation with this thunderbolt:

In London, you are organizing a regular campaign against Anna's child analysis, accusing her of not having been analysed deeply enough, a reproach that you repeat in a letter to me. I had to point out to you that such a criticism is just as dangerous as it is impermissible. I can assure you that Anna has been analysed longer and more thoroughly than, for example, you yourself. Anna's views on child analysis are largely independent of mine; I share her views, but she has developed them out of her independent experience. This incident has left me with an unpleasant impression and has aroused the need to understand more about the mental processes in the English Society, especially in you.

'Jones', Freud wrote to Max Eitingon, 'is a disagreeable person, who wants to display himself in ruling, angering and agitating, and for that his Welsh dishonesty ("the Liar from Wales") serves him well.' Freud was convinced that Jones's hostility to Anna's ideas dated back to 1914, 'when she refused him'. Freud confided in Eitingon his suspicion that Jones was championing Klein because he had no ideas of his own: 'Since his very first work about rationalisation, he has not had any original ideas, and his application of my ideas has stayed on a schoolboy level. Therefore his sensitivity.'

There is no greater insult that a psychoanalyst can direct at a colleague than the accusation of being 'insufficiently analysed'. Jones was stung by Freud's observation because it was true: his analysis with Ferenczi, though intensive, lasted only a couple of months. Jones never quite forgave the Hungarian for having analysed him, and for his greater intimacy with Freud.* Ferenczi was equally suspicious of Jones, warning Freud in 1913: 'It has seldom been so clear to me as now what a psychological advantage it signifies to be born a Jew. You must keep Jones constantly under your eye and cut off his line of retreat.' Jones had spread rumours about Ferenczi's state of mind, and in his biography of Freud wrote that Ferenczi 'towards the end of his life developed psychotic manifestations that revealed themselves in, among other things, a turning away from Freud and his doctrines. The seeds of a destructive psychosis, invisible for so long, at last germinated. The lurking demons within, against whom Ferenczi had for years struggled with great distress and much success, conquered him at the end.' Jones was later accused of blackguarding him by Ferenczi's friend and compatriot, the analyst Michael Balint.

Freud, who had dropped many intimates before (Josef Breuer, Wilhelm Fliess, Jung), and always claimed that these friendships ended because of 'scientific' differences, eventually

* Freud wrote 400 letters to Jones over thirty years but sent 2,500 to Ferenczi. 'I cannot help but wish', wrote Freud, 'that [Karl] Abraham's clarity and accuracy could be merged with Ferenczi's endowments and to it be given Jones's untiring pen.'

turned his back on the lovable, foolish Ferenczi, who had begun practising 'mutual analysis' with his patients. Worrying though this was, it was his unsoundness on the Oedipus complex that finally led to his banishment. 'Our friend', said Freud, 'slowly drifted away from us.' Freud wrote to Jones in September 1932, eight months before Ferenczi's death:

> To be sure, Ferenczi's change is most regrettable, but there is nothing traumatic about it. For three years already I have been observing his increasing alienation, his unreceptiveness about his technical errors, and what is probably most crucial, a personal hostility toward me. His regressive intellectual and affective development seems to have a background of physical decline. His perceptive and good wife let me know that I should think of him as a sick child.

Ferenczi died in 1933, aged fifty-nine, of pernicious anaemia.* Freud discarded Ferenczi – whom he once loved like a son – when he became tiresome, sick and heretical, but Jones, irritating and bumptious though he was, was just too useful.

---

* Called 'pernicious' because it was so often fatal. Just a year after Ferenczi's death, George Hoyt Whipple, William Parry Murphy and George Richards Minot shared the Nobel Prize in Medicine 'for their discoveries concerning liver therapy in cases of pernicious anaemia'. Concentrated liver extract contains large quantities of vitamin B12, deficiency of which (through malabsorption) causes pernicious anaemia. This disease is now easily treatable with vitamin B12 injections.

18

In July 1929, Wilfred Trotter took a call from Buckingham Palace, requesting his opinion on King George V's persisting illness.

'We'll send a car.'

'No, that won't be necessary,' said Trotter, 'I can take the 14 bus.'

Only two days before, the king had attended a service of thanksgiving at Westminster Abbey for his 'recovery' from his prolonged illness. This ceremony was, however, somewhat premature. Even dull old George could see the absurdity of it, snapping at his personal physician, Lord Dawson, on the journey from the abbey to the palace: 'Fancy a thanksgiving service with an open wound in your back!'

Bertrand Dawson, Lord Dawson of Penn, was the most eminent British doctor of the period between the wars. He was a medical politician (twice President of the British Medical Association, eight times President of the Royal College of Physicians) and a highly successful consulting physician with a large clientele of the rich and famous. According to his biographer Francis

Watson, 'he liked good living, good manners, and the cultured hospitality of prosperous and leisured patients'. Dawson's bedside manner was impeccable; he was said to possess a 'Himalayan calm' and pulled off the difficult trick of being both genial and dignified. He had a genius for inspiring confidence in his patients: 'Never, never', he would admonish his students, 'let fear enter.' Dawson, however, had his detractors; Canon F. A. Iremonger, the Dean of Lichfield, wrote that Dawson 'seemed to me almost too handsome, too *soigné*, too much a man of the world', while his black hair, according to the surgeon R. Scott Stevenson, 'owed much more to Art than to Nature'.*

On 21 November 1928, the king, a diligent if banal diarist, wrote: 'Feverish cold, they call it, and I retired to bed.' This 'feverish cold' soon developed into full-blown pneumonia and septicaemia. George, a heavy smoker, was prone to 'bronchitis' and chest infections, and his health had been precarious since he fractured his pelvis in 1915.† This being still the pre-antibiotic era, there was no specific treatment, apart from 'ultraviolet ray therapy', administered with a mercury lamp 'to stimulate the vitality of the tissues'. When faced with a very sick and very august patient, the natural inclination of doctors is to spread the responsibility – and any future blame – as widely as possible. Dawson called in eleven doctors, including the Regius Professors of Physic at Oxford and Cambridge, and issued daily press bulletins. Rich, powerful and royal

---

* Damian Lewis, the handsome, *soigné* actor, is Dawson's great-grandson.
† During an inspection of troops in Flanders, his horse, startled by the sudden bursting into sound of a military band, reared and fell backwards, crushing the king's pelvis.

patients are often prey to the delusion that eminent doctors achieve their eminence because of their clinical abilities. Sir Humphry Rolleston, Regius Professor of Physic at Cambridge, for example, was famously pedantic; a friend and colleague wrote that he 'was never very helpful in consultation, for he always remembered so many possible alternatives'.

After three weeks, the king was no better, still septic and delirious. During these anxious weeks, Dawson's clinical acumen was the subject of much malicious gossip. An apocryphal (and bizarrely racist) story did the rounds in the London clubs that he had once treated a patient for jaundice before realising that the man was *Chinese*. It was rumoured that a mob of doctors and medical students were planning to gather outside Dawson's house to demand that he call in the famous chest surgeon Arthur Tudor Edwards. Even Margot Asquith quipped: 'The King told me that he would never have died if it had not been for that fool Dawson of Penn.'

Dawson suspected that the king had an empyema – a complication of pneumonia, where an abscess develops between the ribs and lung. On 12 December, he summoned all his Himalayan calm and pierced the back of the king's right lung with a large needle and syringed out sixteen ounces of pus. That evening, the chest surgeon Hugh Rigby carried out an operation to drain the empyema. Under intense pressure, and the object of scurrilous *ad hominem* criticism, Dawson had held his nerve. On 9 February 1929, the king was moved to Bognor on the Sussex coast to convalesce – Dawson persuaded him that the sea air would hasten his recovery. His attention to his royal patient was comprehensive and holistic: he tested the water supply and examined the drains; he had the drive levelled; he arranged for a special 'health-giving' glass ('vitaglass') to be fitted in the windows of the king's bedroom. Three days after his arrival in Bognor, Dawson permitted the patient his first cigarette in over two months.

Shortly before leaving Bognor in May 1929, the town successfully petitioned George V to have the suffix 'Regis' attached to its name in honour of its role in his recovery. There are several variations of the 'Bugger Bognor' story. I like this version: when asked by his private secretary, Lord Stamfordham, whether he would assent to this honour, the king replied with the much-quoted obscenity. Stamfordham informed the delegation that His Majesty would be graciously pleased to grant their request. In his 1983 biography of the king, Kenneth ('Climbing') Rose wondered 'would that whimsical alliteration have been attached to his memory had he convalesced at Ramsgate or Cleethorpes, Scarborough, or Torquay?'

The *British Medical Journal* celebrated the king's recovery: 'Only the combination of a sound constitution, the will to live, and perfectly co-ordinated medical care could have achieved this.' This was vapourish toadying; George V was a terrible patient: ungrateful, irritable, and prone to fits of depression and self-pity. After three months of relative calm, the king (now in Windsor Castle) relapsed, with recurrence of the chest abscess. On 31 May he laughed so hard at a ribald joke told by the Labour politician Jimmy Thomas* that the

---

* Thomas, from Newport in South Wales, rose from railwayman to cabinet minister and royal intimate. George V liked him so much that he invited him to stay every year. Thomas was often accused by his enemies

abscess burst; the wound continued to ooze pus and the king became feverish.

Just days after Jimmy Thomas's side-splitting joke, fifteen of the doctors and nurses involved in the king's care were bestowed with honours, with MBEs for the nurses and knighthoods and baronetcies for the doctors. Dawson, a peer since 1920, was made a Privy Counsellor, an unprecedented honour for a doctor.* He knew very well, however, that these awards, not to mention the service of thanksgiving a few weeks later, were at best premature and at worst hubristic. In the days after the event at Westminster Abbey, Dawson, now very anxious indeed, consulted widely. On 12 July, Sir Hugh Rigby (as he was now styled) advised Dawson that further surgery would be necessary, and in a tacit admission that he was out of his depth, suggested that Wilfred Trotter might 'assist' him. *John Bull* magazine noted Trotter's arrival at the palace with approval:

> Mr Wilfred Trotter, who was called in for the latest operation on the King, has always enjoyed a higher reputation inside the medical profession – which after all, really knows best in these matters – than with the public.
>
> For a long time there have been many doctors ready to say that Wilfred Trotter is the best surgeon in the world.

---

of affecting exaggerated working-class mannerisms and of deliberately dropping his aspirates. Leon Trotsky once described him as 'an absolutely unprecedented lackey'.

* A doctor was then regarded by aristocrats as somewhere above a ghillie, but certainly not a *gentleman*. Queen Victoria used to put her personal physician Sir James Reid in his place by announcing 'the gentlemen *and* Dr Reid will join us after dinner'.

He is a little man, clean-shaven, with bowed shoulders, who looks like a retired butler – an intelligent retired butler.

On 15 July, Rigby, 'assisted' by Trotter, operated; the procedure took just forty minutes, and was carried out in the king's bedroom. Dawson issued a statement later that morning: 'The operation on His Majesty the King has been performed. Portions of two ribs were removed, in order that a circumscribed abscess, 1½ inches across should be directly drained and treated. The condition of His Majesty is satisfactory.' The king made a complete recovery; he resumed his preferred activities of shooting,* smoking, stamp-collecting, and being regaled by Jimmy Thomas.

In 1962, R. Scott Stevenson, who knew most of the doctors involved, wrote: 'Sir Hugh Rigby was a pleasant personality, a careful, rather diffident surgeon and he obviously was not drastic enough when he operated on George V's empyema. After drifting for six months with a discharging sinus, the empyema was cured in a week when Wilfred Trotter treated the king as he would have done any other patient in hospital.' Trotter, who told Dawson that it was 'a perfectly straightforward case', was offered a baronetcy but declined. 'With Trotter,' wrote Ernest Jones, 'rank, authority, veneration, counted for nothing.'

While Trotter disappeared out the back gate of Buckingham

---

* After killing 4,000 pheasant in one day in 1913, the king admitted to his son the Prince of Wales that he 'perhaps went a little too far'.

Palace to catch the 14 bus home, Dawson was hailed as 'the doctor who pulled the King through'. He even made the cover of *Time* magazine: 'Lord Dawson has this in common with Eve: whereas she was made from Adam's side, he was made a privy councillor [*sic*] by the side-piercing of George V. He is the perfect British doctor.'

The king enjoyed only five more years of indifferent health, falling mortally ill at Sandringham in December 1935 with heart failure and emphysema, or 'bronchial catarrh'. Dawson once again presided over his treatment, but on this occasion, there was no prospect of recovery. On the evening of 20 January 1936, Dawson wrote his now-famous bulletin: 'The King's life is moving peacefully towards its close.' After the death of George V, Dawson's peerage was upgraded to a hereditary viscountcy.* He died in 1945 aged eighty, full of years and honours; his funeral service was held at Westminster Abbey, conducted by his old friend the Archbishop of Canterbury, Cosmo Lang, who called Dawson 'my dear Preserver'. He left instructions that a post-mortem examination be carried out on his body, 'a rightful tribute which the dead should give the living'.

Rumours about Dawson's role in the king's final illness had been in circulation for some time, with the much recited clerihew, said to have been composed by Dawson's 'friend'

---

* The viscountcy died with him as he had no sons.

and rival, the surgeon Lord Moynihan of Leeds,* his fellow
medical peer:

> Lord Dawson of Penn
> Has killed many men
> That is why we sing
> 'God Save the King'

The rumours were finally given some substance in 1986,
when Francis Watson wrote an essay for *History Today* entitled
'The Death of George V'. His respectful, rather dull biography
of Dawson had appeared many years before in 1950; now
seventy-nine, Watson would die less than two years later. He
was reluctant, he wrote, to describe in the biography the true
circumstances of the king's death, because so many involved
were still alive, including Lady Dawson, who begged him not
to write about it.

Watson had access to Dawson's private diary, which con-
tained this account of the king's final hours: 'Hours of waiting
just for the mechanical end when all that is really life has
departed only exhausts the onlookers. I therefore decided to
determine the end and injected ¾ of a gram of morphia and

---

* Moynihan, while visiting the operating theatres at UCH, once told
Trotter that his brains were outstanding, but he had no technique. Trotter
graciously replied that he valued 'so great a compliment from such a
source'. Trotter's pupil the surgeon Julian Taylor recalled that 'the great
man purred, but a little doubtfully, I think just conscious that there was
a hint of obliquity in the exchange of compliments, but unfortunately
having no inkling that he was in fact being told that his surgery must still
be in the elementary stages of carpentry'.

shortly afterwards 1 gram of cocaine into the distended jugular vein.' Dawson was preoccupied by 'the importance of the death receiving its first announcement in the morning papers rather than the less appropriate evening journals'. Having given the lethal injection, he telephoned his wife, instructing her to ask the *Times* to hold the publication of the morning edition as the king's death was imminent. Dawson wrote his final bulletin: 'Death came peacefully to the King at 11.55 pm.'

Dawson stayed up all night waiting for the embalmers to arrive from London; they got lost on the way to Norfolk, finally arriving at 6 a.m. He carefully supervised every detail of their work, being mindful, wrote Francis Wilson, of 'such unfortunate accidents as that to the coffin of the Duke of Teck which, after a death from acute abdominal sepsis, "burst open with a loud report" during the funeral procession'.

Dawson's reputation took quite a dent following these posthumous revelations, with the former President of the Royal College of Physicians Sir Douglas Black calling his actions 'evil'. And then a new rumour began to spread that Dawson had also played a part in the death in 1938 of George V's sister, Maud, Queen of Norway. On a trip to England, Maud became suddenly ill, underwent an exploratory abdominal operation, and died four days later. Dawson wrote to her doctors in Norway: 'you will agree that the Queen's sudden death was a relief, and which saved her from these last painful stages of the disease both you and I know only too well.' The 'disease' was presumably cancer: did Dawson once again deploy his trusty mixture of morphia and cocaine into a royal jugular vein?

Although Dawson's suave paternalism was typical of doctors at that time, his besetting sin was arrogance – hardly surprising, given that he had risen to become a peer and a Privy Counsellor, and grandly saw himself as a 'statesman'. He was accused too of hypocrisy because he had opposed Moynihan in the House of Lords in a debate on euthanasia. He was not, he said, opposed to euthanasia *per se*; he was opposed to its *legalisation*: 'This is something which belongs to the wisdom and conscience of the medical profession and not to the realm of the law.'

Lord Dawson of Penn: 'too handsome, too *soigné*, too much a man of the world.'

19

In the year after Trotter's cure of George V, Freud too was asked to consult on a royal patient. In early February 1930, Princess Alice of Battenberg was admitted with a diagnosis of schizophrenia to the Schloss Tegel clinic in Berlin under the care of its director, Ernst Simmel. Alice was forty-four, wife of the exiled Prince Andrew of Greece and mother of five, the youngest being Prince Philip, the future Duke of Edinburgh. In the late spring of 1929, Alice had an acute psychosis. She and her family were living at the time in a house in Saint-Cloud outside Paris, loaned to them by Princess Marie Bonaparte, the wife of Andrew's brother, Prince George of Greece. Shortly before this episode, Alice – who had been raised as a Lutheran – had been received into the Russian Orthodox Church. Had she lived in the Middle Ages, Alice's psychosis might have been seen as religious ecstasy: she claimed divine healing powers and was convinced that Christ had chosen her as His earthly bride; her hallucinations were described as 'hyperlibidinal'. Prince Andrew, convinced that his wife's disturbance was a 'hormonal' problem, summoned Alice's Greek gynaecologist

Nikólaos Louros, who correctly diagnosed schizophrenia. Marie Bonaparte, who had been in analysis with Freud and was now a psychoanalyst herself, persuaded Alice – telling her that Christ Himself had recommended it – to agree to admission to the Tegel clinic.

Princess Marie Bonaparte (1882–1962) was the great-grand-niece of Napoleon. Her maternal grandfather, François Blanc, was a multimillionaire who owned the casino at Monte Carlo; his daughter Marie-Félix died soon after giving birth to Marie, who thus inherited a huge fortune. It was to her that Freud directed his famous question – 'that has never been answered, and which I have not yet been able to answer, despite my thirty years of research into the feminine soul, is "What does a woman want?"' Bonaparte became Freud's patient in 1925, seeking treatment for 'frigidity', which she defined as the inability to achieve orgasm in the missionary position. (Despite this frigidity, the princess had numerous lovers, most notably Aristide Briand, eleven times Prime Minister of France during the Third Republic.)

Frigidity had become something of an obsession for Bonaparte; she was convinced that a common (and overlooked) cause was an excessive distance between the clitoris and vagina. Filled with a Trotter-like experimental spirit, Bonaparte carried out a research project in 1923, measuring this distance in two hundred and forty-three Parisian women (rumoured to be mainly her friends and acquaintances), and correlating it with the women's ability to achieve orgasm. She published her findings in 1924 under the pseudonym 'A. E. Narjani' in *Bruxelles-Médical* (a Belgian medical journal) as 'Considerations on the Anatomical Causes of Frigidity in Women'. Those women with a clitorido-vaginal distance of less than 2.5 cm she classified as *paraclitoridiennes*, those greater than 2.5 cm, *téléclitoridiennes*. She interviewed 'some' of the women and reported that those who required clitoral stimulation to reach orgasm were *all* téléclitoridiennes. Bonaparte concluded that there were two types of female frigidity: *libidinal* frigidity, where sexual desire is simply absent, and *vaginal* frigidity, where desire is present, but there is too great a distance between the clitoris and the vagina. Women with 'libidinal' frigidity, she recommended, should undergo psychoanalysis, while those with 'vaginal' frigidity should undergo surgery to shorten the distance between clitoris and vagina.

The princess came to Freud 'in search of the penis* and orgiastic normality'. She was the only patient that Freud ever agreed to analyse for *two* hours every day. He was particularly

---

* The Romanian artist Constantin Brâncuşi caused a scandal with his 1916 bronze sculpture 'Princess X', which he claimed to be a portrait of Marie Bonaparte, but which looks remarkably like an erect penis. In 1909, Brâncuşi had been asked by the princess to carve a bust of her, but he had 'a horror and miserably low opinion' of such sculptures. Bonaparte was naturally undeterred, and, according to Brâncuşi, she 'coquettishly asked me to make an exception'. The artist relented but came to detest the princess for her vanity: 'she was looking in the mirror all the time, even during lunch, discreetly placing the mirror on the table.' Brâncuşi initially produced the relatively conventional 'Woman Looking at a Mirror', but destroyed it in favour of 'Princess X'. When this piece was exhibited at the Salon des Indépendants in Paris in 1920, Brâncuşi was forced to withdraw it by the scandalised organisers.

struck by one 'dream' recounted by the princess. In this dream, she was back in her Parisian childhood home, where she disturbed a couple having sexual intercourse. Freud immediately decided that this was no *dream*, but a real memory of 'the primal scene'. She recalled more details: she had seen a maid fellating a man who had 'a horse-like face'. Freud suggested that the man's equine features must mean that he was a *groom*: sure enough, the princess unearthed an eighty-two-year-old Corsican called Pascal (what a pity his name wasn't Horsley), who had indeed been a groom in her family's service, and who, when pressed by the princess, confessed that he had had an affair with the nanny, and that they had doped little Marie with a bromide called 'syrop de flon'. (I suspect Pascal would have confessed to *anything* to placate his royal interrogator.) She returned triumphantly to Freud with this discovery.

Princess X by Brâncuși.

While in Vienna, Bonaparte sought out the famous gynaecologist Josef Halban. He took her ideas on the anatomical
causes of frigidity so seriously that together they experimented
on 'fresh' corpses to develop a surgical technique for reducing
the clitorido-vaginal distance. (Bonaparte brought a whole new
dimension to the phrase '*my* gynaecologist'.) She told Freud –
who was horrified – that she experienced 'orgasmic pleasure'
when handling a scalpel. Bonaparte and Halban developed a
procedure they called 'the Narjani-Halban Klithorikathesis':
the ligament suspending the clitoris (the *ligamentum sus-
pensorium*) is cut, allowing the clitoris to be bent towards
the vaginal orifice, following which the surrounding skin is
stitched tight. Halban performed the operation only five times;
the princess was the patient for two (or possibly three) of
these procedures. It seems that rich aristocrats could then ask
doctors to do almost *anything*. In his scholarly paper 'Sexual
surgery through the ages', the Dutch sexologist J. J. Drenth
drolly concluded that 'Marie Bonaparte was auto-mutilating
with the help of her gynaecologist'. Predictably, the princess
'venerated' the sexuality of cultures that practised female
circumcision; she was first told about this custom in 1935 by
Jomo Kenyatta, the future president of Kenya, then a graduate
student of the anthropologist Bronisław Malinowski at the
London School of Economics.

Despite Professor Halban's ministrations, the princess's
frigidity was no better. She continued in analysis with Freud,
and became friendly with one of his patients, the American
doctor Ruth Mack Brunswick. She instructed Bonaparte in
auto-erotic technique, telling her that she was prouder of her

masturbation than of 'ten doctoral degrees'. In 1929, the princess began analysis with Rudolf Loewenstein (also her son Peter's* analyst), who soon became her lover. By now, she too, had jumped the couch, and had started seeing patients herself. She briefly considered going to medical school but decided that this would be very hard work and rather time-consuming – why bother when one could become an analyst merely by the imprimatur of Freud himself?

When Sándor Ferenczi died in 1933, Freud suggested to Jones that Bonaparte should replace him as vice-president of the International Psychoanalytical Association. For once, Jones summoned the courage to say no: 'My opinion of her is that she has the highest technical ability, admirable energy and selfless devotion to our cause. I think, however, that her judgements are apt to be impulsive and to need a steadying influence.'

The Berlin Tegel clinic, established in 1927, was run on psychoanalytic lines, and the doctors there had little or no experience of treating psychosis. Even if psychoanalysis had been of any use in psychosis (which it wasn't), Princess Alice could not engage with it, as she was profoundly deaf. Nevertheless, Bonaparte, an intimate of Freud's and a benefactress of the clinic, had to be indulged. When Alice arrived at Tegel, she was floridly psychotic and malnourished, having starved herself for days at a time as an act of self-punishment. Simmel, faced with a

---

* Freud managed to dissuade Bonaparte from initiating an incestuous relationship with Peter – who admitted to being sexually attracted to her – which she thought might cure her frigidity.

deaf, hallucinating, semi-starved princess, had no idea what to do. In desperation, he travelled to Vienna to seek advice from Freud, who had visited the Tegel clinic on several occasions – he stayed with Simmel while in Berlin to have work done on his mouth prosthesis after his cancer surgery. Freud would not, as a rule, take on psychotics because psychoanalysis had nothing to offer, and because he was *afraid* of these patients. He confessed to his personal physician Max Schur: 'I do not like these patients. I am annoyed by them. I feel them to be so far distant from me and from everything human. A curious sort of intolerance, which surely makes me unfit to be a psychiatrist.'*

The Bonaparte connection, however, persuaded Freud to get involved; she was the wealthiest, the most fabulous, the most aristocratic of his circle of intimate women friend-analysands.†

He had a long conversation with Simmel, following which he recommended that Princess Alice should undergo 'an exposure of the gonads to X-rays, in order to expedite the menopause'. This bizarre advice had its roots in Freud's personal experience. In November 1923, some months after his first cancer operation, he underwent the 'Steinach' operation, which was essentially a one-sided vasectomy. The Austrian endocrinologist Eugen Steinach based this procedure on his questionable studies on

---

* The psychoanalyst Helene Deutsch told a story about how Freud, completely at sea, once referred a patient to an old pupil, explaining in a letter that he had no idea what was wrong, that the woman concerned was a 'crazy hen'. Freud had simply witnessed, and failed to recognise, a manic attack in a patient with bipolar disorder.
† Bonaparte replaced Lou Andreas-Salomé as Freud's favourite. He told her: 'Lou Andreas-Salomé is a mirror – she has neither your virility, nor your sincerity, nor your style.'

rats. He claimed that vasectomy (or ligation of the *vas deferens*) caused atrophy of the sperm-producing ('reproductive') cells, but proliferation of testosterone-secreting ('puberty-gland') cells, resulting in a rejuvenating increase in vigour and sexual potency of elderly rats. Steinach was not a surgeon, but he had little difficulty in persuading the urologist Robert Lichtenstern to carry out this procedure. The first three subjects were vasectomised without their knowledge while undergoing surgery for other reasons. Steinach claimed that these patients 'changed from feeble, parched, dribbling drones, to men of vigorous bloom'. Freud underwent the operation hoping to arrest the progress of his cancer. Although he confessed that the procedure had not achieved this, he maintained his belief in its scientific validity. Many prominent men (most notably W. B. Yeats) were 'Steinached'. Yeats, who underwent the procedure at the age of sixty-nine (following which he was dubbed 'the gland old man'), produced some of his best work in the years that followed.

The Steinach operation was, of course, quackery; unilateral vasectomy does not cause these hormonal changes or such dramatic benefits to health. Nevertheless, demand was so great that Steinach came up with an equivalent treatment for women: low-dose radiation of the ovaries. This idea came from yet another animal study: he had irradiated the ovaries of young female rats and erroneously concluded that radiation eliminated the 'reproductive' part of the ovary while sparing the 'puberty-gland'. He believed that the removal of the 'reproductive' part – just like vasectomy in the male – would stimulate growth of the 'puberty-gland' and increase hormone production. Steinach was also persuaded by his own anecdotal experience of a few women who had undergone X-ray treatment for uterine tumours and had reported a marked and unexpected improvement in their general health. Although radiation was even then known to be harmful, many women were also Steinached, most notably the novelist Gertrude Atherton, who claimed miraculous results: 'I had the abrupt sensation of a black cloud lifting from my brain, hovering for a moment, rolling away. Torpor vanished. My brain seemed sparkling with light.'

Freud recommended ovarian radiation 'in order to expedite the menopause'. Induction of a premature menopause, he reasoned, would ameliorate Alice's 'hyperlibidinal' state; he did not consider the possibility this might only exacerbate her psychosis. Freud's ex cathedra advice to carry out a futile and potentially dangerous procedure on a patient he had never seen, with a condition in which he had no expertise, was acted on: Alice duly underwent ovarian irradiation, carried out by a Dr Erich von Schubert. She was briefly better after this 'treatment', and took her own discharge, returning to Saint-Cloud in April 1930. The improvement didn't last long; on 2 May, she had become so disturbed that she was forcibly sedated and admitted as an 'involuntary' patient to the Bellevue sanatorium in Kreuzlinger in Switzerland – Vaslav Nijinsky was a fellow patient – under the care of the 'existential' psychoanalyst Ludwig Binswanger, also a friend of Freud's. During her two-and-a-half years there, her condition steadily worsened. She briefly escaped but was apprehended at the local railway station. She was eventually released, only to be admitted to another sanatorium in Italian South Tyrol, where she spent two months. She spent the next five years apart from her family, wandering aimlessly and anonymously around Europe. She did not meet her husband, Prince Andrew, again until 1937, when they attended the funeral of their daughter Cecilie in Darmstadt in Germany. Cecilie, her husband Georg, Grand Duke of Hesse, and their two children had perished in a plane crash near Ostend in Belgium.

Freud never advised again in a case of psychosis.

The ecstasy of Princess Alice.

20

In 1930, Wilfred Bion, a surgical houseman at UCH, assisted Wilfred Trotter with a craniotomy: 'I remember the near horror with which I saw him enter a skull with powerful blows of a mallet on the chisel he held. Such was his control that he could and did penetrate the hard bone and arrest the chisel so that it in no way injured the soft tissue of the underlying brain.' Bion had started his medical training at UCH in 1924, when he was already twenty-seven; he enrolled there with the intention of becoming a psychoanalyst. While still in his teens, he had joined the Tank Corps, winning the DSO (Distinguished Service Order) for his actions during the Battle of Cambrai in 1918.* After demobilisation, he went up to Oxford where he read history, and experienced nightmares and bouts of sweating that would now be attributed to Post-Traumatic Stress Disorder.

At UCH, Bion witnessed the contrasting styles of Trotter and another senior surgeon, Julian Taylor:

* Bion was recommended for the Victoria Cross, but when asked by a general if he wanted the honour, he replied: 'Oh yes, Sir, very much… well, not really, Sir.'

Taylor found it difficult to tolerate fools gladly. This was particularly noticeable to me from my centrally placed position of the fool. He could not tolerate the response to his inquiry 'What is your trouble?', 'It's my kidneys doctor.' 'Kidneys! What do you know about kidneys!' It offended both his medical knowledge and his sense of propriety. The patient, frightened at having given offence to such an eminent authority, would close up and volunteer no further suggestions lest a storm be evoked. Trotter, on the other hand, listened with unassumed interest as if the patient's contributions flowed from the fount of knowledge itself. It took me years of experience before I learned that this was in fact the case. Trotter's undisturbed friendly interest had the effect of eliciting further evidence from the patient; the fount of knowledge did not dry up.

It was said that when Trotter did a skin graft it 'took'; if Taylor did a skin graft – with equal or maybe even greater technical brilliance and accuracy – it did not take; the body rejected it; it was sloughed off.

Taylor, who had been his pupil, worshipped Trotter, so much so that, according to his *British Medical Journal* obituary, Taylor 'unconsciously imitated that great man in manner, in outlook, and even in walk'.* He did not, however, emulate Trotter's gentle approach to history-taking, nor his patience.

---

* Fritz Wittels wrote how Freud's disciples copied him: 'Some of them imitate his handwriting, some round up their speech or their gestures in his way, shake hands as he did, or occasionally hold an index finger at the upper front teeth as he sometimes did after the operation on his jaw.'

R. Scott Stevenson recalled that Taylor 'was opinionated, and made no concessions to please doctors or patients'.

Bion went on to realise his ambition of becoming an analyst, regarded by many as the most original English psycho-analytic thinker. 'The purest form of listening', he memorably wrote, 'is to listen without memory or desire.' Although Bion underwent long training analyses with John Rickman and, later, Melanie Klein, he acknowledged in his 1985 memoir *All My Sins Remembered* that Trotter – who taught him that the patient was 'the fount of knowledge' – was the greatest influence on his psychoanalytic career: 'I loved Trotter though I could never have dared to admit it.'

He may have *loved* him, but Bion mysteriously failed to acknowledge Trotter's influence on his own work on group psychology. Was this because Trotter belonged to the notoriously philistine and unempathetic profession of surgery? Even Bion's daughter Francesca was puzzled by this: 'Trotter makes observations which remind one strongly of my father's later views.' Bion's 1979 observation – 'I do not see why Man should not be another of Nature's failed experiments' – is remarkably similar to Trotter's prediction, in *Instincts of the Herd*, that 'man will prove but one more of Nature's failures'. Bion used *Learning from Experience* – a favourite phrase of Trotter's – for the title of his 1962 book. The psychologist Nuno Torres wrote that 'Trotter did a series of "mental grafts" on Bion's view of the world, and they "took".'

The Trotter cult had steadily grown at UCH throughout the 1920s. When Jones remarked to him that it must be wonderful to be a senior figure in such a great institution, Trotter dryly replied: 'I can hardly share your romantic illusions; you see, I married the lady.' In those days, senior surgeons like Julian Taylor generally deported themselves like James Robertson Justice's Sir Lancelot Spratt in the *Doctor* films, but Trotter did not conform in any way to this stereotype. He was humble; he didn't care for money or titles; he treated students and patients with what was at the time an unheard-of courtesy; he was both a technically gifted surgeon and a superb diagnostician; his only piece of original research had been rewarded with the Fellowship of the Royal Society; he was a best-selling author and a prose stylist; his rare pronouncements were noted for their wit and brevity.

Surgery is now so much a matter of teamwork that the notion of the great man – there were no great *women* – is an anachronism. When Trotter practised, however, the surgeon was almost entirely responsible for the outcome of any operation. Anaesthesia was rudimentary, and 'intensive care' had yet to be invented. Surgeons were then granted more leeway than other doctors with their temperament, on the grounds that the self-belief required to do the job inevitably came with some degree of arrogance. If the great man threw his instruments in frustration, or shouted at the theatre nurses, he was forgiven, because he alone carried the great burden of responsibility, because the line between boldness and arrogance was slim. Because they had to be decisive, because they had to move on quickly from errors and even catastrophes, surgeons had to have an almost superhuman composure. The surgeons who combined such composure with charisma were worshipped; Trotter uniquely managed to possess these qualities without acquiring arrogance. R. Scott Stevenson, who worked at UCH for eight years, wrote that Trotter 'commanded the affectionate veneration generally reserved for the dead'.

Unusually for a surgeon (for it is generally a career-ending handicap), Trotter was a late riser, a habit that inspired the ditty: 'comes at ten instead of nine, gigantic growths to undermine'. The students and junior doctors shared the Trotter stories and the Trotterisms ('Mr Anaesthetist, if the patient can keep awake, surely you can'). Some of them, like Julian Taylor, began to imitate his walk, his mannerisms, even his voice. 'There are many men', wrote his obituarist in the *British Medical Journal*, 'in whose conversation his habits of speech may still be heard. Some even may be recognised by their curiously softened and lazy-sounding sibilants.' A few, like Wilfred Bion, *loved* him: 'Wilfred Trotter was small and neatly but powerfully built. His strong hands had a beauty which could not by any stretch of the imagination be regarded as the product of a manicurist's cosmetic skill.'

Trotter's genius was for the clinical, not the experimental. Although Robin Pilcher described him as 'a surgeon of unusual virtuosity and versatility', Trotter always maintained that technique was, for a surgeon, a secondary concern, that judgement and diagnostic acumen were more important. 'A thoughtful consideration followed by a practical conclusion', recalled Julian Taylor, 'was his usual method, and never the one without the other where a patient's welfare was concerned.' Taylor distilled the essence of his clinical genius:

The peculiar quality of his approach to the sick was a gentleness that had nothing of the feminine, nor roots in affection for his fellows. It made of every patient a worshipper, of every doctor a lifelong adherent, and of every junior an envious and despairing disciple. His operative methods matched the perfection of the rest. Simplicity of equipment, exclusion of the unnecessary, deliberation, manual ambidexterity, and the gentlest of touches made for a style in which there was no element of display. No one ever happened to operate so simply and effortlessly as Trotter. It was a great art concealing a greater.

Freud is often credited with persuading doctors to 'listen', as if such close attention was something he had invented. As Wilfred Bion witnessed, Trotter did this naturally, instinctively; the irascible Taylor, who had no such patience, wrote how Trotter would listen 'attentively to the longest and most rambling story alike from the neurote and the husky old slum lady, with the same courtesy that he probably paid to duchesses'.

As Trotter had no interest in travel or scientific meetings, his name was virtually unknown outside England. 'Trotter was not attracted', wrote his colleague Sir Francis Walshe, 'to those public expositions of his thought and work that scientific societies provide, and he showed no eagerness to forward his views or to press their acceptance through this medium.' Such reticence would now be incompatible with a career in academic surgery.

In 1931, his health visibly failing – a matter he refused to discuss – Trotter took the unprecedented step of giving up his private practice to concentrate entirely on teaching: in that pre-NHS era, this work was unsalaried. In 1935, he was *persuaded* to accept the chair of surgery at UCH when the incumbent, one Professor Choyce, fell ill. 'The place was revivified,' wrote a colleague. Surgical training in those days was a haphazard affair; Trotter, unusually for such a senior surgeon, stayed for the entirety of any procedure he supervised. That this notoriously remote and reserved man should decide to spend the remainder of his career teaching surprised some at UCH; if he was sometimes bored, he didn't show it: 'He was most easy and accessible,' wrote T. R. Elliott, 'even to bores who never felt his judgement on them.' Recalling his teaching methods, R. Scott Stevenson wrote that Trotter 'had a low, quiet voice. He had little use for the conventional textbooks of surgery, but instead emphasized fundamentals by showing new angles of approach, and taught his students to develop their own powers of observation and thought. He taught his assistants mainly by dropping hints that ran contrary to prevailing ideas.'

Trotter enjoyed only two years of his professorship before illness forced him to retire.

21

In 1931, Ernest Jones published a short book entitled *The Elements of Figure Skating*; a second, much expanded edition was published in 1952. (I have a mental image of him in the classic pose of Henry Raeburn's *Reverend Robert Walker Skating on Duddingston Loch*.) Jones recalled that he had first learned to skate during the two bitterly cold winters between 1893 and 1895, when the River Towy near his boarding school, Llandovery, froze over:*

> For months on end one could skate for miles up and down the river. This enjoyment fused in a curious fashion with the romantic phase of adolescence that was already developing. I conceived the idea that the most delightful experience in the world would be to waltz on ice with a Viennese maiden with an appropriate music emanating from an enchanted island in a lake.

* Jones is a notoriously unreliable witness. The River Towy froze over in 1878, but not again until 1940. There is no record of the river freezing over between 1893 and 1895.

Jones took up skating again in middle age, practising hard in the London rinks and on the frozen lakes of Switzerland during winter holidays. Having concluded that there was no satisfactory instruction book for the beginner, he decided to write one himself. Even though he had written several books on psychoanalysis, Jones was particularly proud when a patient told him that 'there's a good book on skating by a man of your name'.

Always competitive, Jones proclaimed that this was 'the best book' on the subject. He won a silver medal in competition at his home rink (the Grosvenor), served as a judge for the 'Third Class Test', and gave demonstrations on technique. Jones saw skating as a networking opportunity; he became friendly with such fellow skaters as the publisher Sir Stanley Unwin (who would publish the 1952 edition of his book), and Sir Samuel Hoare, who, as Home Secretary, later granted entry visas to Freud and his entourage in 1938. (Jones, recognising Hoare's vanity, had congratulated him on his skating.) His most unlikely skating chum was Sonja Henie, the three-times Norwegian Olympic gold medallist and later a major film star. Photographs of the diminutive Henie (who had a sexual appetite to match Jones's) suggest that they would have made an attractive couple on the ice.

Wilfred Trotter's son Robert recalled that Jones's skating skills were not quite in Henie's league:

My uncle took up skating late in life and used to get much pleasure out of sedate but skilful pirouettings at the now defunct rink in Grosvenor House. He became as competent a performer as could be expected of middle-aged joints. It was perhaps typical of his somewhat intellectual approach to life's problems that he found the easiest way of learning to skate was to write a book about it. The result was a clear and logical account of the procedure, which has evidently been of assistance to would-be performers since a new and larger edition was later called for. My only criticism is that my uncle's prose style, usually straightforward and unpretentious, here lapses at times into what can only be described as archness.

Jones's book began: 'This book is addressed by a beginner to beginners, and the distinctive feature of it is its psychological approach to the problems in studying Figure Skating.' The tone, however, was more erotic than psychological: 'Skating combines and surpasses the joys of flying and dancing; only in a certain type of dream do we ever attain a higher degree of the same ravishing experience of exultantly skiing the earth.' Continuing in the same vein, he gushed: 'All art, however refined, disguised and elaborated its technique, takes its ultimate source in love for the human body and the desire to command it.' Jones gave detailed advice on 'the art of falling', advising that the skater should practise in the bedroom, 'with an ample supply of cushions and eiderdowns'. In this safe environment, one could 'learn to slither'.

Even Freud, weary of the endless phallic interpretations of his favourite pastime, once irritably snapped that 'sometimes, a cigar is just a cigar'. Not so for Jones: 'The two qualities – apart from physical appearance – of chief importance aesthetically

205

are a sense of life and a sense of rhythm. First consider the former. A stiff, over-careful skater makes a lifeless impression. It is largely a psychological problem, one with which an inspiring instructor is sometimes able to cope. Similarly, the matter of rhythm is really one of personality.'

After his marriage in 1919 to Kitty Jokl, the man once dubbed 'Erogenous Jones'* – who was serially unfaithful to Loe Kann, who had affairs with several patients and the wives of friends, who probably committed several sexual offences – seems to have settled for the deep comfort of the marriage bed and forsaken all others. There is not a whiff of scandal from the remaining thirty-nine years of his life, not a single rumour or cryptic remark; even the stream of intimate letters from infatuated patients dried up. Jones – astonishingly – appears to have been completely faithful to Kitty. Did he make a conscious decision that with the advent of middle age, he would have to choose where to spend his energies?

How little we know our parents, how remote their lives before our arrival. Mervyn Jones seems to have had little knowledge of his father's frantic erotic life. Ernest was a stern domestic figure – more grandfather than father – who was forty-three

* This nickname was bestowed on Jones by Alexander Faulkner Shand (1858–1936). A barrister, he was a founding member of the British Psychological Society in 1901. Camilla, Queen Consort, is his great-granddaughter.

when Mervyn was born. 'But you know how it is when you are married,' Kitty recalled on the occasion of Jones's centenary in 1979. 'You give up a part of your personality to your partner. He was a good husband and father, although an authoritative one. I was reminded of the Swiss Official who married us and addressed him as: "You, the Master of the house." He certainly was that.' Mervyn wrote that his father, so preoccupied with sex in his work and his premarital life, forbade all talk of it at home: 'To say nothing of sex itself, divorce and marital infidelity were subjects avoided in the family circle. In everyday life his attitudes were prim and even prudish.' He strongly disapproved of homosexuality, so much so that in 1922, he persuaded the governing committee of the International Psychoanalytical Association (known as the *Verein*) to introduce a rule barring homosexuals from becoming members of any psychoanalytical association. 'In most cases,' said Jones, 'they are abnormal.'* Psychoanalysis may have been modern, even *avant-garde*, but Jones was at heart an Edwardian, who, according to Mervyn, 'disapproved of Shakespeare in modern dress, cocktails, and women who wore trousers'. Mervyn did, however, get some insight, as a boy, into his father's work when he sneaked into his consulting room: 'the drawers of his desk, as I discovered when I took a peep, were crammed with obscene verses and pornographic drawings produced by patients.'

---

* This homophobia was not shared by Sigmund Freud. In 1935, he wrote a now famous letter to the mother of a gay man: 'Homosexuality is assuredly no advantage, but it is nothing to be ashamed of, no vice, no degradation; it cannot be classified as an illness.'

22

n 1934, the twenty-five-year-old Archie Cochrane entered the
UCH medical school to complete the two remaining years of
his training. In his memoir, *One Man's Medicine*, he praised
the 'wonderful collection of teachers I found there: Thomas
Lewis, George Pickering and Wilfred Trotter', but found the
indifference to evidence in medicine 'irritating' and 'depressing'.
Cochrane started 'a sort of club of individuals who would ask
consultants what was the evidence that their treatment was
having any effect. We found this great fun. There was so little
evidence available.'

Thirty years before at UCH, Ernest Jones was shocked
when his house physician Ivor Tuckett explained the evidence
base for medical treatments at the time:

> My naiveté received a smashing blow in the first week when
> Tuckett calmly stated that in the whole Pharmacopeia only
> four drugs could claim to have scientific evidence for any
> therapeutic effect at all. And so he went through the whole
> of medical teaching, sifting traditional beliefs, pious hopes,

and superstitious opinions from the definite basis of tested knowledge. It did me the world of good, and I have never lost that perspective of the probable as compared with the possible.

This 'smashing blow' to his naiveté did not have any permanent effect on Jones, who admitted that he was 'not over-liberally endowed by nature' with scepticism, a quality that in Trotter was 'all-embracing'.

Empirically trained scientists are rarely sympathetic to psychoanalysis. Cochrane was an empiricist who had been failed by psychoanalysis; this personal experience inspired his life's work and, indirectly, the foundation of evidence-based medicine, where his name lives on in the Cochrane organisation.* Born to a wealthy Scottish family in Galashiels, Cochrane (1909–88) took a first in Natural Sciences at Cambridge. He decided to study medicine and began working on tissue culture research at the Strangeways Laboratory in Cambridge. He did not enjoy laboratory work and had grown increasingly anxious about his sexual problem: 'I was

---

* Founded in 1993 (five years after Archie Cochrane's death) by Sir Iain Chalmers as the Cochrane Collaboration, now simply known as 'Cochrane'. Chalmers founded the organisation in response to Cochrane's rebuke that 'it is surely a great criticism of our profession that we have not organised a critical summary, by specialty or subspeciality, updated periodically, of all relevant randomised controlled trials.' Cochrane, which consists of over fifty global groups and 37,000 volunteers, prepares, maintains and distributes summaries of randomised-controlled trials and meta-analyses of medical interventions. Although it has its detractors, Cochrane is one of the great pillars of evidence-based medicine.

incapable of ejaculation, despite desire and erection.' He consulted several doctors in Cambridge and London but found neither sympathy nor relief. In desperation, he travelled in 1931 to the Kaiser Wilhelm Institute in Berlin, which then had an international reputation for medical research. A young American, who was in analysis with Theodor Reik,* was staying at the same Berlin hostel:

> He was being psychoanalysed and we spoke at length about it. I had been strongly influenced by Freud. I found his hypotheses fascinating. The trouble was the lack of supporting, and in particular, experimental evidence. The main evidence in support of Freud's theories was the success of therapy. The idea became increasingly attractive to me to test his principal hypothesis by seeing if the technique could help my own troubles, while at the same time learning more about psychoanalysis and seeing whether the hypothesis could be tested in other ways. It seemed much more attractive than tissue culture; so I made my second mistake.

---

* The same Reik who had analysed Frank Ramsey. He moved from Vienna to Berlin in 1928. In 1925, Reik, a lay analyst, had been briefly suspended from practising by the Viennese authorities following a tip-off by fellow analyst Wilhelm Stekel. The following year, he was sued for 'quackery' by an American patient, Newton Murphy. Murphy, himself a physician, had come to Vienna hoping to be analysed by Freud, but Freud was fully booked and passed him on to Reik. Freud wrote his 1926 book *The Question of Lay Analysis* partly as a defence of Reik.

Cochrane was impressed by the fact that Reik had analysed the Cambridge don Richard Braithwaite, a man he knew and admired. They agreed a fee: 'We discussed terms, and I found that I could just afford his help if I cut my standard of living. We started out with a promise that I would resume medical studies as soon as possible, while he would recommend me to be accepted as a psychoanalyst if he found me suitable. It all seemed very reasonable.' Cochrane soon regretted his choice of analyst: 'This is not because he was not an able man. I still respect him, but he was the most intuitional analyst of them all, and I was always asking, "But where's the evidence?" This made transference, as they call it, difficult.' To complicate matters, Reik decided to move back to Vienna, as Berlin had become too dangerous for Jews. Cochrane gamely followed, and enrolled at the medical school, which had reciprocal arrangements with Cambridge. Like Frank Ramsey and Lionel Penrose before him, Cochrane found that he could live very cheaply in the city; he enjoyed the opera, the theatre and the social life, but not the medical school:

The teaching of medicine in Vienna was second rate. It was almost entirely by lectures and extremely dogmatic. Patients were sometimes documented at lectures, but students were not allowed to touch them, only in psychiatric wards, where I was allowed to talk to patients. I suppose I learnt a certain amount. In comparison with other branches of medicine, psychoanalysis seemed to have a slight advantage: the analysts at least had ideas, even if these lacked proof.

He attended one of Freud's seminars – Freud had been granted an honorary chair by the university in 1902* – but was disappointed: 'He was dogmatic and did not encourage discussion.'

Cochrane's analysis was equally frustrating. The analysis was conducted in German, which Cochrane now spoke with 'an aristocratic accent'. Reik explored his childhood, the early death of his father and brothers, his circumcision; they 'played the game of free association'. Vienna was now getting to be as dangerous for Reik as Berlin, so he moved again, this time to the Hague in Holland. Despite the lack of progress with his analysis, Cochrane yet again followed Reik, and was accepted by Leiden (this was now his *third* medical school), where he threw himself into his studies and social life but made just as little progress there with Reik as he had in Vienna or Berlin. He had now spent two and a half years, in three countries, undergoing analysis; without his private income, he would have given up long before. Cochrane was relieved when Reik finally suggested that he should return to London to finish his medical training. Although they parted on good terms, it had taken a long time for Cochrane to take the hint. Reik, whose plan to move to England was blocked by Ernest Jones,† eventually emigrated to the US, where he had a long

---

* Unlike Trotter, Freud struggled to achieve this title. He was finally granted his chair through the intercession of one of his patients, Marie Ferstel. She struck a bargain with the Minister of Public Instruction, Wilhelm von Härtel, persuading her aunt to donate a painting by Arnold Böcklin (*Die Burgruine*) to the new Modern Gallery in Vienna, in return for his recommending to the emperor, Franz Joseph, Freud's appointment as professor.

† Freud wrote to Jones in November 1933 about Reik, 'who is at present

and successful career. Many years later, Cochrane wrote of his experience:

> I had explored the psychoanalytic field both theoretically and practically. I had found it fascinating as regards new hypotheses but lacking in experimental proof. I also found that its attempt to found its proof on clinical effectiveness was doubtful. This was not based only on my own experience but on that of many people under analysis I had met. I formed the provisional hypothesis that analysis could treat hysteria, a disappearing disease, but little else.

~

While at UCH, Cochrane attended a rally in London in support of a nationalised health service: 'I decided to go alone with my own banner. (I had some trouble even in those days in fitting into organized groups.) After considerable thought I wrote out my slogan: *All effective treatment must be free.*' After serving with an ambulance unit during the Spanish Civil War, Cochrane returned to UCH, graduating in 1938. He spent much of the Second World War as a prisoner of war, having been captured in Crete while serving with the Royal Army Medical Corps. Cochrane eventually became an

---

in Vienna, very discouraged and without prospects, and who absolutely demands that I interest you in his fate. The exigencies of these times have not had a very favourable effect on his mental peculiarities.' Jones responded to this lukewarm request: 'If only one knew of some way of finding him a research post. He is in every way unsuitable for therapeutic work, where his irresponsibility towards his patients and unscrupulousness towards his colleagues have so often been demonstrated.'

epidemiologist with interests in tuberculosis and pneumo-
coniosis (coal miners' lung).

His short 1972 book *Effectiveness & Efficiency* was an
unlikely bestseller; he once claimed that he had written most
of it in three hours. Cochrane observed that the NHS (then
a youthful twenty-four years old) was already under strain
because it gave 'a blank cheque both to the demands of patients
and the wishes of doctors' and didn't properly evaluate the
evidence for medical treatments. Taking an example close
to his heart, he wrote: 'Present-day psychiatry is basically
inefficient in that it encourages the use of therapies, many of
which are of unknown effectiveness, and which may possibly
be dangerous. They have failed to evaluate psychoanalysis
and psychotherapy.'

Cochrane argued that randomised controlled trials* should
be used to identify treatments that *worked*; that the NHS
should provide *only* interventions proven to be effective; and
that access to such treatments should be equitable. Now, this
argument seems uncontroversial and self-evidently *right*, but
fifty years ago, it was almost revolutionary, and paved the
way for the emergence of evidence-based medicine (EBM) in
the early 1990s. Psychoanalysts are generally unsympathetic
to EBM, which they regard as an attack on their hermeneutic

---

* Regarded as the gold standard for trials of new treatments, particularly
drugs. Patients recruited to such trials are randomly assigned to the new
drug or to a dummy, or placebo. Neither the patient nor the doctor conducting the trial knows which one they have been given ('double blind').
This randomisation and blinding eliminates most (but not all) causes of
bias and error.

system, their 'way of knowing'. A common criticism of EBM is that its obsession with measurement and metrics led doctors to neglect those things that can't be measured, such as compassion. But this is to misunderstand EBM, the explicitly stated aim of which is to combine scientific evidence, clinical judgement and patients' values. EBM assumes that scientific knowledge is never 'complete' and is ultimately fallible; it teaches doctors humility, to accept the limitations of their craft.

Cochrane's sexual problem was never cured, but eventually – in 1965 – he found what he believed was the cause, when his sister was diagnosed with the hereditary disorder acute intermittent porphyria – the ailment that is thought to have caused the madness of King George III.* Cochrane's wandering around Europe after Theodor Reik may have failed to elucidate – let alone cure – his problem, but it did focus his attention on why evidence *matters* in medicine. Freud was indifferent to the outcome of therapy; his patients and their problems were simply the raw material for his ideas and his writing – he didn't really care whether they got better or not, and this indifference has persisted within psychoanalysis to this day.

---

* The 'who-killed-Cock-Robin?' school of medical history, with its speculative, retrospective diagnoses, is a rather dubious endeavour; there is no convincing evidence, for example, that George III had porphyria. Cochrane's self-diagnosis of porphyria as the cause of his sexual problem is equally unconvincing; anorgasmia is not a typical feature, and he displayed none of the other symptoms of the disorder.

Cochrane's inherited wealth gave him the luxury of not having to conform to the prevailing medical orthodoxies; he pursued what interested and engaged him and was indifferent to professional advancement. He wrote his own obituary for the *British Medical Journal*: 'At first, like many of his generation, he was bemused by Freud and Marx. Unlike most of them he spent a year with the International Brigade during the Spanish civil war and started a training analysis in Vienna. Unconvinced by either experience he returned to medical research.'

Archie Cochrane, aged twenty-two,
at Cambridge.

23

A delicate young man who had survived such chronic ill health in childhood and adolescence might have been expected to pursue a more contemplative career than surgery, but it was this very work that gave Wilfred Trotter's writing its vigour, its sharpness, its common sense, its connection with 'real' life. Medicine, he wrote, was 'in that very small class of professions that, in this tame world, can still be called jobs for men. By that I mean professions in which it is possible for people – men and women – to pursue the dying ideal that an occupation for adults should allow of intellectual freedom, should give character as much chance as cleverness, and should be subject to the tonic of difficulty and the spice of danger.'

Addressing a group of UCH students starting their clinical training in 1932, Trotter offered this unusual advice (unusual because the instillation of conformity is one of the chief functions of medical schools): 'Uniformity of thought is increasingly the apparent goal and demand of civilization; education has no use for the fires of rebellion. Still there burns on in most of us a small wild spark. I advise you to nourish it as a precious possession.

Do not, however, be under any misapprehension. Really to think for oneself is as strange, difficult, and dangerous as any adventure.'

Trotter told his students that they were moving 'from the world of science to that of a practical art'. Then, as now, anatomy and physiology were of little assistance in navigating this unfamiliar country; and then, as now, medicine was neither science nor art, but a craft, or 'practical art', like 'those of the farmer, the builder, the blacksmith, the joiner, the sailor'. Medicine was too proud to accept this, and this snobbery has led to much misunderstanding about doctoring:

> In these days of the rapid progress of science it is tempting and fatally easy to become contemptuous of the practical arts. In the practical arts man made his first serious attempt at the continuous storage of knowledge and the establishment of a progressive culture. Half-seen truths and obscure intuitions cannot be preserved, but can be given permanence when embodied in rules of action and sanctioned by tradition. It was in such rules that the earliest practical discoveries of man were kept alive. We complain of the invincible conservatism of such traditional arts as medicine and agriculture. As long as a body of knowledge exists as an art, conservatism, whatever its defects, is a quality of functional value and indispensable in the circumstances. Conservatism then is a functional in a practical art, but in science it is meaningless and always and wholly harmful. The bulk of a doctor's activities remain then in the region of art. Fashion and the popular voice tend always to exaggerate

the conquests of science, and to press the frontier far beyond the line of its actual advance. A practical art which pretends to be an applied science does not thereby show itself to be progressive, it shows itself to be quackery.

Practical arts, he said, preserved 'the accidental fruits of experience and the creations of genius' and 'must be sparing of theory and keep closely with the facts'. The practical arts *had* to be conservative because 'there is no unequivocal difference between the change that was progress and the change that was decay. New knowledge was therefore accepted as reluctantly as old custom was given up.' Nowadays, neophilia is one of the besetting sins of medicine.

The *patient* was the centre of Trotter's medicine: 'The well-equipped clinician must possess the qualities of the artist, the man of science, and the humanist, but he must exercise them in so far as they subserve the getting well of the individual patient.' Trotter told his students that they had to be both *taught* and *trained*: teaching was the imparting of knowledge, but training was 'the cultivation of aptitude'. He anticipated the now universally accepted idea – propagated by the likes of Daniel Kahneman – of human reasoning as fatally flawed, 'an instrument with an error deplorably great'. Yet it is *only* this error-prone instrument that can make what Trotter called 'the fundamental observation of medicine: my clinical instinct tells me that this patient is ill'.

He defined the aptitudes that doctors must cultivate. The first is *attention*: 'giving one's whole mind to the patient without the interposition of anything of oneself. It sounds simple but only the very greatest doctors fully attain it.' As Wilfred Bion observed, Trotter had a genius for listening. The second is *intuition*, which 'is only inference from experience stored'. Experience, however, is an *active* process: 'An event experienced is an event perceived, digested, and assimilated.' The third aptitude is the art of handling living flesh: 'the sick body denies its secrets to the mutton fist as it does to the beefy mind.' The fourth – and most important – aptitude is that of handling the sick man's mind. For this, the doctor must convince the patient of his *interest*: 'To the deep unreason with which all patients approach the medicine man, his interest is more potent than knowledge and skill, the latest development in science, or the utmost virtuosity in art.' How I wish I had known this when I qualified as a doctor nearly forty years ago: how many things we are told when young that we only recognise the truth of when it is too late.

Trotter argued that doctors needed to cultivate these aptitudes *and* harness science. He warned, however, that the doctor must work in the real world, where scientific certainty is often elusive: 'the last thing a doctor is free to do is to exercise the scientific suspense of judgement, and he scarcely ever makes a decision that is justifiable on strictly scientific grounds. The advice to think scientifically would seem, therefore, to risk paralysing his judgement rather than activating it.' The doctor, a practical artisan, must instead develop 'a soundly cultivated judgement', which, he conceded, is 'difficult to specify and much more difficult to secure'. Medical *science* and medical *practice* are different spheres and should not be confused. Reading Trotter now, it is almost as if he is addressing the future, cautioning the Evidence-Based Medicine zealots to temper their enthusiasm for data with nuance and reflection, to value the practical art as much as the applied science: 'The affectation of scientific exactitude in circumstances where it has no meaning is the fallacy of method to which medicine is most exposed.'

As Archie Cochrane clearly saw, the medicine of that time was loaded with authoritative and hieratic opinions 'often contradictory of one another'; most of these opinions had never been subjected to proof or disproof. Science is measurement, but measurement is boring and difficult, and, as Trotter noted, even 'the able observer is apt to be impatient of the drudgery of scientific proof'. After Galen's* death in AD 216, medicine went into decline for a thousand years. Trotter attributed this sclerosis partly to various pseudo-systems of 'dogmatic rationalism'. Many such systems (all 'gruesome balderdash') came and went: Georg Ernst Stahl (1659–1734), for example, advanced an animistic theory that regarded bodily disease as arising from 'misbehaviour of the soul'; John Brown (1735–88) divided diseases into 'sthenic' and 'asthenic', to be treated respectively with opium and alcohol; for Boissier de Sauvages (1706–67), all diseases were caused by 'gastrointestinal irritation' and should be treated by starvation and bleeding. These 'rationalistic' systems were all influential and all 'singularly ineffective, if not harmful', and did not bear 'any close relation with medical discovery'. Discovery, he observed, 'has been the result of action rather than thought. Fact has led to fact, observation to observation, experiment to experiment.'

* Aelius Galenus, Greek physician.

223

'But why think, why not try an experiment?' the surgeon John Hunter famously asked the vaccine pioneer Edward Jenner in 1775, replying to a request for his opinion on some abstruse biological question. 'Thinking', for Hunter, meant these pseudo-rationalistic systems. Trotter argued that medicine needed both thought and experiment. The problem, however, is that medicine is a *craft*, 'admirably adapted for the conservation of knowledge, but in its very nature ill-suited for the discovery of new truth'. He cited the example of scurvy: James Lind described the cure of the disease by lemon juice in 1753, but it took another 154 years for Holst and Frølich* to prove him correct: 'an active clinical science, by its situation so favourably placed for a direct attack, could have saved some of these long and costly years.'

Trotter correctly predicted that 'great discoveries will continue to be unexpected', and that there would be 'a bitter war of attrition' on cancer. His death in 1939 coincided with the beginning of a fifty-year golden age of medicine, which saw the arrival of antibiotics, the discovery of the DNA double helix, effective treatment for tuberculosis, vaccines against the great infectious killers like diphtheria, influenza and polio, organ transplantation, CT and MRI scanning, cardiac bypass surgery, intensive care, endoscopy. The 'bitter war of attrition' on cancer grinds on.

---

* Axel Holst and Theodor Frølich, the Norwegian researchers who, using an animal model (guinea pigs) of scurvy, proved that the condition was diet-related.

Six months before he died, Trotter, now suffering from advanced kidney failure, gave a lecture at St Mary's Hospital in London on 'Has the Intellect a Function?' He listed three approaches to the pursuit of knowledge: the practical arts, the natural sciences, and philosophy. The edifices built by Aquinas, Marx and Hegel, he argued, were no better than the pseudo-rationalistic medical systems; indeed, they were 'more deadly than cholera or bubonic plague and far more cruel'. Philosophy, he said, 'desires its conclusions to *feel* true, science that they should come true; philosophy needs certitude, science needs verification. Science has no certitudes because its conclusions are based not on internal conviction, but wholly on observed experience.' Science's most impressive aspects, according to Trotter, were 'first, its detailed trustworthiness in practice, and second, its *provisional quality*'. Science must always return to the facts, but philosophy is 'free from these scruples'. Philosophy, he concluded, 'has evolved innumerable systems of doctrine, each rationally proved by its founder to be true, and all inconsistent with one another. An experiment that has gone on failing for two and a half millennia may well make us wonder whether the apparatus is adequate or the method sound.'

The label that most irritated Trotter was 'philosopher'; he once told Julian Taylor that he was tired of being fêted with this title, preferring to be praised for his 'practical contribution to a patient's recovery'. He may have been an intellectual, a *thinker*, but Trotter was not a philosopher; the practical arts and the natural sciences advanced knowledge, but philosophy had failed. Freud foolishly claimed to be a scientist, but his own pseudo-rationalistsic system, built on 'internal conviction' and his own, singular experience, was that of a philosopher.

Wilfred Trotter: Master of his craft.

24

Sometime late in 1936, Ernest Jones received three visitors at his consulting rooms: Laurence Olivier, Peggy Ashcroft, and the director Tyrone ('Tony') Guthrie. Guthrie was preparing his production of *Hamlet* for the Old Vic, with Olivier in the title role; they called on Jones for advice on Hamlet's psychology. He had first written about the play back in 1910,[*] arguing that the Prince of Denmark was driven by his Oedipus complex. Hamlet, according to Jones, is like all men, and wants to make love to his mother and kill his father. Like all men, he represses these desires; then his uncle Claudius does these very things. If Hamlet were to kill Claudius, these repressed desires would surface; he has a vague intuition of this, which prevents him from acting:

[*] 'The Oedipus-Complex as an Explanation of Hamlet's Mystery', in the *American Journal of Psychology*. Jones later revisited the theme in print on several occasions, eventually publishing a book, *Hamlet and Oedipus*, in 1949.

In reality his uncle incorporates the deepest and most buried part of his own personality, so that he cannot kill him without also killing himself. This solution, one closely akin to what Freud has shown to be the motive for suicide in melancholia, is actually the one that Hamlet finally adopts. The course of alternative action and inaction that he embarks on, and the provocations that he gives to his suspicious uncle, can lead to no other end than his own ruin and, incidentally, to that of his uncle. Only when he has made the final sacrifice and is at death's door is he free to fulfil his duty to avenge his father, and to slay his other self – his uncle.

Jones was flattered by Olivier's interest. As a medical student, he had fancied himself as a stage performer; there was always something of the actor manqué about him. Jones's student party piece was a selection of recitations – for which he affected a Cockney accent – from Kipling's *Barrack-Room Ballads*, which went down a storm in the annual medical school revue, or 'smoking concert', held, bizarrely, in the dissecting room. The performance was so well received that Jones was asked to appear at Cardiff's Park Hall, where, before an audience of two thousand, he forgot his lines: 'The audience encouraged me by clapping, and I moved on to the next verse. When I broke down in this also they lost their sympathy and the rest of the recitation didn't go down well.' Characteristically, Jones learned from this humiliation, and vowed that he would never again appear before an audience so poorly prepared.

In his 1982 memoir *Confessions of an Actor*, Olivier wrote about his meeting with Jones:

He had made an exhaustive study of Hamlet from his own professional point of view and was wonderfully enlightening. I have never ceased to think about Hamlet at odd moments, and ever since that meeting I have believed that Hamlet was a prime sufferer from the Oedipus complex – quite unconsciously, of course, as the professor was anxious to stress. He offered an impressive array of symptoms: spectacular mood swings, cruel treatment of his love, and above all a hopeless inability to pursue the course required of him. The Oedipus complex, therefore, can claim responsibility for a formidable share of all that is wrong with him.

Guthrie was equally convinced, telling the *New York Times*: 'This self-conflict is fascinatingly explained by Ernest Jones. His "Hamlet and Oedipus" brings psychoanalysis to bear, and offers what is to me by far the most interesting and convincing explanation of the central puzzle of the play – Hamlet's procrastination in the matter of vengeance.'

Up to then, John Gielgud's Hamlet was regarded – in the words of the critic James Agate – as 'the high water-mark of English Shakespearean acting'; Gielgud was romantic and exquisite, Olivier virile and modern. The Shakespeare scholar Robert Shaughnessy wrote that critics of Guthrie's *Hamlet* were 'universally unaware of the production's Oedipal dynamics and much more impressed by Olivier's astounding athleticism, vigour and masculinity'. Harcourt Williams, Guthrie's predecessor at the Old Vic, thought Olivier 'a shade too acrobatic'. The production ran from 5 January to 20 February 1937; when

Guthrie staged it in Denmark that June, Olivier insisted that Cherry Cottrell (who played Ophelia) be replaced by his new lover, Vivien Leigh. In his memoir, Olivier couldn't resist cracking the hammiest of all actorly jokes: 'As one of my predecessors is reputed to have said in reply to the earnest question "Did Hamlet sleep with Ophelia?" "In my company, always."'*

Jones's influence might not have been immediately obvious in Guthrie's 1937 stage production but it was certainly clear in Olivier's 1948 film version, for which he won Oscars for best picture and best actor. 'The figure seen haunting the battlements of Elsinore', wrote the novelist Sylvia Townsend Warner, 'is that of Dr Ernest Jones.' In *The Great European Stage Directors* (2018), Roberta Barker and Tom Cornford wrote that the film 'is obsessively Freudian in its scenography, with Hamlet probing the passageways and staircases of his own consciousness and mounting his mother on a conspicuously vulval bed'. Phallic imagery is everywhere, with towers, pillars and swords; Hamlet and Gertrude kiss like young lovers, not mother and son. This Oedipal fever was only heightened by the fact that, at forty, Olivier was a rather mature Hamlet, while Gertrude (played by Eileen Herlie†) was a mere twenty-nine; Olivier had initially considered casting another actor for the leading role in his film but concluded that it would be 'simpler'

---

* Variations of this anecdote appear in countless theatrical memoirs; there are as many versions of it as the 'Bugger Bognor' story.
† Herlie had played Gertrude in a 1945 Stratford production, with yet another older (by four years) Hamlet, Peter Glenville. She reprised the role on Broadway in 1964 with Richard Burton: he was her first *younger* Hamlet, albeit by a mere eight years.

if he played Hamlet himself. Olivier consoled himself that elderly Hamlets were a theatrical tradition: 'It was an ancient custom for the most ancient actor-managers to play Hamlet; I am sure Irving was in his sixties before finishing with the part. I was on the cusp of forty.'

In a 1966 television interview with Kenneth Tynan, Olivier acknowledged the influence of Jones's thesis on his film version of *Hamlet*: 'I thought it was the absolute resolution of all the problems concerning Hamlet. At least, it gave one a central idea which seems to fill the great vacuum left by all the crossed ideas about Hamlet, what he really was, what he really wasn't, whether he was a man of action, whether he wasn't a man of action. He could safely be a man of action under the auspices of that particular idea, that he couldn't kill the king because, subconsciously of course, he was guilty himself.' In *Confessions of an Actor*, however, Olivier recalled only the man of action, with a detailed description of the complicated stunt in the final scene, when Hamlet kills Claudius: 'After a few seconds there was a little stunned clapping. One of the lads muttered to another beside him, "Good old Larry, he gets on with it."'

Having solved the riddle of Hamlet, Jones was convinced he'd also decoded another of Shakespeare's titular characters, and shared this insight at a second meeting, as Olivier recalled:

There was a dichotomy of purpose between Ralph Richardson's Othello and my Iago. Tony Guthrie and I were swept away by Professor Jones's contention that Iago was subconsciously in love with Othello and had to destroy him. Unfortunately, there was not the slightest chance that

Ralph would entertain this idea. In a reckless moment during rehearsals, I threw my arms round Ralph and kissed him full on the lips. He coolly disengaged himself from my embrace, patted me gently on the back of the neck and, more in sorrow than in anger, murmured, 'there, there now, dear boy, *good* boy...'*

Freud, too, was obsessed with *Hamlet*; he saw a parallel in the Rat Man, with his 'paralysis of the will' and 'fantasies of revenge'. He was not taken seriously, however, by Shakespeare scholars because he subscribed to the 'Oxfordian' theory, which holds that Edward de Vere, the 17th Earl of Oxford, was the author of the works attributed to William Shakespeare.† Both Jones and James Strachey tried unsuccessfully to persuade Freud that this theory, which appealed to his love of riddles and cryptic writings, was bunkum. Jones speculated that Freud's belief in the Oxfordian theory was itself Oedipal, the

---

* Anthony Quayle (who played Cassio) had a slightly different recollection of this kiss, and the subsequent exchange between Richardson and Olivier:

'What are you doing, cocky?'

'We thought, that is, Tony and I thought, that as I am being taken away, it might be a good idea if I were to bend over and give you a kiss.'

'Indeed? Then let me give you due warning that if you do so, I will get straight back up and walk off the stage.'

† After the death of Jones's daughter Gwenith in 1928, Freud wrote a spectacularly clumsy and insensitive letter, suggesting to Jones that he might distract himself by investigating the Oxfordian theory as laid out in J. Thomas Looney's *Shakespeare Identified* (1920): 'I am very impressed by Looney's investigations, almost convinced.' When the grief-stricken Jones replied that the theory was not highly regarded in literary circles, Freud harrumphed: 'I was dissatisfied with your information about Looney.'

projection of a subconscious desire to alter his own paternity, so that he became the son of his half-brother Emanuel, a more successful businessman than his father, Jacob.

The psychoanalytic interpretation of fictional characters is one of the more endearingly batty Freudian enterprises. If we accept Jones's claim that Hamlet can be explained by his Oedipus complex, we must also accept that Shakespeare (or the Earl of Oxford) somehow *knew* of the existence of this complex, and wrote the play armed with this knowledge. This, however, does not sit comfortably with psychoanalytic dogma, which holds that Freud *discovered* the Oedipus complex during his 'self-analysis', and that this complex was, and is, *universal*. By this reasoning, Rosencrantz has an Oedipus complex, as does Laertes; even Claudius has an Oedipus complex. The psychiatrist Anthony Daniels pointed out the absurdity of Jones's claim: 'For a doctor to try to examine and diagnose Hamlet as if he were a real person is for him to make a category mistake: non-existent people cannot suffer from real disorders (though the reverse is not true: real people can suffer from non-existent ones.)'

Jones's *Hamlet* thesis was mocked as early as 1911 by the American psychiatrist James Hendrie Lloyd in an address to the Philadelphia Neurological Society: 'The Prince did not know what ailed him. Moreover, Shakespeare himself did not know what it was; the commentators do not know what it was; nobody knows what it was but Jones, and he has discovered it by the methods of psychoanalysis, applied to the play after three hundred years.'* Even Mervyn Jones joined the mockery:

> It may or may not be true that all men are born to grapple with the Oedipus complex, but Freud was content to detect it among the bourgeoisie of Vienna without asking whether it was as clearly present in proletarian Glasgow, let alone among the Yoruba or the Navajo.† (However, if Freud and Jones were right in seeing the Oedipus complex as the key to the problems of a Danish prince called Hamlet, this does lend force to their assertion.)

Or, as a Freudian might argue, was this public and gratuitous ridicule of Jones (and the rival father figure, Freud) by his son a typically Oedipal act of revenge, and thus incontrovertible *proof* of the existence of the Oedipus complex?

---

* 'An extremely vulgar attack,' Jones told Freud.

† The Polish-born anthropologist Bronisław Malinowski's *Sex and Repression in Savage Society* (1927), based on his studies of the indigenous inhabitants of the Trobriand Islands (an archipelago off Papua New Guinea), challenged the universality of the Oedipus complex. Malinowski 'discovered' that the Trobriand Islanders had a matriarchal society, where boys were disciplined by their maternal uncles, not their fathers, and therefore had an 'avuncular', rather than Oedipal, complex, with the desire 'to marry the sister and kill the maternal uncle'. Ernest Jones strenuously rejected Malinowski's argument (which was as absurd as Freud's), insisting that Freud had established the Oedipus complex as 'a universal *fons et origo*'. Malinowski later became a close friend of Marie Bonaparte; it was 'Malino' who sent his graduate student Jomo Kenyatta to tell her all about female circumcision.

25

On 17 February 1937, while Tyrone Guthrie's production of *Hamlet* was still playing at the Old Vic, Dr Melitta Schmideberg gave a paper at the British Psychoanalytical Society (with Ernest Jones in the chair) entitled 'After the Analysis – Some Phantasies of Patients'. Melitta was then thirty-three, a doctor and psychoanalyst, who with her husband, Walter (also a doctor and psychoanalyst), had followed her mother Melanie Klein to London, arriving in 1932. Joan Riviere was appalled by this paper, writing to James Strachey: 'Melitta read a really shocking paper on Wednesday plainly attacking "Mrs Klein and her followers" and simply saying we were all bad analysts – indescribable.' Melitta mocked her own mother, whom she referred to as 'Mrs Klein': 'Analysis is regarded as an atonement, as a cleansing process, as a religious exercise. Getting on in the analysis means doing one's duty, obeying one's parents, learning one's prayers, defecating.'

At the age of only fifteen, Melitta, encouraged by her mother (who was then analysing her), had started attending meetings of the Hungarian Psychoanalytical Society in Budapest; she qualified as a doctor in 1927 in Berlin, and by 1929 was in a training analysis with Karen Horney. With the rise of Nazism, the German-speaking Jewish analysts were beginning their exodus. Melitta, still close to her mother, chose London. Even though Melanie and Walter (who had been treated in the 1920s at the Tegel clinic in Berlin for alcohol and drug dependence) didn't get on, it all went well for a while – the Schmidebergs regularly took her on weekend drives around the south of England. But everything changed in April 1934, when Klein's eldest son, Hans, was killed while on a walking holiday in the Tatra mountains between Slovakia and Poland. Although this tragedy was almost certainly an accident, Melitta was convinced that Hans had committed suicide, and blamed her mother. In Nicholas Wright's 1988 play *Mrs Klein*, Melitta is given this line: 'Hans died because he couldn't bring himself to hate you. I can, I do.' Melanie Klein was 'too distraught' to attend Hans's funeral in Budapest, and fell into a deep depression, exacerbated by the split from her lover, the journalist Chezkel Kloetzel.

Melitta's loathing of her mother was encouraged by her new analyst, Edward Glover, the dour, caustic Scot who had been Jones's second-in-command at the society for many years; Glover became a surrogate father, openly holding Melitta's hand at international psychoanalytic conferences. He wrote a thinly disguised portrait of Klein in his 1940 book, *An Investigation of the Technique of Psycho-Analysis*: 'She had a high opinion of herself as a mother, but was, in fact, self-aggrandising, tyrannical, and selfish.' Glover told anyone who would listen that Klein claimed to be 'the most important person since Jesus Christ'. Melitta publicly accused Klein of depriving her of psychoanalytic referrals, and adopted the decidedly unusual tactic of heckling her mother at scientific meetings, on one occasion screaming at her 'where is the father in your work!' before stamping her feet and storming out. Her abuse of her mother became so intense that Jones suggested to Melitta that she should consider moving to the US, while advising Klein that she should take a defamation case against Melitta and Glover.

The doctrinal and personal disputes within the society reached boiling point with the arrival of Anna Freud and several other Viennese analysts in 1938. (Most of the other European analysts went to the US because they distrusted both Jones and Klein, and because there was a greater demand there for their services.) There was also a simmering resentment of Jones, who, supported by Glover, had run the society as a personal fiefdom for over two decades, and who, with subtle (and not so subtle) hints, let it be known that he controlled the supply of psychoanalytic patients. Jones, by making the society the regulating body for psychoanalysis throughout the British Empire, also exerted control of the societies in several other countries and, in a brilliant political stroke, made it mandatory for all English-speaking psychoanalysts (including the Americans) to take out a subscription to the *International Journal of Psychoanalysis* – the journal of the British Society.

And so began the long internecine war within the British Psychoanalytical Society; this conflict has been called, with typical English understatement, 'the Controversial Discussions'.

These 'discussions', which lasted from 1943 to 1946, were preceded by a phoney war during the late 1930s and early 40s, when several 'extraordinary business meetings' were held. There were three factions: the Freudians, the Kleinians, and a non-aligned 'Independent' group. The main issue at stake was whether the training of analysts should be conducted on Anna-Freudian or Kleinian principles; Jones's autocratic control of the society was of lesser importance.

At one of these extraordinary meetings, on 11 March 1942, with Jones in the chair, Melitta launched yet another blistering attack on her mother and her supporters:

The excessive positive transference they show, the over sensitiveness with which they react to the slightest criticism of Mrs Klein, and the corresponding hostility towards non-Kleinian analysts is striking. The system of analysis and control analysis has become a key factor in the Kleinian game of power politics. Its role is reminiscent to that confession used to play in the Catholic Church. It yields power and information. The latter can be used for political purposes. The Kleinians shelter behind ambiguity and vagueness. Anybody who attempts to disentangle their views is sure to be told that he misunderstood them. They are satisfied with hurling their accusations at their critics, and *make no attempt* to provide lucid explanations. They lack the most elementary scientific discipline. In a manner somewhat reminiscent of Dr Goebbels, they try to impress us by repeating time after time the same slogans, by putting forward exaggerated claims and dogmatic statements, by accusing their opponents and intimidating the hesitants, by a constant play of emotions of every sort, instead of presenting and substantiating their theories according to scientific standards.

When Melitta eventually concluded this philippic against her mother, Jones remarked dryly: 'Dr Schmideberg has really admirably illustrated the difficulty of discussing these matters without personal attacks.' Eva Rosenfeld, who was in analysis with Klein, recalled: 'At the meetings I could only see something quite terrible and very un-English happening, and that was a daughter hitting her mother with words and this mother being very composed, quite quiet, never defending herself, but having such power in that society, being so powerful that it really didn't matter what Melitta said.'

Ever since the Freuds' arrival in London in 1938, Jones had begun to feel ambivalent about Melanie Klein. While he liked her personally, and found her theories persuasive, he felt threatened by this protégé who had become the dominant figure in *his* society. He was also aware that this war was – unwittingly – *his* fault, for it was he who had placed the two main adversaries in the society: *he* had invited Klein to London, *he* had engineered the Freuds' flight from Vienna. Klein insolently rebuked Jones for providing a refuge for the Freuds, which, she told him, had done 'much harm to psychoanalysis'. As president, he was officially neutral; he tried to convince both women that he was on *their* side. On 21 January 1942, for example, Jones wrote to both Klein and Anna Freud; he told Freud that Klein had 'neither a scientific nor an orderly mind, her presentations are lamentable, and she is also in many ways neurotic'; he told Klein that Freud was 'an indigestible morsel'.

The English analysts resented Anna Freud and the Viennese arrivals who now made up one third of the society; James Strachey complained that 'these wretched fascists' and 'bloody foreigners' had invaded their 'peaceful compromising island'. Many feared for their livelihoods; Barbara Low (a Freudian) complained bitterly – in an unedifying slanging match – that Joan Riviere (a Kleinian) wouldn't refer patients to her. After much venting at the extraordinary meetings, the discussions proper began in January 1943. What 'scientific differences' could possibly cause such bitterness and personal animosity? Anna Freud laid out her position: 'For Mrs Klein object relationship begins with, or soon after birth, whereas I consider that this is a narcissistic and auto-erotic phase of several months' duration which precedes what we call object relationship in the proper sense.' Jones listed the fault lines as: 'the early development of sexuality, especially in the female, the genesis of the superego and its relations to the Oedipus complex, the technique of child analysis and the death instinct.' No doubt the Arrians and the Athanasians subscribed to their beliefs with equal conviction. What is striking about the dispute is the repeated use of the word 'scientific' – scientists do not, as a rule, cling to speculative ideas with such dogmatic intensity; differences are resolved by collecting more data. The word 'scientific' was bandied about by the likes of Melanie Klein, Joan Riviere and James Strachey, none of whom had any scientific training or knowledge of statistics and experimental method, who did not understand that at the core of science is *doubt*. This long war was a theological, not a scientific, dispute.

Before the Controversial Discussions got underway, Melanie Klein left London for the Perthshire town of Pitlochry, where she spent the spring and summer of 1941. Short of cash and keen to get out of London, she was persuaded by the parents of a patient, a ten-year-old boy who had been evacuated to Scotland, to join him there so that his analysis could continue. This boy has been immortalised in the psychoanalytic literature as 'Little Richard'. He was first brought to Klein because of school refusal and agoraphobia. Between 28 April and 23 August, Little Richard underwent ninety sessions of analysis in a converted Girl Guide hut in Pitlochry. The boy had very reasonable grounds for his anxiety in the spring of 1941: not only had he experienced the Blitz, he had also found his father slumped on the bathroom floor after a heart attack, tea dribbling from his mouth. His fears turned out to be entirely justified – the family's London home was later bombed, a fact that Klein did not mention in her account of the case, *Narrative of a Child Analysis*.

In the early 1980s, Klein's biographer Phyllis Grosskurth tracked down Richard, then in his fifties. 'I remember her', he recalled, 'as short, dumpy with big floppy feet. Melanie had a rather loose lower lip. It always seemed to hang a bit, and her mouth never seemed to be closed. She had a strong accent.' Klein (who referred to herself as 'Mrs K.' in the *Narrative*) used toy battleships to draw the boy out. When Richard (who was precociously bright) talked about the Germans seizing the French port of *Brest*, 'Melanie seized on b-r-e-a-s-t, which of course was very much her angle. She would often talk about "the big Mummy Genital" and "the big Daddy Genital", or the "good Mummy genital" or the "bad Daddy genital". I can't remember what other things she had to say. It was very much a strong interest in genitalia.' Klein shared her interpretations with Little Richard as the analysis progressed. Here is a typical 'Mrs K.' interpretation:

> Richard turned to the map and expressed his fears about the British battleships being blockaded in the Mediterranean if Gibraltar were taken by the Germans. They could not get through Suez. Mrs K. interpreted that he worried unconsciously about what might happen to Daddy when he put his genital into Mummy. Daddy might not be able to get out of Mummy's inside and would be caught there, like the ships in the Mediterranean.

For Klein, Richard's anxiety about the war raging outside was really all about the conflict *within*: he had projected his Oedipal hatred of his father on to the blameless figure of Adolf Hitler. When she used phrases such as 'Hitler-daddy' and 'Hitler-penis', Little Richard, according to Klein, would 'become very anxious and start pacing around the room'. (The urge to run *from* the room must have been overwhelming.) He told her that he 'couldn't listen to this', that he was 'an innocent child', and that he wanted to leave. Richard was clever and rebellious; he used a variety of tactics against Mrs K.:

242

denying her 'interpretations', laughing at her, even humouring her by pretending to play along. But in the end, admitting defeat, Little Richard told Mrs K. that psychoanalysis was '*very wrong*'.

During the three years of the Controversial Discussions, Jones absented himself, pleading a series of illnesses – all thought to be psychosomatic; because his London home had been bombed, he had to move to the Plat in Sussex. Melanie Klein, in a letter to Sylvia Payne, suggested that her daughter was deranged, cryptically referring to 'Melitta's illness', which '*should not be mentioned*'. She realised that Jones was not to be trusted: 'I shall never forgive Jones for being so weak, so undecided and actually treacherous.' The Stracheys and the Stephens did not take sides, hoping for a peaceful settlement. James Strachey pleaded for 'patience, moderation, open-mindedness, and compromise'. He wearily summed up the dispute: '"Your views are so *defective* that you are incompetent to carry out a training analysis or for the matter of that any analysis at all," says one protagonist. "Your views are so *false* that you are incompetent to carry out a training analysis or for the matter of that any analysis at all," says the other protagonist.' In a 1942 debate, Karin Stephens made the reasonable observation that with so many of the society's members 'in the patient-analyst relation with one another, adult equality relations are hardly possible in such circumstances'. During one heated exchange (ironically on 'hatred and aggression'), the members didn't notice the loud sound of exploding bombs dropped by the Luftwaffe.

Melitta and Walter Schmideberg.

In November 1946, a 'gentleman's agreement'* was eventually reached. Trainees could choose from an 'A' group of Kleinian trainers, a 'B' group of Freudians, or a 'middle' group of Independents. Although the gentleman's agreement was officially a draw, the Kleinians had won, but at great cost

* Ironic, as the main protagonists were women; Edward Glover complained bitterly (before resigning) that the society was 'woman-ridden'. Jones, when choosing whom to admit to the society, had a strong preference for women.

244

to the society, which barely survived this period of collective psychosis. Jones returned to London, but the Controversial Discussions filled him with 'a melancholy weariness'. He had a heart attack in October 1944, following which he stepped down as president. The war over, Jones naturally maintained good relations with both Melanie Klein and Anna Freud, particularly the latter, whose imprimatur and support he needed for his biography of Sigmund Freud, which was dedicated to Anna, 'true daughter of an immortal sire'. Edward Glover, having resigned from the society, remarked of Jones: 'Give the devil his due, Jones was a clever little man. He used to say I was a divinely normal person, and when I left the society, he said I was a paranoid character.' (Accusing an opponent of being mentally ill was a tactic that Jones used on several occasions.)

Anna Freud withdrew to her clinic in Hampstead, a rival court where she reigned for many years; when she attended psychoanalytic congresses, she was usually flanked by Dorothy Burlingham and Marie Bonaparte. Melanie Klein grew ever more imperious as the years passed. She discarded old supporters like Joan Riviere and protégés like Paula Heimann; Wilfred Bion became her favourite in the last decade of her life. The young R. D. Laing, the future favourite psychiatrist of the counterculture, attended one of her seminars in the 1950s, and found her 'physically repellent with the jewellery and heavy makeup'; he spoke of her 'adamantine dogmatism', and how her supporters were 'beaten down into complete submission'.

Anna Freud and Melanie Klein would have been horrified by the observation that they had a great deal in common. The bitterness of the Controversial Discussions was equalled only by the triviality of their differences and the bizarre family dynamics of the principal protagonists. The conflict over training is puzzling, as both Klein and Freud worked almost exclusively with children, and nearly all the trainees would go on to work with adults. Anna and Melanie remained committed to their competing theories heedless of later advances in child psychology and development. Although they were both uncredentialled, they demanded, and were granted, leadership roles in the training of English psychoanalysts. One of the many ironies of the Controversial Discussions was the vehemence of the views expressed on training by people who had never undergone any training themselves. (Klein, for example, could not understand why she was not accorded the same professional privileges as doctors, such as admission rights to hospitals.) The smooth transition of these careless, foolish, relentlessly self-obsessed people from analysand to analyst is grimly comic. Ernest Jones, who always advised would-be analysts to qualify first in medicine, distrusted these couch-jumpers. Sigmund Freud had no such qualms and ushered into the new profession via the back door his own daughter, Princess Marie Bonaparte, Lou Andreas-Salomé, the Stracheys, Dorothy Burlingham and Joan Riviere. There is something almost heroic about their indifference to experience, apprenticeship, knowledge, judgement, responsibility; they simply averted their gaze when their interventions went awry. To this day, psychoanalysis is a haven of dilettantism: many neo-Freudians work both at the couchside and in the academy.

Melitta could not stomach the defeat and moved to New York in 1945; she divorced Walter, who died of alcoholism in

1954. She and Melanie were never reconciled. In 1949, at the International Psychoanalytical Congress in Zurich, Melitta and Melanie passed each other, but did not speak; when the Congress was held in London in 1953, Melitta walked past the seated figure of her mother, both pretending not to see the other. Melanie Klein died on 22 September 1960. Melitta did not attend the funeral at Golders Green Crematorium: she was elsewhere in London that day, giving a lecture. Several witnesses mentioned her flamboyant red boots.

Melanie Klein's seventieth birthday party, Kettner's restaurant, 1952. Standing (from left): Melanie Klein, Ernest Jones, Herbert Rosenfeld, Joan Riviere, Donald Winnicott. A nervous-looking James Strachey sits in front of Joan Riviere.

26

On 15 March 1938 – three days after the Nazi annexation – Ernest Jones arrived in Vienna. He went straight to the offices of the International Psychoanalytic Press (the *Verlag*), where he ran into SA troops – 'villainous-looking youths armed with daggers and pistols'. They had arrested Freud's son Martin, and then briefly detained Jones, who was released after an hour, having loudly insisted (in his fluent Prussian-accented German) that he was a British citizen. Arriving at Freud's apartment, he ran into yet another SA gang; they were temporarily stunned into shamed silence when the sick old man appeared: 'he had a way of frowning', wrote Jones, 'with blazing eyes that any Old Testament prophet might have envied.' Freud was determined to stay in the city that had been his home for seventy-nine years. He underestimated the Nazi threat to the Jews, insisting that the Catholic Church – not Hitler – was 'my true enemy'. Even after Hitler became German chancellor in 1933, Freud maintained that 'legalised persecution of the Jews would immediately result in the intervention of the League of Nations'. Although Jones typically claimed credit for persuading the reluctant Freud to leave Vienna, it was the arrest and brief detention of Anna by the Gestapo that convinced him. 'It was', wrote Jones, 'the blackest day in Freud's life.'

Princess Marie Bonaparte arrived on 17 March and immediately took charge, leaving Jones free to return to London, where he obtained travel permits for Freud and his extended entourage (family, sister-in-law, maid, his personal doctor Max Schur, Schur's wife and children). The princess stayed for three weeks: she paid the extortionate tax – the *Reichsfluchtsteuer* – imposed by the Nazis on Austrian Jews fleeing the country;* she organised the packing of Freud's papers, his collection of antique figurines, and the famous couch. Her imperious manner and high connections opened many doors; Nazi officials were impressed and slightly intimidated. She did not hesitate to drop very big names: Roosevelt and Mussolini, she told them, would take a dim view of any mistreatment of Professor Freud.

For two nervous months between March and June 1938, Freud, now housebound and without patients, whiled away the days by translating (from French to German) Bonaparte's short book about the illness of her dog, *Topsy: The Story of a Golden-Haired Chow*. Freud – assisted by Anna – had worked, intermittently, on this task for some time; now he gave the book his full attention. 'I love it,' he wrote to the princess, 'it is so movingly genuine and true. It is not an analytic work, of course, but the analyst's thirst for truth and knowledge can be perceived behind this production, too.' *Topsy* has been

---

* This tax was 20 per cent of all property; for the Freuds, this amounted to $4,824.

interpreted variously as a metaphor for Europe's sickness in the 1930s, for Freud's cancer, for Bonaparte's fear of ageing, death and loneliness. In his introduction to a 1994 English translation of *Topsy*, Gary Genosko wrote: 'Many of the parallels between the illnesses of Topsy and Freud have been documented. Both suffered from tumours of the right side of the oral cavity which made chewing difficult; both were treated by palliative surgery, Roentgen rays and radium. The fact that Topsy won her battle against cancer must have expressed for both Marie Bonaparte and the Freuds the wish that Freud would yet recover.'

Bonaparte's 'kind young servant' first alerted her to the dog's 'small growth under the right lip'. Her vet removed this lesion, and gave the specimen to the princess, who naturally had connections in the highest echelons of French academic histopathology: 'One of my friends, a doctor and biologist, took charge of the sections.' (A recurring theme in Bonaparte's life is her access to eminent doctors, and their willingness – no, *eagerness* – to oblige her.) There was an anxious wait while the specimen was examined microscopically by her tame pathologist: 'There, as I waited, in my woman's heart, more specially isolated that year than ever before, a passionate affection, all of a sudden, declared itself for Topsy, who, until now, had been but a graceful toy to me.' She was devastated by the diagnosis: 'a lympho-sarcoma, a tumour that will develop, grow, spread elsewhere, ulcerate, suffocate her and condemn her in but a few months to the most atrocious of deaths.'

Could the princess, with her many medical connections, save Topsy? 'Somewhere in Paris,' she wrote, 'there is a huge house where steel apparatus of a fiendish appearance glitters in the dim light of armour-plated rooms. They produce mysterious rays which sometimes heal poor human suffering from the most horrible of all diseases. Why have I not yet interceded for Topsy with the god who reigns over these realms?' The 'god' in question was Professor Antoine Lacassagne, director of the Pasteur Institute, to which the princess had been a generous donor. She persuaded him to take on Topsy, who thus became the first dog to undergo radiation treatment for cancer: 'Topsy, if she can be healed, has as much right to life as I. At last I dared take Topsy to the divinity of the Rays. He said he would try to cure her.'

While Topsy submitted uncomplainingly to hour-long sessions of radiation, the princess mused on their relationship, on Topsy's barrenness, on death: 'Despite the gulf that separates our races, Topsy, you are still my sister, my terrestrial sister. I, Topsy, have given two scions to the human race. I have passed on the life I received; not you. My life, like yours, Topsy, is declining. When you are dead, Topsy, I shall have you wrapped in a white sheet, and softly laid on a bed of fine sand, remote and deep in the clayey soil of my garden.' Topsy's survival appeared doubtful: 'Her body is growing thinner and thinner; morning after morning, Topsy is taken to the Temple of the Rays, her thin body is fastened to a plank.'

Fortunately for Topsy, lymphosarcoma is a radio-sensitive tumour; she survived, declared cured five years later by Lacassagne. This recovery, however, then prompted the princess – always difficult to satisfy – to ponder on the inevitability that Topsy 'will have to grow old. Then her grace, before her, will die. She will lose her teeth.' And then a new lip swelling raised the possibility of recurrence. Lacassagne spoke frankly to Bonaparte:

> 'Among the humans that we treat,' he said in his slow and steady voice, 'at least fifty per cent never recover. They are condemned to a horrible end. To kill them would be an act of mercy. But one cannot. So – if I loved an animal as you love Topsy, I should leave her the benefit of being an animal. I would not torment her with cruel and useless treatments. I would let her enjoy the end of her life happily, and when she really begins to suffer, I would administer euthanasia.'

But Topsy, in the time-honoured fashion of doughty fighters, proved the doctors wrong: 'The swelling in Topsy's lip has suddenly dissolved. It was only an oedema caused by the rays. Topsy is probably cured, and will never know in her new-born joy of living that she touched the frontiers of death.' Topsy lived out her days in the princess's beautiful house in Saint-Cloud, summering in Saint-Tropez. The dog was immortalised not only by her owner, but also by the sculptor Oscar Nemon, whose 1931 likeness of Topsy is now in the Ashmolean Museum in Oxford.*

---

* Nemon was the favourite sculptor of the psychoanalytic movement, producing a bronze statue of Freud (now situated at a road junction in Hampstead) and a bust of Melanie Klein. Klein hated the twice life-size likeness and hid it in her attic before eventually destroying it. Nemon was sanguine about this act of desecration: 'My impression was that Melanie had a noticeable tendency to pomposity and was easily capable of self-righteous behaviour. Maybe these qualities were manifest in my work and caused her some discomfort.'

Topsy is the child that never grows up, never deserts, and, unlike her analysands, doesn't prattle: 'Near her, I find rest from human beings, so wearisome, so heavy. You don't talk, Topsy, nor do you trouble my contemplation by the recital of your woes, your quarrels.' The princess worried that those 'poor humans who have to bang on sheet iron or rust, in the metallic hell of a factory' might not be sympathetic to the problems of a princess and her pampered chow: 'You don't know, Topsy, what stretches beyond over the walls of the gardens.' Referring briefly to her husband (Prince George of Greece*), Bonaparte wrote that 'he has his occupations and will soon leave again'. People come and go, but 'Topsy, who has reconquered life, is for me a talisman that conjures away death'.

Ernest Jones's relationship with dogs was not quite so magical as Bonaparte's. In 1912, when they lived in Toronto, Loe's little dog, to whom she was 'passionately attached' (the dog had become a child substitute after her miscarriage), was bitten by a rabid dog. No expense was spared: 'We are having him treated, at home,' he told Freud, 'by Pasteur serum sent from Philadelphia. This has to be sent twice a day for three weeks, and at present we are in a state of anxiety owing to the regularity and mistakes of the agents. Unfortunately, it will be several months before the danger will be past, and consequently the anxiety.'

---

* Their marriage never recovered from the wedding night, when Prince George informed her that his paternal uncle, Prince Waldemar of Denmark, was the love of his life. 'I hate it as much as you do,' he told his new bride, 'but we must do it if we want children.'

In 1927, Anna Freud's beloved German shepherd, Wolf, bit Jones: 'He flew at me and tore a piece of my thigh. Sigmund Freud, who was present, sagely remarked that dogs instinctively recognise those who dislike them or are afraid of them, and at once treat them as enemies.' Did Wolf have some strange canine intuition of Jones's previous intentions towards Anna?* Freud wrote to his friend Max Eitingon: 'I had to punish Wolf for that, but did so very reluctantly, for he – Jones – deserved it.'

Wolf features prominently in the Freuds' family mythology. Anna walked Wolf every day to the Prater, Vienna's large public park. One morning, startled by a soldier on exercises firing a blank, the dog bolted, and Anna lost him. When she eventually returned to the family apartment, Wolf was there before her, having arrived by taxi. The driver told Anna that Wolf had jumped into his cab, resisted removal, and lifted his head to reveal a collar medal with his address, 'Prof. Freud, Berggasse 19'. Clement Freud recalled a walk with his grandfather and Wolf in Vienna, when they came across a man having an epileptic fit. Rather bizarrely, the onlookers – instead of providing first aid – put coins into the man's hat as a gesture of sympathy. When asked by Clement why he hadn't contributed, Freud replied: 'He did not do it well enough.'

---

* Wolf may have detected Jones's 'permanent dislike of wolf-like dogs, particularly Alsatians', a phobia dating from his boyhood night terrors 'of wolves who might descend on me from nearby woods. It was no doubt a projection on to my innocent father of some oral-sadistic phantasies.'

Freud's favourite dog Jo-Fi (also a chow) was acquired from Dorothy Burlingham in 1930. Jo-Fi spent the day with Freud in his consulting room, lying at the foot of the analytic couch. The dog was very useful in bringing sessions to a conclusion, as she invariably stirred herself at exactly fifty minutes. Jo-Fi died in 1937,* and was replaced by another chow, Lun. When Freud arrived in London via Paris on 6 June 1938, Lun had to go into a quarantine kennel for six months. On 2 December 1938, the *Daily Mail* carried the headline 'Freud's Pet Dog is Released from "Prison"', accompanied by a photograph of Lun being greeted by Anna and Marie Bonaparte. The dog's release was reported also by the *Evening Standard* and several other newspapers in London, Paris and Brussels. In the weeks before his death, Freud was heart-broken when Lun withdrew from him; the dog could not tolerate the stench from his master's necrotic cancer.

In the 2004 two-part television film *Princesse Marie*, the title role is played – with her usual icy hauteur – by Catherine Deneuve, who captures the princess's self-regard and aristocratic entitlement. When she bares her soul (and her breasts) to Freud, he tells her – somewhat regretfully – that he is an old man, and moreover, a *petit-bourgeois*. Freud, wrote Jones, was 'monogamic [*sic*] in a very unusual degree'. One unintentionally comic scene has Bonaparte visiting a mental hospital in London.

* After Dorothy Burlingham's death in 1979, Anna Freud bought a chow puppy, which she named Jo-Fi.

Arriving in her chauffeur-driven Rolls-Royce, she is met at the entrance by the hospital's white-coated director. He escorts the princess along a procession of grotesques, including a woman whose hands are raw from compulsive hand washing. The director admits to Bonaparte that even after three months of analysis, this patient is no better. The princess, addressing the director as if he were an idiot child (for such is the insolence of great wealth and privilege), tells him that it obvious to *her* what is causing this woman's compulsion: she is trying to wash away a childhood fantasy of wanting to caress her father's testicles.*

Royal and fabulously wealthy, the princess indulged (nearly) all her whims, from the serial relocation of her clitoris to the radiation of her chow; the only caprice denied her was incest. Foolish and self-obsessed though she may have been, if I could undergo analysis in any period of history, with any analyst, I would undoubtedly choose to be a patient of Princess Marie Bonaparte's in the 1930s. She conducted her analytic sessions in the beautiful garden at Saint-Cloud; the patients – who had been collected by her chauffeur in one of her fleet of splendid cars – lay on a couch, she behind on a chaise-longue. No doubt Topsy was close by. During the summers, which she spent in

---

* This scene was based on Bonaparte's visit to the Hôpital Sainte-Anne in Paris, where she tried to convince the psychiatrist Henri Claude (who was sympathetic to psychoanalysis) that a young woman's phobia of touching soap in the bath was caused by this suppressed childhood wish. Claude, who told her she was talking nonsense, was pursued down the corridor by the princess, shouting at him: 'But you *cannot* behave this way!'

Saint-Tropez or Greece, she brought her analysands with her, arranging their travel and accommodation. Pleasant though this might have been, I suspect that she would have looked down on my plebeian origins and been bored by my mundane preoccupations.

Princess Marie Bonaparte and Topsy.

27

Although Ernest Jones knew the Home Secretary Sir Samuel Hoare as a fellow skater, he persuaded Trotter to get him a formal letter of introduction to Hoare from the President of the Royal Society, Sir William Bragg. In the saintly way of eminent scientists, Bragg asked him: 'Do you really think the Germans are unkind to the Jews?' When Jones went to the Home Office, Hoare immediately agreed to grant permits for Freud, his family, servants, personal physician, and even a few of his pupils and their families. Meanwhile, in Vienna, Dr Anton Sauerwald, the Nazi official assigned to the Freuds, although an anti-Semite, treated Freud well: he had studied chemistry under the Jewish Professor Herzig, a man he deeply admired, and a close friend of Freud's. Sauerwald was so taken by Freud's personality that he was prompted to read his work, which he found as impressive as the man; he was charmed too, by Marie Bonaparte and Anna Freud. Sauerwald put himself in some danger when he signed a document confirming that Freud had no foreign assets, despite knowing that Freud (with the help of Marie Bonaparte) had secretly transferred funds in the form of gold out of Austria. On one occasion, Martin Freud witnessed Sauerwald politely knocking at the door of the Freud apartment, only to be pushed aside by an SS officer, who told him, 'We do not knock at doors.'

The Nazis persecuted the Viennese Jews with labyrinthine bureaucracy. They insisted that before being granted an exit visa and the *Unbedenklichkeitserklärung* (certificate of 'innocuousness'), Freud would have to sign this statement:

> I Prof. Freud, hereby confirm that after the Anschluss of Austria to the German Reich I have been treated by the German authorities and particularly by the Gestapo with all the respect and consideration due to my scientific reputation, that I could live and work in full freedom, that I could continue to pursue my activities in every way I desired, that I found full support from all concerned in this respect, and that I have not the slightest reason for any complaint.

As he signed, Freud sarcastically told Sauerwald: 'I can heartily recommend the Gestapo to anyone.' Freud left Vienna on 4 June 1938, taking the train* to Paris, where he stayed with Marie Bonaparte, before sailing from Calais to Dover. Jones used his connections with the Home Secretary and the

---

* Between the years 1887 and 1899, Freud suffered from a train phobia (siderodromophobia). Naturally, he self-analysed this phobia, and according to Jones, 'It turned out to be connected with the fear of losing his home (and ultimately his mother's breast) – a panic of starvation which must have been in its turn a reaction to some infantile greed. Traces of it remained in later life in the form of slightly undue anxiety about catching trains.'

Lord Privy Seal to ensure Freud's luggage was not searched, and – to put the press and gawpers off the scent – that his train arrived at a different platform in Victoria station. He took care of everything, from arranging accommodation to organising the delegation from the Royal Society, who turned up a few days later at the rented house in Primrose Hill to offer Freud their fellowship.

Freud was very reluctant to leave Vienna, not least because it would mean finding new doctors. On Jones's advice, he tried to contact Wilfred Trotter for advice on his cancer treatment. Trotter wrote to him on 15 August:

Dear Professor Freud

It was with great regret that I had already left London when you tried to reach me on the telephone. I have been brought here [his house in Blackmoor, Hampshire] to make my convalescence after a long illness and shall not be in London for a month. Although I am very sorry I have lost the opportunity of giving you any help I could, I am afraid I should not be a very useful counsellor as I am no longer in the active practice of surgery. I have had some talk with Ernest Jones about your illness and from what he was able to tell me I formed the opinion that, in this country at any rate, you should be in the charge of a dentist and surgeon acting in consultation. The names that were mentioned between us were those of Warwick James the dentist and Julian Taylor the surgeon. I know both these men well and worked in collaboration with them. My opinion of both in the matter of skill and judgement is very high and I think they would make as strong a combination as could be found in this country. I hope you will not consider this letter and these remarks an intrusion; but I have felt a certain responsibility since my talk with Jones, and especially since I learnt you had failed to find me on the telephone.

May I add that I am deeply anxious that this country should give you of its best.

Believe me

Very sincerely yours

Wilfred Trotter

Freud duly replied on 21 August:

Thank you for your kind letter. I deeply appreciate your interest in my case and my person and I trust I will be able to see you when you are back in London, to renew an acquaintance started at Salzburg in 1907 or 8, do you remember?

As it turned out, Freud did not call on the services of Warwick James or Julian Taylor. When Freud's cancer returned, Hans Pichler, his Viennese surgeon, assisted by his London-based former pupil George G. Exner, carried out a major operation at the London Clinic on 8 September 1938, cutting through the cheek to access the tumour. Pichler – bizarrely – was driven all the way from Vienna by his fellow Nazi party member, Dr Anton Sauerwald. Sauerwald had secretly visited Freud in London a few weeks before to discuss the closing of his bank accounts and a plan whereby Marie Bonaparte would buy the remaining stock of books held by the *Verlag* in Vienna. Freud, now aware that his cancer had returned, persuaded Sauerwald to fetch Pichler from Vienna. (Marie Bonaparte later remarked that the English doctors were all afraid of Freud.)

Freud was extremely weak after this procedure, writing to Marie Bonaparte that the operation was 'the most severe since 1923 and has cost me a great deal'. Pichler's intervention, however, was to no avail, for there was recurrence of the cancer in February 1939. Although retired from surgical practice, Trotter was one of several doctors who visited Freud during this month. Marie Bonaparte (now almost a permanent house guest) summoned Professor Antoine Lacassagne (Topsy's radiation specialist) from Paris. He returned the next month to supervise radiation treatment, but Freud's cancer was more resistant than the chow's. He distracted himself from his cancer with the writing, translation and publication of his final work, *Moses and Monotheism*. In this book, Freud claimed – rather sensationally – that Moses was born an Egyptian, *not* a Jew,* that he had been killed by his followers, and that collective guilt for this slaying led to a religious neurosis among the Jews. (The Bible states that Moses lived to the age of one hundred and twenty, but Freud believed the Old Testament scholar Ernst Sellin, who argued that Moses was murdered.) The Jewish linguist and writer Abraham Yahuda visited Freud and begged him not to publish it; the book was later panned by biblical

---

* An old Jewish joke tells the story of the bright Yiddish boy who, when asked who the mother of Moses was, answers, without hesitation, 'the princess'. No, he is told, the princess only took Moses out of the water. 'That's what *she* says [*sagt sie*],' replies the boy.

experts and Egyptologists. Kitty Jones (assisted by Ernest) was tasked with the English translation, but was dilatory, which greatly irritated Freud, who was desperate to see the book published before he died. Mervyn Jones recalled: 'In connection with Freud's book *Moses and Monotheism*, which my mother had translated, my father endeavoured to convince my uncle during a stroll in the garden that monotheism was a historic advance on polytheism. Trotter listened patiently and then pronounced: "The improvement is purely mathematical."' In June 1939, Freud wrote to Trotter to thank him for his medical services and for his advice on the English translation of *Moses and Monotheism*. Trotter replied: 'Like the rest of the world I was already in your debt. It is a source of pride that this personal obligation has been so generously added.'

Anna Freud seems to have blamed Trotter for her father's swift deterioration during his final illness and was convinced that Pichler might have saved him. Her biographer, Elisabeth Young-Bruehl, wrote: 'Learning to live with her grief was a long ordeal; learning to control her anger, her feeling that her father's death was linked to Dr. Trotter's break with Dr. Pichler's treatment plan was a more pressing project.' Two months after her father's death, she wrote to A. A. Brill: 'The operations always saved his life again for a period, and the radium failed to do so. If we had stayed near his old surgeon, he might have kept him alive longer.' Decades later – in 1980 – she wrote to the Argentinian José Schavelzon (who was researching for a book* on Freud's cancer): 'I believe that the long duration of the illness was due

* *Freud, un paciente con cancer (Freud, a cancer patient)*, 1983.

to Dr. Pichler's great care. He had decided to remove every new sign of growth, even if precancerous, immediately and not to wait for full development. When we emigrated to England, the surgeon there [Trotter] changed the method, waited for full development, and that led to a very quick end.'

During the last year of his life, Freud received many famous visitors at his Hampstead house. (Despite being in his eighties and dying of cancer, Freud was given a mortgage by Barclays Bank to buy this property.) Isaiah Berlin, who collected famous acquaintances* like George V collected stamps, called in October 1938. Berlin, still only twenty-nine, had been a Fellow of All Souls, Oxford, since 1932, the first Jew to be elected to the fellowship. Freud asked Berlin what he did; when Berlin replied that he taught philosophy, Freud replied, 'then you must think me a charlatan'. The interview got off to an awkward start: Berlin failed to identify the origin of one of Freud's classical figurines, and confessed that no, he didn't know princess Marie Bonaparte or indeed any members of the Greek royal family. 'I see you are not pretentious,' replied Freud after Berlin's ignorance of the first question, and 'I see you are not a snob', after the second. Freud mused about setting up practice in Oxford; Berlin told him there would be great demand for his services there. Martha Freud (making a rare appearance)†

* This long list included Nehru, Stravinsky, Pasternak, Wittgenstein, Virginia Woolf, Churchill and Picasso.
† Martha remains a shadowy figure in the huge Freudian biographical literature, rarely mentioned. Their only recorded quarrel was whether

brought in the tea and moaned to Berlin that her husband ('this monster') forbade the lighting of Sabbath candles on Friday night. 'Religion', Freud responded, 'is a superstition.' After tea, Berlin joined the Freuds and their fifteen-year-old grandson, Lucian, in the garden, in an atmosphere that Berlin recalled 'was pure Vienna, circa 1912'. Freud, he told his biographer, Michael Ignatieff, was 'not a genius, but an old Jewish doctor, clever, malicious and wise'.

Lucian Freud met Berlin again fifty-eight years later, in 1996, when he painted a portrait of the now grand old man. The National Portrait Gallery had invited Freud to choose any sitter; he picked Berlin. Freud (seventy-four) and Berlin (eighty-six) met for more than a dozen sittings. They hit it off, gossiping about mutual friends, but Berlin was tired and ill, and dozed for much of the time. The portrait was never finished, and Berlin died the next year.

Lucian was very proud of being Sigmund Freud's grandson. His life-long estrangement from his younger brother Clement* was said to have been caused by the latter's taunt that Lucian was not Ernst's biological son, and thus not Sigmund's grandson. (A quick comparison of photographs of Lucian and Sigmund's father, Jacob, shows the absurdity of this slur.) Lucian, ever contrary, claimed that it was Sigmund's zoological

---

mushrooms should be cooked with or without the stalks.
* Clement – who was born Clemens – became a television and radio personality, restaurateur, journalist and Liberal MP. He once remarked that the only time he had ever been 'outgrandfathered' was when Winston Churchill (grandson of the Prime Minister) was allocated a grander hotel suite when they visited Peking in the 1970s as part of a parliamentary delegation.

research (on the sex organs of eels), and not psychoanalysis, that he was most proud of. He was taken to see his grandfather's body and recalled 'a sort of hole in his cheek like a brown apple. That was why there was no death mask made, I imagine. I was upset.'

Forty years later, some critics speculated whether Lucian's *Naked Man with Rat** was inspired by his grandfather's famous patient; they were disappointed to learn that the painter had never heard of the Rat Man. The year after completing *Naked Man with Rat*, Lucian produced a nude portrait of his eighteen-year-old daughter, Rose Boyt; he painted seven of his fourteen acknowledged children in this manner. The same critics tried to explain the 'Freudian significance' of this invasion of his children's privacy, with its echoes of Sigmund Freud's prolonged analysis of his youngest daughter.

Arthur Koestler called to see Freud in the autumn of 1938. He was thirty-three and had recently completed his first novel, *The Gladiators*. Koestler, a Hungarian Jew, was appalled when Freud told him that the Nazis were 'abreacting the aggression pent up in our civilization', and that he didn't really blame them. Koestler's mother, Adele, with whom he (Koestler) had a relationship of mutual loathing, had been a patient of Freud's in 1890. Adele, then a wealthy young woman living in Vienna, went to see him with a persistent tic. Fifty years later, she

---

* The rat, cradled in the naked man's right hand, was drunk for the sittings, having been given half a crushed sleeping tablet diluted in Veuve Clicquot.

told her son that Freud was 'a disgusting fellow', who had massaged her neck and asked her 'scandalous and outlandish questions about sex'. Adele's uncle had also consulted Freud, before committing suicide in 1900. Given his family history, Koestler might not have been well disposed to Freud, but was impressed despite himself: 'though small and fragile, the dominating impression was not that of a sick octogenarian, but of the indestructible vitality of the Hebrew patriarch.'

The Austrian novelist Stefan Zweig worshipped this dying patriarch: 'it was my first experience of a true sage, exalted beyond himself, to whom neither pain nor death any longer counted.' Zweig brought Salvador Dalí to see Freud in July 1938; the young artist was a great admirer; surrealism, after all, owed much to psychoanalysis, which inspired a great deal of bad art. Dalí made several sketches of Freud. A month before meeting him, Dalí had had an epiphany about Freud:

> Several years after my last ineffectual attempt to meet Freud, I made a gastronomic excursion into the region of Sens in France. We started the dinner with snails, one of my favourite dishes. All of a sudden I saw a photograph of Professor Freud on the front page of a newspaper which someone beside me was reading. I immediately had one brought to me and read that the exiled Freud had just arrived in Paris. We had not yet recovered from the effect of this news when I uttered a loud cry. I had just that instant discovered the morphological secret of Freud! Freud's cranium is a snail! His brain is in

the form of a spiral – to be extracted with a needle! This
discovery strongly influenced the portrait drawing which I
later made from life, a year before his death.

Freud did not initially warm to Dalí, telling him that he preferred classical painting, but wrote to Zweig the next day:
'I really owe you thanks for bringing yesterday's visitor. For
until now I have been inclined to regard the surrealists, who
apparently have adopted me as their patron saint, as complete
fools. That young Spaniard, with his candid fanatical eyes and
his undeniable technical mastery, has changed my estimate.
It would be very interesting to investigate analytically how he
came to create that picture.'

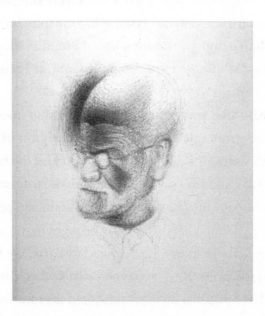

Dalí's sketch of Freud.

Virginia and Leonard Woolf called on 28 January 1939. Although the Woolfs' Hogarth Press published Freud, Virginia was the only prominent Bloomsberry who was not converted to psychoanalysis. After reading his *Collected Papers* in 1924, she wrote in her diary: 'We are publishing all of Dr Freud, and I glance at the proof and read how Mr A. B. threw a bottle of red ink in the sheets of his marriage bed to excuse his impotence to the housemaid, but threw it in the wrong place, which unhinged his wife's mind – and to this day she throws claret on the dinner table. We could all go on like that for hours; and yet these Germans think it proves something – besides their own gull-like imbecility.'

Leonard told Freud about a newspaper report he had read concerning a man convicted of stealing books from Foyle's, among them a volume by Freud. He was fined by a magistrate who told the thief that he would have preferred to punish him by forcing him to read the full twenty-four volumes of the *Complete Edition*. Freud was amused by this story; his books, he said, had made him not famous, but *infamous*. Leonard, who had been disappointed by previous encounters with celebrities, finding them 'disappointing or bores, or both', recalled that Freud had 'an aura, not of fame, but of greatness'. This aura was invisible to Virginia, who saw instead 'a screwed up shrunk very old man, with a monkey's light eyes'.

Freud and Jones wrote less frequently to each other when they both lived in London. Six months before he died, Freud wrote his last letter to Ernest Jones (to the end, addressed as

270

'Jones'): 'I still find it curious with what little presentiment we humans look to the future. But our impotence forces us to accept everything that fate brings.' Jones wrote his final, typically deferential, letter to Freud three weeks before the Master's death: 'it has been a very interesting life and we have both made a contribution to human existence – even if in very different measure.' Sigmund Freud died on 23 September 1939. His doctor, Max Schur, gave him a slightly higher dose than normal of morphine, following which Freud fell into a coma. Some assisted dying campaigners have cited this as an act of euthanasia, but Schur was simply treating his pain. Near the end, he described his world as 'a little island of pain floating in a sea of indifference'. It was fitting that Freud died in England, the country – said Jones – that 'had given him more courtesy, more esteem and more honour than his own or any other land'.

Wilfred Trotter died nine weeks later, on 25 November. He had suffered from painful bouts of obstruction from kidney stones for many years; this eventually led to renal failure, which in those pre-dialysis, pre-transplant days was fatal. Loe Kann wrote to Bessie ('Owlie') on the day of Trotter's death about her premonition:

Dear Owlie
Since I gave you the little pearl ring (when you left Toronto) until this day you have been the most loving and perfect wife to one of the greatest, most lovable men in the world. What this has meant in joy and suffering only you can

know. Today and in the future this suffering may obscure everything – after which you will carry on with your indomitable courage.

And now I'm going to sleep – I was literally in that room with you for the last two nights. And at 6 this morning, I thought I heard an air-raid warning – but I was wrong. I stood at the open window, listening and waiting. Do you believe in telepathy?

Loe, who, according to Jones, was given 'ten years to live at the outside' by Trotter in 1906, attended his funeral thirty-three years later.

Wilfred Trotter's death was marked by obituaries in all the major medical journals, and even a short one by Ernest Jones in the *International Journal of Psychoanalysis*, on the grounds that 'he was one of the first two or three in England to appreciate the significance of Freud's work'. Henry Head, whose work on nerve physiology had been trashed by Trotter, wrote a letter of condolence to Bessie: 'Although I cannot use my hands to write, I must dictate a few words of sympathy with you in your loss. Your husband was the most original and the most brilliant surgeon I have ever worked with, and he made the most complex operation appear to be the simplest in surgery. But apart from his professional skill we loved him for his wisdom and for his ironical outlook on life.'

The funerals of both Freud and Trotter were held at Golders Green Crematorium.* Stefan Zweig gave a eulogy for Freud

---

* Freud's ashes were placed in an antique Greek urn given to him by Marie

in German, Ernest Jones in English. Jones quoted – naturally – from *Hamlet*: 'And so we take leave of a man whose like we shall not know again. From our hearts we thank him for having lived; for having done; and for having loved.' History does not record who spoke in praise of Trotter.

No good deed, says the cliché, goes unpunished. Freud's nephew Harry, an officer in the US army, had Anton Sauerwald arrested in 1945 and charged with war crimes; Harry was convinced that he had robbed the Freuds and destroyed the *Verlag*. (Harry, according to the Freuds' maid Paula Fichtl, was 'not very bright'.) Sauerwald languished in jail while he recovered from pulmonary tuberculosis, and was eventually tried at Nuremberg, where he was acquitted of all charges in 1949, after both Anna Freud and Marie Bonaparte had written letters to the court in his support. Sauerwald had no further contact with the Freuds and died in Innsbruck in 1970.

Bonaparte. The urn was severely damaged during an attempt to steal it in 2014. The urn, which contains the ashes of both Sigmund and Martha Freud, is now protected by a glass casing and a guard. Visits to 'Freud Corner' can only be made while accompanied by a member of the crematorium staff.

28

Ernest Jones's biography of Freud was, like James Strachey's *Standard Edition*, the work of his old age. In the preface, Jones – in a veiled reference to Trotter – wrote: 'my own hero-worshipping propensities had been worked through before I encountered Freud.' Given the hagiographical tone of the biography, this claim rings a little hollow. Although *The Life and Work of Sigmund Freud* was a critical and commercial success, later scholars of psychoanalysis are ambivalent about it: it is just too *readable*. These neo-Freudians look down their noses at Ernest Jones; they don't like the disobliging fact that the spreading of the word required the services of this fixer, seducer and opportunist. Freudian theory, being so self-evidently true, should not have required the rattling of the stick inside the swill bucket.

Wilfred Trotter gave a lecture in 1932 on 'The Commemoration of Great Men.'* He speculated that 'a future and

---

* The Hunterian Oration at the Royal College of Surgeons, honouring the memory of the surgeon and anatomist John Hunter (1728–93).

more realistic age may reach the conclusion that the time to celebrate its heroes is while they are alive, and not to wait with our remarkable patience until they are safely dead'. He might have been amused, had he survived a few years longer, to learn that his brother-in-law would be honoured in this manner, with the institution, in 1944, of the annual Ernest Jones Lecture by the British Psychoanalytical Society.* This honour was partly an attempt to heal the deep divisions within the society in the wake of the Controversial Discussions. Trotter's son Robert attended several of these annual lectures: 'It used to give one something of a jolt to see my uncle in the flesh at these gatherings with their distinctly posthumous air.' Perhaps he was echoing his father, who observed: 'It is unfortunately very much easier to recognize a man's greatness after he is dead and when we are freed from the distraction of the actual presence, which unhappily tends so often to be odd, angular, and even quarrelsome.'

The only footage of Jones available on YouTube (107 views) is a 1956 television interview with Lionel Trilling, conducted in the library of the New York Psychoanalytical Association; this staged conversation was part of the celebrations marking the centenary of Freud's birth. A bust of the great man (with trademark penetrating gaze) sits sternly behind them, almost hovering. Jones is stiff, formal, dyspeptic-looking; indeed, he is

* Last given in 2020 by Baroness Helena Kennedy KC, who took as her subject 'Law and the Politics of Disruption: how the rise of populism challenges the rule of law.'

'odd, angular, and even quarrelsome', rarely making eye contact with his oleaginously deferential interviewer. Apart from a slight rolling of his 'r's, his accent has no trace of South Wales; his diction and vocabulary are almost antique, and there are no jokes. Jones is formally attired, with a rose in his buttonhole. His face is lined and gaunt; he is seventy-seven, and would die less than two years later, in February 1958. 'I have never met a normal person,' he testily informs Trilling, 'everyone I have met has neurotic symptoms.' Although the Controversial Discussions were still a vivid and bitter memory, he praises both Anna Freud and Melanie Klein. 'Life', he concludes, 'is something to be endured on the basis of reality.' Trilling later wrote about this encounter: 'Dr Jones was in his seventy-eighth year. Only a few days before his flight to New York he had been discharged from the hospital after a major operation for cancer; during the flight he had suffered a haemorrhage.'

Although Jones suffered a second heart attack in June 1957, he attended the International Psychoanalytic Congress in Paris that August. He was still President of the International Psychoanalytical Association, in which capacity he attended a fête put on by Marie Bonaparte, where he danced with the princess. Several who were present commented on his pallor and a bleed in his right eye. Jones had recently completed his biography of Freud, a task that, according to Melanie Klein, had kept him alive. Anna Freud, who was moved by the tenderness Jones had shown to her father in the biography, thought that this work changed Jones in the last decade of his life; his insecurity, his resentment of his peers and his feeling of being unappreciated gradually disappeared.

In early 1958, what Jones had thought was 'a nasty gastric flu' turned out to be multiple cancer deposits in the liver. Max Schur recalled that Jones was almost proud when he told him of his cancer: 'it was as though he had said "now I am really like Freud".' Mervyn visited his father on the day before he died; typically, Ernest was dictating a piece to Kitty, insisting that *he* had been the first person outside Vienna to champion Freud's ideas: 'When the sentence was read over to him, he decided that it was unfair to Jung. I suggested giving Jung a footnote: "too important", my father said.' Mervyn had travelled to London from a by-election in Rochdale (which he was covering for

The President: Ernest Jones.

Tribune) to see his father, who was dying in his *alma mater*, UCH. Ernest's dying was clearly something of an inconvenience:

> That was my last memory of him. Ernest Jones died the next day.
>
> Despite the defeat at Brighton, the issue of nuclear weapons was in the forefront of politics. At Rochdale, both Labour and Liberal candidates came out for renunciation of the bomb; Labour won the seat, with the Tories coming a pitiable third.

Mervyn later regretted this filial impiety: 'Freud once said that the most important event in any man's life is the death of his father, and so assuredly it was for me. I mourned my father deeply, and I mourn him still.'

Jones survived long enough to witness the golden age of psychoanalysis in America, when university departments of psychiatry were dominated by Freudians, when New York City alone had four times as many analysts as the whole of Britain. Freud would have been perplexed: although an Anglophile, he never hid his contempt for the United States. Even if Edward Glover disdainfully noted in 1946 that 'bowdlerised' Freudian theories had 'made their way to the maid's pantry', psychoanalysis in England remained confined to the squares of Bloomsbury, where it offered the rich a means of managing their anxiety in the new, confusing, secular, atomised, spiritually rudderless age. Glover would never have to listen to common folk recounting their banal dreams. Psychoanalysis never established itself there as it did in America, because, as Trotter once wrote, the English have 'an almost sullen indifference to great projects and ideals'. England could never have produced, or taken seriously, a Freud.

Freud may have been a great man, but by his own admission, he was unfit to be a psychiatrist, and was not even a good psychoanalyst,* while Trotter, in the words of Robin Pilcher, was 'the perfect example of a good doctor'. I searched hard for Trotter, but only a few humble artefacts survive; Jones, in contrast, popped up often, and in the most unlikely places, while Freud, as Auden wrote, is 'no more a person now but a whole climate of opinion'. Apart from the admiration of Ernest Jones, Trotter and Freud had much in common: they wrote exceptionally well and had a personal charisma that attracted ardent admirers. But while Freud *needed* disciples, Trotter was embarrassed by such attention; while Freud treated only the fee-paying Viennese bourgeoisie (and later the rich from anywhere), Trotter treated the duchess and the 'husky slum-lady' alike; while Freud craved honours and titles, Trotter declined them; while Freud based his practice on his own speculative theories, Trotter's exquisite surgical technique was a humble 'practical art'; while Freud was indifferent to the outcome of therapy, Trotter's *only* concern was the patient's recovery; while the name of Freud is known to anyone who can read, Trotter is forgotten – the students and

* Freud once admitted to Abram Kardiner: 'In the first place, I get tired of people. Secondly, I am not basically interested in therapy. I am also too patriarchal to be a good analyst.'

trainees who imitated his gait and speech are all dead. Fame, as Anthony Daniels observed, is often bestowed on the least deserving. This neglect would not have troubled Trotter; he had little regard for the world's coarse thumb and finger. A quintessentially English figure, he may have been self-effacingly modest, but he knew his own worth: he was, in his own phrase, one of that 'small band of the heroically gifted'. In 'The Commemoration of Great Men', he seemed to anticipate his own impending insignificance:

> From the moment of a man's death the memory of him begins to fade, for he has entered on a new state about which the only certainty is that it has nothing to do with life. Nothing can arrest this decline, no memorial can do more than delay it and as it delays distort. In all our commemorations, whether by word or by plastic art, we make our own pictures and drift increasingly away from the actual man.

The new high-rise UCH building on the Euston Road opened in 2005; the old Victorian-Gothic hospital in Gower Street (the Cruciform Building), where Trotter once reigned, is now owned by University College London, and houses several research centres, including the Wolfson Institute for Bio-medical Research. The UCH medical school merged with the Middlesex Hospital medical school in 1987, and later with the Royal Free Hospital medical school in 1998, to create the University College London (UCL) medical school. I wrote to the UCL medical school, who confirmed that 'the William [*sic*] Trotter Prize was founded as a prize for the highest marks in Surgery in the final year examination. A prize was awarded up until 2021 when the money in the endowment finally ran out.'

Wondering whether Trotter was still honoured at UCH, I wrote to one of the surgical professors there. He made detailed inquiries and was eventually informed:

Dear Professor

Your email has been forwarded to UCL Records, as we manage the UCH collection.

Searching the catalogue, we do not have any hospital records for Wilfred Trotter.

I can't imagine that Trotter would have been in any way disturbed by this oblivion.

29

Beginning in the early 1890s, Sigmund Freud experienced a prolonged spiritual crisis, and what emerged from this crisis was psychoanalysis. In his correspondence with his close friend the surgeon Wilhelm Fliess, Freud developed his ideas on infantile sexuality, the Oedipus complex, the unconscious, and the meaning of dreams. Freud's self-analysis – the psychoanalytic equivalent of Jesus's forty days in the desert – was the *fons et origo* of this new religion. He constructed the edifice of a grand complete theory of the human psyche around the flimsy frame of his own life. In an intense period, lasting from 1898 to 1905, Freud wrote the books that made him famous.

Shortly after moving into the apartment at Berggasse 19, Freud wrote to Fliess: 'Do you suppose that someday one will read on a marble tablet on this house: Here on July 24, 1895, the secret of the dream revealed itself to Dr Sigmund Freud?' His analysis of his own dreams would be the model for *all* dreams: 'He discovered psychoanalysis in his sleep,' wrote Adam Phillips. Dream analysis had been a paid occupation since Artemidorus of Ephesus wrote his *Interpretation of Dreams* in the second century AD. Freud claimed that dreams represented unconscious desires, whose meaning could be interpreted. Because human beings had always believed that dreams must have a *meaning*, this idea had great appeal. Neuroscience, however, does not give much credence to his claims: dreaming seems to be essential for psychological health, but Freud's idea that dreams can be symbolically decoded is dismissed by most sleep scientists. (Many of our dreams are, in fact, quite transparent, and do not require 'interpretation'.)

Freud's feelings towards his parents became the Oedipus complex, which was experienced by *all* sons. 'A single idea of general value dawned on me,' he wrote to Fliess. 'I have found in my own case the phenomena of being in love with my mother and jealous of my father, and I now consider it a universal event in early childhood.' Although Freud, being familiar with the classics, chose Oedipus, he could just have easily chosen – had the circumstances of his childhood been different – the equally implausible Cronus, who castrated his father Uranus and devoured his children.

Freud's patient population in *fin-de-siècle* Vienna, consisting largely of 'hysterical' bourgeois young women, was an equally flimsy foundation for his ideas. Freud's patients were atypical in this regard (Charcot's hysterics were largely poor and illiterate), but being fee-paying, they were a self-selecting group. 'Hysteria' (or conversion disorder) is now uncommon; much of what came to his consulting room was a product of the sexually repressive culture that prevailed in that city at that time. In his autobiography, Stefan Zweig wrote how 'the fear of everything physical and natural dominated the whole people, from the highest to the lowest with the violence of an actual neurosis'. Young women 'were hermetically locked up under the control of the family, hindered in their free bodily as well as intellectual development. The young men were forced to secrecy and reticence by a morality nobody believed or obeyed.' Freud assumed that the psychodynamics of this highly selected patient pool could be extrapolated to all of mankind, but this assumption was a very great leap.

Freud did not have a vocation for medicine: 'Neither at that time, nor indeed in my later life, did I feel any predilection for the career of a doctor.' As a boy, his passions were archaeology, classical history, languages and literature. At the age of seventy, he wrote:

> After forty years of medical activity, my self-knowledge tells me that I have never really been a doctor in the proper sense. I became a doctor through being compelled to deviate from my original purpose; and the triumph of my life lies in my having, after a long and roundabout journey, found my way back to my earliest path. I scarcely think, however, that my lack of genuine medical temperament has done much damage to my patients.

Freud, though he always claimed to be a scientist, was at heart a literary scholar; the Nobel laureate Francis Crick once remarked that he was 'not a scientist, but rather a physician who had many novel ideas and wrote unusually well'. Freud admitted, for example, that Ludwig Börne's 1823 essay 'The

Art of Becoming an Original Writer in Three Days' inspired the idea of free association. He was nominated on several occasions for the Nobel Prize in both Literature and Medicine, but did not win;* he was, however, awarded the Goethe Prize in 1930 for the excellence of his writing. When Havelock Ellis described him as an artist rather than a scientist, Freud bristled, regarding this as an attempt to discredit his work, but he suspected that Ellis was right. Recalling his training in 'hard' science with the physiologist Brücke, Freud reflected regretfully: 'It still strikes me as strange that the case-histories I write should read like short stories and that they lack the serious stamp of science.'

Psychoanalysis may no longer be the dominant force it once was, but Freud remains one of the great intellectual figures of the twentieth century. The triumph of his life was to persuade many people that his personal conviction – or, as Wilfred Trotter called it, his 'prophetic intuition' – was correct. He did this because he was, as the psychiatrist and writer Anthony Storr pointed out, a guru, with many of the characteristics of those unusual people: he claimed special insight based on personal revelation; this revelation came to him following a period of spiritual crisis; he generalised from his own experience; he was intolerant of criticism; he

---

* The Nobel Prize in Medicine was awarded on just two occasions for work on mental illness: in 1927 to Freud's old friend Julius Wagner-Jauregg 'for his discovery of the therapeutic value of malaria inoculation in the treatment of dementia paralytica', and in 1949 to António Caetano de Abreu Freire Egas Moniz 'for his discovery of the therapeutic value of leucotomy [lobotomy] in certain psychoses'.

had personal charisma; he had absolute certainty about his ideas. He had the advantage, too, of good timing: after the carnage of the First World War, intellectuals concluded that both religion and philosophy had failed. Freud's new system of thought filled the vacuum and explained the horror; its narrative of human life offered an alternative to religion. Even if he was 'wrong', his greatness is undiminished: Trotter did not change the world, but Freud did. His converts were relatively few, but they were mightily influential, a very elite herd indeed. 'Freud was a genius, there's no denying it,' mused his most famous patient, the Wolf Man. 'All those ideas he combined in a system: even though much isn't true, it was a splendid achievement.'

Freud made one great error: he maintained to his dying day that psychoanalysis was a science. Anthony Storr summed it up well: 'If Freud had been content to maintain that psychoanalysis was a hermeneutic system, a historical way of interpreting human behaviour in terms of past events and influences, he might have kept the respect of scientists.' Many others, such as Peter Medawar, Karl Popper and Vladimir Nabokov were not so generous; Medawar famously called psychoanalytic theory 'the most stupendous intellectual confidence trick of the twentieth century'. Medawar's accusation, however, was unfair: it was not a confidence trick, because tricksters *know* they are cheating: Freud believed in his own theories with absolute conviction. But, as Primo Levi wrote, 'There is trouble in store for anyone who surrenders to the temptation of mistaking an elegant hypothesis for a certainty.' Still Freud clung on to the notion of psychoanalysis as 'a new science'.

In *The Future of an Illusion* (1927), he wrote this remarkably self-deluding passage:

> But scientific work is the only road which can lead us to a knowledge of reality outside ourselves. It is an illusion to expect anything from intuition and introspection; they can give us nothing but particulars about our own mental life, which are hard to interpret, never any information about the questions which religious doctrine finds it so easy to answer.

Freud conveniently forgot that his most famous ideas came from 'intuition and introspection' and his 'own mental life'. The paradox (and tragedy) of psychoanalysis is that it was founded by a man with scientific training who claimed that it was a science, but who didn't abide by the rules of science.

While Darwin's great idea has been supported by many decades of empirical observation, psychoanalysis does not have such scientific prestige. Although it was the dominant model within American psychiatry from the 1940s to the 1970s, psychoanalysis was eventually toppled when it became gradually evident, after many decades of toil at the couch-side, that it didn't cure even the relatively benign neuroses it confined its efforts to. Freud turned his back on the mad, the schizophrenic, the locked-up lunatics, and actively discouraged psychoanalysts from treating them. They were left in the madhouses to the mercies of doctors like Julius Wagner-Jauregg. The asylums remained full throughout the glory years of Freudianism.

As early as 1921, Emil Kraepelin wrote a remarkably prescient critique of Freud's ideas:

Here we meet everywhere the characteristic fundamental feature of the Freudian method of investigation, the representation of arbitrary assumptions and conjectures as assumed facts, which are used without hesitation for the building up of always new castles in the air, ever towering higher, and the tendency to generalisations beyond measure from single observations. I must finally confess that with the best will I am not able to follow the trains of thought of this 'metapsychiatry', which, like a complex, sucks up the sober method of clinical observation. As I am accustomed to walk on the sure foundation of direct experience, my Philistine conscience of natural science stumbles at every step on objections, considerations, and doubts, over which the lightly soaring power of imagination of Freud's disciples carries them without difficulty.

Trotter was one of the first empiricists to demonstrate that many scientific 'discoveries' do not withstand the icy attention of replication. Freud thought that empirical research to confirm, or replicate, his 'discoveries' was redundant, because these discoveries were so self-evidently *true*, and had been established so conclusively. In the 1950s, the Menninger Clinic in Houston, Texas, began a long-term study of forty-two patients undergoing formal psychoanalysis. An Archie Cochrane-style randomisation to a placebo was, of course, impossible. A final report was eventually published in 1972, by which time several of the original researchers had died. The results were underwhelming: after years in analysis, many patients were no better; those who did improve were 'better-functioning' at the outset of the study. Like any other talking therapy, most patients found it, in varying degrees, helpful and comforting. Psychoanalysis has a brilliant riposte, however, to the accusation of ineffectiveness: it was never meant to *cure* you.

The Canadian psychiatrist Joel Paris, who trained as a psychoanalyst, wrote of his suspicion, as a young doctor, of 'fables with happy endings' – case histories (such as Freud's Rat Man) where the patients become 'remarkably better as soon as therapists help them to achieve some crucial insight'. Paris's own experience convinced him that such happy endings were rare. He followed up over many years a group of his own patients; most had improved, but those who had minimal therapy did just as well as those who had spent years in analysis, and childhood trauma didn't have a consistent relationship with later neurosis. Paris had his own moment of mid-life revelation when he concluded that Archie Cochrane was a better guide to the practice of psychiatry than Sigmund Freud.

The debate around the effectiveness of psychoanalysis rages on. Unfortunately, the kind of evidence Archie Cochrane demanded of psychoanalysis is not available and will never be available. The randomised controlled trial may be a very useful method of assessing new drugs, but its application to a therapy as individualised as psychoanalysis is dubious. All we can conclude is that most talking therapies help, to a greater or lesser degree, people with psychological distress.

The compassion of the therapist seems to be more important than the school they subscribe to or the method they use. As Wilfred Trotter observed, the doctor's *interest* trumps all other considerations. Even Archie Cochrane, who urged doctors to 'randomize until it hurts', who lamented the lack of empirical evidence for psychoanalysis, recognised the power of this interest. He recounted this episode from his time as the only doctor in a prisoner-of-war camp:

The Germans dumped a young Soviet prisoner in my ward late one night. The ward was full, so I put him in my room as he was moribund and screaming and I did not want to wake the ward. I examined him. He had obvious gross bilateral cavitations and severe pleural rub [a sign of pleurisy]. I thought the latter was the cause of the pain and the screaming. I had no morphine, just aspirin, which had no effect. I felt desperate. I knew very little Russian then and there was no one in the ward who did. I finally instinctively sat down on the bed and took him in my arms, and the screaming stopped almost at once. He died peacefully in my arms a few hours later. It was not the pleurisy that caused the screaming, but loneliness. It was a wonderful education about the care of the dying. I was ashamed of my misdiagnosis and kept the story secret.

In her old age, Melitta Schmideberg told the Freudian scholar David Cohen that she had long before realised that 'talking and chicken soup were as effective as complicated analytic techniques'. Melitta's remark summarises what was later called the 'Dodo bird verdict':* the *type* of talking therapy doesn't matter, but the *interest* of the therapist does. If the therapist regards the Oedipus complex as a useful concept, why fret over whether this complex exists or not?

Defenders of psychoanalysis argue that the Freud bashers (their favourite pejorative term for their opponents), in their hysterical hatred of psychoanalytic theory, have failed to acknowledge the positive aspects of his legacy, that they have thrown the baby out with the bath water. This baby, unfortunately, is a very feeble foundling. The Freudians argue that whatever one's views on the Oedipus complex, or infantile sexuality, Freud's discovery of the unconscious and his emphasis on empathetic listening to people remain important. But Freud did not 'discover' the unconscious mind – Goethe and Schopenhauer had written about this concept long before him – and while listening attentively to patients is certainly important, it is hardly comparable to natural selection or relativity as an original idea, particularly when some doctors who had never heard of Freud did this naturally and effortlessly. Wilfred Bion's approach to his psychoanalytic patients was inspired not by Freud, but by a *surgeon* – Trotter.

The so-called Freud bashers are very often apostates – disillusioned ex-Freudians such as Jeffrey Masson and Frederick Crews; their critiques read like the memoirs of cult escapees. Freudians use a standard arsenal of rebuttals: *ad hominem* accusations of the critic suffering from 'resistance', and – if the

---

* In *Alice's Adventures in Wonderland*, the Dodo proclaims: 'Everybody has won, and all must have prizes.'

critic is an analyst – of being 'insufficiently analysed'. Joel Paris wrote that these counterarguments were practical examples of Leon Festinger's concepts of cognitive dissonance and belief perseverance, similar to the rationalisations made after the world continues to exist by those who have prepared for its end.

Karl Popper dismissed psychoanalysis as a pseudoscience because its hypotheses cannot be refuted empirically; *all* scientific hypotheses, he argued, are potentially refutable. In the hermetically (and hermeneutically) sealed psychoanalytic bubble, irrefutability was built in: the philosopher Frank Cioffi observed that 'the need to avoid refutation' accounted for 'a host of peculiarities in psychoanalytic theory and practice which are apparently unrelated'. The social anthropologist Ernest Gellner saw a common thread in Freudian and Catholic apologetics – *ineffability*: 'it's a mystery'.

Peter Swales, once the Rolling Stones' promoter before he became the 'guerrilla historian of psychoanalysis', elaborated a gnostic vision of psychoanalysis where Freud had sold his soul to the Devil. Reading the vast academic psychoanalytic literature, which has consumed rivers of ink and filled several libraries, is, indeed, like descending into a kind of secular hell, or being lost in a strange, frightening, medieval country, full of witches, minor demons, monsters, labyrinths; Freud's architecture of the psyche bears as much relation to reality as Tolkien's map of Middle-earth. The simplest events and objects are imbued with a malign significance; everything is in code and riddles. Families, far from being the centre of comfort and safety, are threatening and treacherous; childhood is no longer a time of enchantment, but is instead, in the words of Adam

Phillips, 'inherently catastrophic'. Freud, a dutiful husband and devoted father, was the presiding deity of a school of thought that posited the family as the source of neuroses.

The mockery of psychoanalysis started as early as 1921, when a Bloomsberryish hoax was perpetrated in Ithaca, New York State. A man claiming to be 'an intimate friend and pupil of Freud' gave a talk to a packed lecture theatre: 'A dreamer does not know what he dreams,' he told the audience, 'but he does not know what he knows and therefore believes what he does not know.' The *Times* gleefully reported that 'a large part of the faculty and undergraduates of Cornell University were hoaxed' and that 'with the help of a few phrases and formulas, anyone can be a Freudian'.

The Freudians may hate mockery, but they fear indifference more. So long as the Freud wars grumble on, psychoanalysis survives. The English Freudian psychologist Harry Guntrip (who, unusually for a psychoanalyst, was a practising Christian) wrote in 1954 that 'The work of Freud will never be safer than when it evokes hostility. What happened to Christianity could equally well happen to psychoanalysis.' Guntrip needn't have worried. Psychoanalysis may have been debunked as a *science*, but still appeals to what Christopher Lasch, in *The Culture of Narcissism* (1979), called 'the hydra-headed narcissism of the affluent bourgeoisie'. Psychoanalysis made solipsism acceptable by giving it a vocabulary and an architecture. This appeal is largely unacknowledged: if you look up 'the psychoanalysis of narcissism', you find a library of material; if you look up 'the narcissism of psychoanalysis', there is almost nothing. Freud's granddaughter Sophie was one of the very few to recognise this narcissism: 'I'm very sceptical about much of psychoanalysis,' she told the *Boston Globe* in 2002. 'I think it's such a narcissistic indulgence that I cannot believe in it.'

'The psychoanalytic session', wrote Ernest Gellner, 'is a masterpiece of combination of a rule-addicted, orderly and individualist ethos, with those of abandon and intense emotion. What could be more appropriate for bourgeois individualists?' Lucian Freud regretted that his grandfather's 'science' had become so debased that it was 'used to pass the afternoon of somebody who could no longer find anyone else to bore'. Adam Phillips has conceded that the main require-ment of psychoanalysis now is that it be *interesting*: 'I read psychoanalysis as poetry. So I don't have to worry about whether it is true or even useful, but only whether it is haunting or moving or intriguing or amusing.'

To his dying day, Ernest Jones believed that psychoanalysis was a science: 'like all true physicians, I have a deep aversion to anything at all resembling quackery, and prefer the certainties of knowledge to the certitudes of enthusiasm.' He referred to Freud's 'discoveries', as if he had identified a new subatomic particle, or the fossil of a hitherto unknown species. Poor Jones, who did not have a sceptical bone in his body, recounted an anecdote that confirms his deafness to mockery: 'an American gentleman', who having listened to Jones summarise for him the main principles of psychoanalysis, asked: 'That's all very interesting. Are you interested in palmistry too?' Jones was desperate to place psychoanalysis on a respectable professional footing. The report published by the British Medical Association in 1929, which recognised psychoanalysis (but *only* the Freudian variety) as a legitimate branch of psychiatry and the British Psychoanalytical Society as its training body, was a victory for Jones, who had written much of the document, including the famous assertion that there was 'no danger in thinking too much about yourself'. The report, in truth, was neutral and lukewarm: 'the Committee has had no opportunity of testing psychoanalysis as a therapeutic method. It is therefore not in a position to express any collective opinion either in favour of the practice or in opposition.' Jones's personal reputation remained salty until quite late in his career; his name was finally dropped in 1932 from a list of 'dangerous people' who were not allowed to speak on the BBC.

Freud and Jones would have been disappointed by how psychoanalysis fared after their deaths, with bitter schisms and rival priesthoods; some of these priests believed in eye of newt, others in toe of frog, united only in their mutual contempt. It has collapsed as a power within psychiatry, so much so that the great Harvard psychiatrist Alan Stone (1929–2022) concluded that the only future for psychoanalysis is as a tool for literary criticism. Psychoanalysis, one hundred years on, has moved on from its messy, protracted divorce from psychiatry and medicine to its new home in the academy. A school of thought that was founded by a highly conventional, self-confessed *petit bourgeois* Viennese neurologist became one of the pillars of Theory, a static, monolithic system curated by people for whom 'science' is a term of derision: psychoanalysis appealed to post-modernist academics precisely *because* of its lack of scientific foundation. The obscurity of the writing that emerged became the model for all academic prose, and many such academics jumped the couch to become analysts themselves. Psychoanalysis-as-theory reached its dismal apotheosis in France in the wake of Jacques Lacan. We have the paradox that psychoanalysis, accessible only to the well-off, became inextricably intertwined, at least in the academy, with modish ideas about social justice. Psychoanalysis, which Desmond Bernal – with preposterous glibness – predicted would explain *everything*, in the end explained nothing.

Wilfred Trotter, a *scientific* sceptic, was wary of *nihilistic* or 'agitated' scepticism, which turns reasonable doubt into unreasonable incredulity: 'The mind likes a strange idea as little as the body likes a strange protein, and resists it with similar energy. The most powerful antigen known to man is a new idea.' Although he argued for evidence, he was open to, and tolerant of, speculative and untested ideas. Such ideas, he argued, 'kept science fresh and living'. Trotter argued for *provisional acceptance*: 'The truly scientific mind is altogether unafraid of the new, and while having no mercy for ideas which have served their turn or show their uselessness, it will not grudge to any unfamiliar conception its moment of full and friendly attention.' Science had, indeed, given psychoanalysis 'its moment of full and friendly attention', and having found it wanting, moved on. In *Instincts of the Herd*, Trotter summed up the difference between the scientific and the psychoanalytic attitude: 'That heavy bodies tend to fall to the earth and that fire burns fingers are truths verifiable and verified every day, but we do not hold them with impassioned certitude, and we do not resent or resist inquiry into their basis.' Now that scientific scepticism is so much part of our culture, it is Trotter who speaks to us: compared to Freud, he has far more useful things to say about science, medicine and even philosophy. Trotter may have been 'heroically gifted', yet it is Freud, flawed and fundamentally in error, a tragic figure whose life's work was a chimera, who is the great man.

Ernest Jones, who once wanted to *be* Trotter, found his purpose and life's work in serving Freud. Disgraced and exiled as a young doctor, he outlived all the other disciples to become the first evangelist of the movement. Psychoanalysis was the banner behind which marched a raggle-taggle army of failed neurologists, curious intellectuals, psychopaths, sexual opportunists, cultural entrepreneurs, eccentric aristocrats, and bored rich dilettantes. It was the making of many of them: Jones's stalker, Joan Riviere, was eventually distracted from torturing him by becoming an analyst herself; it gave a purpose to the feckless younger Bloomsbury sons James Strachey and Adrian Stephen; Anna Freud, the awkward youngest child, found her life's work and her life partner; Melanie Klein, disowned by her own daughter, became the world's most influential child analyst; Princess Marie Bonaparte, who had been obsessed with her pudendal anatomy to the point of self-mutilation, finally found a cause and a 'Great Master'. Psychoanalysis was the solution to the pressing problem of what to do with their lives.

Sources

Most books about Freud and, indeed, psychoanalysis in general, tend to be written by devout believers, many of them practising analysts. It is a strange literature, often deeply partisan with wilful omissions of disobliging facts, or breezy rationalisations of egregious misbehaviour; jaws that should have dropped and eyes that should have popped remained resolutely undropped and unpopped. When I started researching this book, I did not quite realise how vast the psychoanalytic corpus is – like a vast polluted ocean with no visible seabed and no horizon. Reading it was a strange, dissonant experience; although Freudian scholars use terms that *sound* scientific, their work should be read as a form of theology.

The psychoanalytic literature is designed to exclude interlopers. As this is not an academic book for a specialist readership, I have grasped the freedom to edit and shape the primary sources as I see fit. This is not an attempt on my part to corrupt these texts or to bend them to my own agenda; it is solely for the comfort of the reader. When quoting from letters, I have omitted that which is irrelevant, boring or untelling.

As so much of this literature is impenetrable, I have quoted a few texts unchanged to give a flavour of this prolixity; some of these passages gave me the joy of the collector who finds a perfect specimen.

'The material amassed on Freud', wrote the American psychologist Henry Murray, 'is the most precise and penetrating data that exists on the life of any individual in history.' Books by true believers include Ernest Jones's *The Life and Work of Sigmund Freud* (1953–7), Peter Gay's *Freud: A Life for Our Time* (1988), Adam Phillips's *Becoming Freud: The Making of a Psychoanalyst* (2014), and Élisabeth Roudinesco's *Freud: In His Time and Ours* (2014). Paul Roazen's detailed *Freud and His Followers* (1975) is less hagiographical (Anna Freud was scandalised by it); Anthony Storr's *Freud: A Very Short Introduction* (1989) is brief, readable and wise.

Ernest Jones has been the subject of two substantial biographies: *Ernest Jones: Freud's Alter Ego* by Vincent Brome (1983) and *Freud's Wizard: Ernest Jones and the Transformation of Psychoanalysis* by Brenda Maddox (2006). Maddox's book is coloured by the fact (which she admits) that she herself underwent psychoanalysis for several years. Brome's book, unfortunately, contains numerous factual errors. Jones was working on his memoir *Free Associations: Memories of a Psychoanalyst* when he died in 1958; the unfinished book was published the following year, with an epilogue by his son, Mervyn. A new edition was published in 1990, with a revealing new introduction by Mervyn. Mervyn's *Chances: An Autobiography* (1987) is sad, revealing and funny. Jones's long correspondence with Freud is gathered in R. Andrew

Paskauskas's *The Complete Correspondence of Sigmund Freud and Ernest Jones, 1908–1939* (1995).

The best account of Jones's 1906 trial for indecent assault is '"Romancing with a Wealth of Detail": Narratives of Ernest Jones's 1906 Trial for Indecent Assault' by the independent scholar Philip Kuhn, published in *Studies in Gender and Sexuality* (2002, 3(4): 344–378). Kuhn wrote also about the 1908 affair, 'In "The Dark Regions of the Mind": A reading for the indecent assault in Ernest Jones's 1908 dismissal from the West End Hospital for Nervous Diseases', published in *Psychoanalysis and History* (2015, 17(1): 7–57). The only detailed account of Jones's affair with Frieda Gross is by Ken Robinson, also in *Psychoanalysis and History* (2013, 15(2): 165–189): 'A Portrait of the Psychoanalyst as a Bohemian: Ernest Jones and the "Lady from Styria"'. Philip Kuhn wrote about Jones's Canadian period for the *Canadian Bulletin of Medical History* (2018, 35(1): 94–136): 'When Ernest Jones First Arrived in Toronto, or Reappraising the Bruce Letter.' Robert Trotter wrote an amusing and revealing piece about Jones (his uncle) for the *University College Hospital Magazine* in 1959: 'Ernest Jones 1879–1958'. To mark the centenary of his birth, the *International Journal of Psychoanalysis* (1979, 60: 271–287) published a selection of pieces about Jones by his wife Kitty, Anna Freud and William Gillespie.

A surprising source of fascinating details about Loe Kann's later life with Herbert ('Davy') Jones was John Wilsey's *H. Jones VC: The Life and Death of an Unusual Hero* (2002). There is no full-length biography of Morfydd Owen; Rhian Davies's *Never So Pure a Sight: Morfydd Owen (1891–1918)*

A Life in Pictures (1994) is the only book on Owen. I have quoted Donald Hutera's *Times* review (28 August 2015) of Sweetshop Revolution's 'I Loved You and I Loved You'. The most comprehensive paper on delayed chloroform poisoning is 'Clinical evidence for delayed chloroform poisoning' by C. M. Thorpe and A. A. Spence in the *British Journal of Anaesthesia* (1997, 79: 402–409).

Ernest Jones revisited *Hamlet* on several occasions; his final visit was the 1949 book *Hamlet and Oedipus*. Anthony Daniel's amusing trashing of Jones's thesis, 'Dr Jones's Hamlet Complex', appeared in the *New Criterion* in October 2010. Peter Donaldson's 'Olivier, Hamlet, and Freud' in the *Cinema Journal* (1987, 26(4): 22–48) is a scholarly account of Jones's influence on Olivier. Olivier's *Confessions of An Actor: An Autobiography* (1982) recounts his meeting with Jones. Anthony Quayle's anecdote about Ralph Richardson's Othello is in his memoir *A Time to Speak* (1990). Roberta Barker and Tom Cornford wrote about Tyrone Guthrie's Old Vic production of Hamlet in *The Great European Stage Directors* Vol. 3 (2018). Sylvia Townsend Warner's 'Footsteps on the Battlements' is published in the *Journal of the Sylvia Townsend Warner Society* (2021, 1: 45–48). A transcript of Kenneth Tynan's 1966 television interview with Laurence Olivier was published by the *Tulane Drama Review* (1966, 11(2): 71–101). James Hendrie Lloyd's lecture 'The so-called Oedipus-Complex in Hamlet' was published in the *Journal of the American Medical Association* (1911, LVI(19): 1377–1379). Bronisław Malinowski described his search for the Oedipus complex among the Trobriand Islanders in *Sex and Repression in Savage Society* (1927).

'Jones on Ice: Psychoanalysis and Figure Skating', Todd Dufresne's and Gary Genosko's textual analysis of Jones's *The Elements of Figure Skating* appeared in the *International Journal of Psychoanalysis* (1995, 76(1): 123–133).

Professor David Trotter gave me access to archival material about Wilfred Trotter, particularly his letters to Ernest Jones, some of which have already been published in Jones's memoir. This archive also contains newspaper clippings about Trotter's involvement in the treatment of George V, as well as material relating to *Instincts of the Herd in Peace and War* (1916). I have quoted extensively from Trotter's *Collected Papers* (1941). The best biographical pieces about Trotter are by two of his pupils, Julian Taylor and Robin Pilcher. Taylor's essay was published in the *Annals of the Royal College of Surgeons of England* (1949, 4(3): 144–159), and Pilcher's in the same journal (1973, 53(2): 71–83). T. R. Elliott wrote a lengthy piece for *Obituary Notices of Fellows of the Royal Society* (1941, 3(9): 325–344). Other obituaries appeared in the *British Journal of Surgery* (1940, 27(108): 625–628), the *British Medical Journal* (1939 (2): 1117–9), and the *International Journal of Psychoanalysis* (1940, 21: 114). Over the years, many doctors have written about Trotter, including Charles D. Aring in the *Journal of the American Medical Association* (1957, 99(2): 313–316), K. S. George and M. McGurk in the *British Journal of Oral and Maxillofacial Surgery* (2005, 43(6): 500–504), Irving B. Rosen in the *Canadian Journal of Surgery* (2006, 49(4): 278–280), and Ronald A. Malt in the *New England Journal of Medicine* (1957, 257: 933–935). Philip Kuhn kindly shared an unpublished biographical chapter about Trotter.

R. Scott Stevenson's *In a Harley Street Mirror* (1951) contains an amusing vignette on Trotter. Wilfred Bion wrote about Trotter in his second volume of autobiography *All My Sins Remembered* (1985). Nuno Torres explored Trotter's influence on Bion in his chapter 'Gregariousness and the mind' in *Bion's Sources: The Shaping of His Paradigms* (2013).

I have quoted from several commentaries on *Instincts of the Herd*, including Reba Soffer's 'New Elitism: Social Psychology in Prewar England' in the *Journal of British Studies* (1989, 8: 111–140), Gillian Swanson's 'Collectivity, human fulfilment and the "force of life": Wilfred Trotter's concept of the herd instinct in early 20th-century Britain' in *History of the Human Sciences* (2014, 27(1): 21–50), Jaap van Ginneken's *Mass Movements in Darwinist, Freudian and Marxist Perspective: Trotter, Freud, and Reich on War, Revolution and Reaction 1900–1933* (2007), and (best of all) Sir Francis Walshe's introduction to the 1953 edition of the book.

Trotter's famous nerve experiment was published in the *Journal of Physiology* (1909, 38(2–3): 134–241). This paper demolished the previous work of Henry Head and W. H. R. Rivers ('The Afferent Nervous System from a New Aspect', *Brain* 1905, 28(2): 99–115, and the much more detailed 'A human experiment in nerve division', *Brain* 1908, 31(3): 323–450); Sir Francis Walshe famously trashed this paper in *Brain*: 'The anatomy and physiology of cutaneous sensibility: a critical review' (1942, 65: 48–112). T. R. Elliott's obituary of Trotter contains a judicious summary of the work. Other good accounts appear in 'Henry Head's lifelong studies of cutaneous sensation' by Michael Swash in the *Journal of Medical Biography* (2021,

30(1): 57–63), *Freud in Cambridge* by John Forrester and Laura Cameron (2017), and Ben Shephard's *Headhunters: The Pioneers of Neuroscience* (2014). I have quoted from Hugh Morriston Davies's obituary in the *Annals of the Royal College of Surgeons of England* (1965, 36(4): 246–249).

Michael Powell's 'Sir Victor Horsley – an inspiration' appeared in the *British Medical Journal* (2006, 333: 1317–1319), as did Julian Taylor's obituary (1961, 1: 1255–1256). I accessed *Plarr's Lives of the Fellows* of the Royal College of Surgeons of England for details on Rupert Bucknall. Although I have referred to David Eder only fleetingly, he is an interesting figure. John Turner's 'David Eder: Between Freud and Jung' appeared in the *D. H. Lawrence Review* (1997, 27(2/3): 289–309); Mathew Thomson's '"The Solution to his Own Enigma": Connecting the Life of Montague David Eder (1865–1936), Socialist, Psychoanalyst, Zionist and Modern Saint' was published in *Medical History* (2011; 55(1): 61–84).

Freud's Women by Lisa Appignanesi and John Forrester (1992, new ed. 2005) is a great source of useful information on Loe Kann, Lou Andreas-Salomé, Marie Bonaparte, Joan Riviere, Alix Strachey, Dorothy Burlingham and Anna Freud. Michael John Burlingham's *The Last Tiffany: A Biography of Dorothy Tiffany Burlingham* (1989) is a detailed account of the life of Dorothy Burlingham and her children Bob and Mabbie. Burlingham later wrote a more emollient essay, 'The Relationship of Anna Freud and Dorothy Burlingham', for the *Journal of the American Academy of Psychoanalysis* (1991, 19(4): 612–619). Gina Bon, their secretary, wrote about Dorothy and Anna Freud in *American Imago* (1996, 53(3):

211–226). Elisabeth Young-Bruehl's *Anna Freud: A Biography* (1988) is the definitive biography. Anna Freud's collaboration with Joseph Goldstein and Albert Solnit is described in the fathers' rights activist Robert Whiston's 1 September 2009 blog, 'Anna Freud: her secret failure', and in a 20 March 2011 blog, 'Child Custody: Let Doctors Decide?' by the American legal academic M. Gregg Bloche.

The only biography of Joan Riviere is Marion Bower's short and reverential *The Life and Work of Joan Riviere: Freud, Klein and Female Sexuality* (2018); I have also quoted Athol Hughes's 'Joan Riviere: Her Life and Work', from *The Inner World and Joan Riviere: Collected Papers* (1991). A series of obituaries of Riviere (by James Strachey, Paula Heimann, and Lois Munro) appeared in the *International Journal of Psychoanalysis* (1963, 44: 228–235).

Patrick J. Mahony's *Freud and the Rat Man* (1986) is the most comprehensive – if not the most readable – account of Ernst Lanzer. Freud's five-hour lecture on the Rat Man is fictionalised in Anthony Burgess's *The End of the World News* (1982). In the Rat Man chapter, I have quoted from Fritz Wittels' memoir *Freud and the Child Woman* (1995), and Michael Shepherd's *Sherlock Holmes and the Case of Dr Freud (1985)*. Owen Hewitson's essay on Lacan and the Rat Man, 'Reading "The Neurotic's Individual Myth" – Lacan's Masterwork on Obsession' was published in LacanOnline.com on 23 September 2013.

Edward Bernays' *Crystallizing Public Opinion* (1923) is a useful insight into its author. Iris Mostagel's 'The Original Influencer' (*History Today*, 6 February 2019) is a good account of Bernays' 'torches of freedom' stunt. Matthew Freud told his 'any relation?' anecdote in *GQ* magazine (10 May 2021).

Although Cheryl Misak's *Frank Ramsey: A Sheer Excess of Powers* (2020) is good on Cambridge in the 1920s, John Forrester's and Laura Cameron's monumental *Freud in Cambridge* (2017) is the last word on the subject and is also full of delicious detail on the Bloomsberries. Another good account of the Bloomsbury analysts is Douglass W. Orr's short book *Psychoanalysis and the Bloomsbury Group* (2004). Michael Holroyd's hilarious description of his first encounter with James and Alix Strachey appeared in the preface to the revised 1994 edition of *Lytton Strachey*.

Lionel Penrose is the hero of Daniel Kevles's *In the Name of Eugenics: Genetics and the Uses of Human Heredity* (1985). I referenced Sir Cyril Clarke's 'Lionel Penrose: Some aspects of his life and work', published in the *Journal of the Royal College of Physicians of London* (1974, 8(3): 237–250).

Archie Cochrane wrote about his experience of psychoanalysis in *One Man's Medicine* (1989). His gossipy 1987 interview with Max Blythe is available online. I have quoted also from his *Effectiveness and Efficiency: Random Reflections on Health Services* (1972). 'Cochrane's problem: psychoanalysis and anejaculation' (*Australasian Psychiatry* 2007, 15(2): 144–147) reviews the sexual difficulty that first prompted Cochrane to enter analysis. Other useful articles on Cochrane included Sir Iain Chalmers' 'Archie Cochrane (1909–1988)' in the *Journal of the Royal Society of Medicine* (2008, 101(1): 41–44), and Cochrane's self-written obituary in the *British Medical Journal* (1988, 297: 63). Jeremy Howick's

The Philosophy of Evidence-Based Medicine (2011) contains a useful summary of Cochrane's ideas, while Joel Paris's *Fads and Fallacies in Psychiatry* (2013) is good on the rise of evidence-based treatments for mental illness.

I dipped into several dull biographies of George V, including John Gore's *King George V: A Personal Memoir* (1941), Harold Nicolson's *King George the Fifth: His Life and Reign* (1952) and Kenneth Rose's *King George V* (1983). Rose recounts the 'bugger Bognor!' episode amusingly, proving that a skilled biographer can write a good book about a boring person. The best account of the king's illness, however, is in R. Scott Stevenson's *Famous Illnesses in History* (1962). Francis Watson's *Dawson of Penn: A Biography* (1950) contains much useful material, but notably fudges Dawson's role in the king's death in 1936; Watson eventually set the record straight in his article for *History Today* (36(12): 12 December 1986). Dawson made the cover of *Time* magazine on 1 September 1930. Commentaries on Dawson include J. H. Rolland Ramsay's 'A king, a doctor, and a convenient death' in the *British Medical Journal* (1994, 308: 1445) and Michael Cook's 'Another death in the family', posted on mercatornet.com on 8 November 2011.

The best account of Princess Alice's psychosis is Dany Nobus's 'The madness of Princess Alice: Sigmund Freud, Ernst Simmel and Alice of Battenberg at Kurhaus Schloß Tegel' in *History of Psychiatry* (2020, 31(2): 147–162); David Cohen's 'Looking Back: Freud and the British royal family' in the *Psychologist* (2013, 26: 462–463) was also useful. I cited two papers by Chandak Sengoopta on Steinach: 'Rejuvenation and the prolongation of life: science or quackery?' in *Perspectives in*

Biology and Medicine (1993, 37(1): 55–66) and '"Dr Steinach coming to make old young!": sex glands, vasectomy and the quest for rejuvenation in the roaring twenties' in *Endeavour* (2003; 27(3): 122–126).

Célia Bertin's *Marie Bonaparte: A Life* (1982) is remarkably uncritical of its subject, skipping over her involvement in Princess Alice's 'treatment' and making no mention of Brâncuşi's *Princess X*. The story of this sculpture is well told in 'The Controversies of Constantin Brâncuşi: *Princess X and the Boundaries of Art*' by Philip McCouat in his 2015 online piece for the *Journal of Art in Society*. An English translation of *Topsy: The Story of a Golden-Haired Chow* was published in 1994 and tells us far more about Bonaparte than Bertin's biography. Jelto J. Drenth's chapter 'Sexual Surgery Through the Ages, in Varying Cultures' in *Cultural Differences and the Practice of Sexual Medicine* (2020) contains an account of Bonaparte's bizarre collaboration with the gynaecologist Josef Halban. I should mention also Alison Moore's 'Relocating Marie Bonaparte's Clitoris' in *Australian Feminist Studies* (2009, 24(60): 149–165), if only for the title.

Phyllis Grosskurth's *Melanie Klein: Her World and her Work* (1986) is the most comprehensive biography but is unashamedly pro-Klein. Julia Segal's short *Melanie Klein* (1992) is a useful summary of the life and work. Pearl King and Riccardo Steiner's *The Freud-Klein Controversies 1941–45* (1991) is a detailed account of the great schism. Klein's account of the case of Little Richard was published as *Narrative of a Child Analysis: The conduct of the psycho-analysis of children as seen in the treatment of a ten-year-old boy* (1961). Commentaries on the story of Little Richard include Deborah Britzman's 'Melanie Klein, Little Richard, and the Psychoanalytic Question of Inhibition' in *Novel Education: Psychoanalytic Studies of Learning and Not Learning* (2006) and Hilary Clark's 'Complicating Disorder: The Play of Interpretation and Resistance in Melanie Klein's *Narrative of a Child Analysis*' in *Atlantis* (2011, 35(2): 30–39.).

For an insight into the economics of psychoanalysis, look no further than Francis Levy's unintentionally comic 'Psychoanalysis: The Patient's Cure', in *American Imago* (2010, 67(1): 23–71). Janet Malcolm's *Psychoanalysis: The Impossible Profession* (1977) is a revealing insight into the profession in America. Malcolm doesn't mention the fact that she had been in analysis for several years; perhaps she thought her readers would assume that as a New York Jewish intellectual, she *must* have been in therapy.

David Cohen's *The Escape of Sigmund Freud* (2009) contains a detailed account of Anton Sauerwald's role in Freud's flight from Vienna. Michael Ignatieff's *Isaiah Berlin: A Life* (1998) describes Berlin's encounters with both Sigmund and Lucian Freud. Geordie Greig's *Breakfast with Lucian: A Portrait of the Artist* (2013) and Richard Nathanson's online essay 'Lucian Freud, "Portrait with Horses", 1939' are both interesting on the relationship between Lucian and his grandfather. Dalí's insight about Freud's cranium appears in his autobiography *The Secret Life of Salvador Dalí* (1942).

I have quoted from several critiques of psychoanalysis, including Joel Paris's *The Fall of an Icon* (2005) and Ernest Gellner's *The Psychoanalytic Movement: The Cunning of*

Unreason (1985). Anthony Storr's *Feet of Clay: Saints, Sinners, and Madmen: A Study of Gurus* (1996) places Freud firmly in this tradition. Robert Coe's interview with Peter Swales in *Rolling Stone* (27 September 1984) is fascinating, while Raymond Tallis's 'The shrink from hell' in the *Times Literary Supplement* (31 October 1997) is a brilliant trashing of Élisabeth Roudinesco's biography of Jacques Lacan. Oliver Burkeman's 'Therapy wars: the revenge of Freud' (the *Guardian*, 7 January 2016) is a nuanced essay on the psychoanalysis vs cognitive behaviour therapy debate. The Ithaca lecture episode was reported by the *Times* as 'A useful hoax on Freudians' on 17 December 1921.

Other useful books include Roy Porter's *A Social History of Madness: Stories of the Insane* (1987), Frederick Crews' *Freud: The Making of an Illusion* (2017), Peter Medawar's essay collection *The Strange Case of the Spotted Mice* (1996), Anthony Storr's *Churchill's Black Dog and Other Phenomena of the Human Mind* (1988), and Philip Kuhn's *Psychoanalysis in Britain 1893–1913: Histories and Historiography* (2017).

Acknowledgements

I want especially to thank David Trotter, who welcomed me to his home, where I spent two happy days reading material about his grandfather. Thanks to Dr Ken Ó Donnchú of University College Cork who helped me decipher Wilfred Trotter's handwriting. Dr Rhian Davies readily shared her vast knowledge of Morfydd Owen. Philip Kuhn, the independent scholar of the history of psychoanalysis in England, very generously gave me much useful material on Ernest Jones and Wilfred Trotter. Professor Mark McGurk at University College Hospital (UCH) went to great lengths to help me in the search for material relating to Trotter at UCH. Thanks also to Professor Dame Jane Dacre at University College London (UCL) Medical School, and to Dan Mitchell of the UCL Library Special Collections for sourcing some of Trotter's correspondence. I first wrote about Trotter for the *Dublin Review of Books*: thanks to Maurice Earls, co-editor of the *drb*. I wrote about the death of George V for the medical humanities journal, *Hektoen International*. Thanks to Professor Andrew Lees for neurological advice, to Sir Iain Chalmers for helping me find a photograph of the young Archie Cochrane, and to Aidan Doyle and Iain Bamforth for help with proofreading.

My editor Neil Belton has provided unwavering encouragement; I thank him and his colleagues at Head of Zeus, Matilda Singer and Karina Maduro. My thanks to Professor Neil Vickers and the Centre for the Humanities and Health at King's College London, for giving me an academic refuge and access to their wonderful library. Finally, thanks, as always, to Karen, James and Helena.

Image Credits

About the Author

Seamus O'Mahony worked as a hospital doctor for many years in both Britain and his native city of Cork, in the south of Ireland. He is the author of *The Way We Die Now*, which won a BMA Book Award in 2017, *Can Medicine Be Cured?* and *The Ministry of Bodies*.

Index

Images are denoted by *italics*.